A PLUME BOOK

HOW TO RAISE YOUR ADULT CHILDREN

GAIL PARENT is an Emmy Award–winning television writer and producer whose credits include *Tracey Takes On* (featuring Tracey Ullman), *The Carol Burnett Show*, and *The Golden Girls*, among others. Also a bestselling novelist, Parent is the author of *Sheila Levine Is Dead and Living in New York*. She lives in Beverly Hills, California.

SUSAN ENDE, M.F.T., has been a psychotherapist in private practice for twenty-five years and has taught at the California Institute of Technology, Pepperdine University, and California State University, Los Angeles. She lives in Pasadena, California.

HOW TO RAISE
YOUR ~Adult~ CHILDREN

(handwritten editorial insertion: "Adult" with caret ^ between "YOUR" and "CHILDREN")

Real-Life Advice for When Your Kids
Don't Want to Grow Up

Gail Parent and Susan Ende, M.F.T.

A PLUME BOOK

PLUME
Published by the Penguin Group
Penguin Group (USA) Inc., 375 Hudson Street, New York, New York 10014, U.S.A. • Penguin
Group (Canada), 90 Eglinton Avenue East, Suite 700, Toronto, Ontario, Canada M4P 2Y3
(a division of Pearson Penguin Canada Inc.) • Penguin Books Ltd., 80 Strand, London
WC2R 0RL, England • Penguin Ireland, 25 St. Stephen's Green, Dublin 2, Ireland (a division
of Penguin Books Ltd.) • Penguin Group (Australia), 250 Camberwell Road, Camberwell,
Victoria 3124, Australia (a division of Pearson Australia Group Pty. Ltd.) • Penguin Books
India Pvt. Ltd., 11 Community Centre, Panchsheel Park, New Delhi – 110 017, India • Penguin
Group (NZ), 67 Apollo Drive, Rosedale, Auckland 0632, New Zealand (a division of Pearson
New Zealand Ltd.) • Penguin Books (South Africa) (Pty.) Ltd., 24 Sturdee Avenue, Rosebank,
Johannesburg 2196, South Africa

Penguin Books Ltd., Registered Offices: 80 Strand, London WC2R 0RL, England

Published by Plume, a member of Penguin Group (USA) Inc. Previously published in a
Hudson Street Press edition.

First Plume Printing, August 2011
10   9   8   7   6   5   4   3   2   1

 REGISTERED TRADEMARK—MARCA REGISTRADA

The Library of Congress has catalogued the Hudson Street Press edition as follows:

Parent, Gail.
    How to raise your adult children : because big kids have even bigger problems /
Gail Parent and Susan Ende.
        p.   cm.
    ISBN 978-1-59463-069-9 (hc.)
    ISBN 978-0-452-29720-3 (pbk.)
    1. Parent and adult child.   2. Adult children—Family relationships.   3. Adult children
living with parents.   4. Parenting.   I. Ende, Susan.   II. Title.
    HQ755.86.P37   2010
    306.874—dc22   2010016976

Printed in the United States of America
Original hardcover design by Eve L. Kirch

PUBLISHER'S NOTE
Every effort has been made to ensure that the information contained in this book is complete
and accurate. However, neither the publisher nor the author is engaged in rendering
professional advice or services to the individual reader. The ideas, procedures, and suggestions
contained in this book are not intended as a substitute for consulting with a professional.
Neither the author nor the publisher shall be liable or responsible for any loss or damage
allegedly arising from any information or suggestion in this book.

For Saul from Gail

For Richard from Susan

CONTENTS

ACKNOWLEDGMENTS

Gail would like to thank her children Kevin and Gregory Parent, as well as her assistant Myles Gullette. And a very large thank-you to her mother.

Susan would like to thank Adam and Dana for being admirable adult children and Richard for being so wonderful to parent with.

We would both like to thank the people at Penguin, especially our very good editor Meghan Stevenson, as well as Steve Fisher and Alice Martell, who made this book happen.

INTRODUCTION

Should you lend your son money? Do you pay for his medical insurance when he can't? Do you dare to comment on how your child is raising her child? When your adult child gets in trouble and can't afford a lawyer, do you hire one for him? What happens when your gay son and his partner adopt a baby and his partner leaves him? What if your daughter is on her way to becoming obese? There are millions of questions parents have when dealing with their adult children. Until now, there have been very few answers. But this book will tell you how to get along with your grown children and, along the way, help them become strong, independent adults.

The idea for the book was formulated on a trip that we and our husbands took together. The men enjoyed the scenery and we women talked about our children—across seven different countries. Since we missed the scenery, we bought postcards. We wished there were a guide for parents like us, so we decided to write one. That's how *How to Raise Your Adult Children* was born.

Figuring out the right format for the book was the most difficult part of the process. We tried answering the questions together, but that didn't work. Gail tended to have more practical advice. A lot of it came from her mother. As a comedic author, she also wanted to throw in a few punch lines. Susan's answers were serious and rooted in psychology. She knew the behavior problems hidden in every question. We then decided to answer the questions separately, which worked. Many times we agree. Sometimes we don't, but the answers are always presented from two unique points of view.

Where did the questions come from? Everywhere. We started close to home, gathering questions from friends and relatives. Then they told their friends and relatives, who contacted us, until eventually we began to receive questions from strangers. The day we heard that a friend of a friend of a friend had followed our advice and it worked, we knew we were in business.

Writing a book is interesting, fun, and frustrating. But once we got into it, we kept our goal in mind. We wanted people to gain insight and stop walking on eggshells with their adult children. We both knew that what Gail's mother had taught her was true: When kids are little, they have little problems. When they are big, they have big problems. We wanted to be able to help our readers be there for the big problems, but not cause them.

When our children are young, we feed and dress them. When they are old enough, we expect them to feed and dress themselves. We teach them to ride bikes and later to drive cars so they can move further and further away from us on their own steam. We make sure they have the right skills and know the rules of the road before sending them off to practice getting themselves around, independent of us. We worry, but we let them go anyway.

We should do the same thing when our kids are adults, especially regarding money. Money is the currency of adult life. By the time a kid leaves college, he should have mastered the skills of budgeting, financial planning, delayed gratification, working, spending wisely, and saving for a rainy day. College is a good time to practice those skills. We shouldn't send money on demand or bail a kid out of a jam. This is an area parents sometimes forget about when raising adult kids. Our children can't be independent unless they are supporting themselves, and they have to master the skills to do it.

Nor are they independent unless they live on their own. Living with us or in our guest room is not living independently. Living on one's own is a developmental step just the way driving a car is. We need to expect and prepare our children to live on their own after they leave school. It should be part of what a parent teaches his child to do. He can practice in college, when we're usually still paying the bills.

When our children become adults, we need to rethink and rewrite our relationships with them. We need to treat them like adults and expect them to behave like adults. When our children are independent, we have no control over them. Independent children can make their own decisions about their lives, their money, and who they choose as friends and romantic partners.

We also need to accept that when our children are adults, the configuration of the family changes. The children no longer live with us and we are no longer the primary relationship in their lives. They have their own personal lives that are more important to them than their families are.

We and our adult children are separate. Our child is on his own life journey, which is different from ours. His may take him to another state, to a lifestyle different from ours. He is his own person, not an extension of Mom and Dad.

Although we raised him with our values, to be truly separate from us our child has to develop his own value system. His value system will be influenced not only by us but also by his peers and his own reading and thinking. So his values may, in various ways, be different from ours. We need to recognize the differences and accept them, even if we don't like or admire them. If not, we could lose the relationship with our child.

So our primary focus when answering the questions in this book was to point parents in the direction of making decisions to foster their child's independence. It's all too easy to get into the mode of reacting to the problem of the moment without looking at the long-term issues. Unless the house is burning down, in which case we should react instantly and call 911, we should think through decisions before we make them. Fostering independence should be our goal and we should make our decisions from that perspective.

We, like many others, thought that when our kids left home, our parenting days were over. We quickly learned that they weren't. *How to Raise Your Adult Children* is here to help. This book answers questions that most parents never imagined they would have to ask.

HOW TO RAISE
YOUR Adult CHILDREN

CHAPTER ONE

Money

Money is a big subject when it comes to adult children. The question of whether Mom and Dad should pay for something comes up over and over. It's tempting to avoid thinking about money until we have to, then make the most comfortable decision and hope for the best. But that's not the mature way to handle the money subject. A better way is to use some principles to guide our money choices that help our children become maturely functioning adults.

First, a child who is dependent always feels ambivalent toward the person he's dependent on. We may think that if we provide our child with what he needs and make him dependent on us, he will feel secure. But dependence, in reality, means *lack* of security, because the one you're dependent on has control over your destiny. Being dependent means you're not free. Therefore dependence always breeds some resentment.

Parents should want their children to be independent. The reality is that no one is truly independent unless he is financially independent. Being able to fully support yourself boosts self-esteem and self-confidence. Knowing that you can take care of yourself, no matter what, means security.

A parent's goal for his adult child should be financial independence. But even if we agree to this precept, we can get lost putting it into action. The pitfall for the child is that being taken care of financially feels familiar and appealing. Being on his own can be frightening. So why not go with the known rather than the unknown? Why not hold on to Mom and Dad's purse strings? Although our child may seem to have a healthy thrust toward financial autonomy, he may also have a hidden wish to be taken care of. We have to remember that the purse strings, like the umbilical cord, need to be cut. And since the purse is ours, we have to do the cutting.

The pitfall for us as parents is the fantasy that if our child needs our money, he will love us and be grateful. Actually, it's just the opposite. The parent who provides the money is the source of the child's shame and self-doubt. Really, it's a vicious cycle—if the child doesn't have confidence in himself, he falls back on dependence, and being dependent fosters insecurity and anxiety . . . and so the circle goes around.

Second, the boundaries between a parent's money and an adult child's should be clear. Children are not entitled to Mom and Dad's money. They are not even entitled to inherit it. Parents can do whatever they want to with *their* money. Likewise, parents are not entitled to their child's money. Parents are not entitled to spend all their money, even if it's on their child, and then expect him to support them. In the same vein, children are not entitled to tell parents how to spend their money nor are parents entitled to tell their child how to spend his.

Third, our expectations regarding money should be known. If parents plan to pay for college, they should tell their kid. But if parents can't or don't want to, they should be precise about what they will spend, if anything, and expect the child to deal with the limitations—for example, by getting a job during high school or college. The same goes for weddings. Going into debt to pay for a wedding is irresponsible.

But what if you want to give your kid money? It's better to give a gift than a loan. Children who need money are not likely to be able to pay off a loan. It's human nature to be anxious about a debt you can't pay and to want to stay clear of the person you owe money to. It is also important to remember that parents should not give what they can't afford.

Parents also need to be vigilant about not using money for control. Parents shouldn't want to control their adult children and shouldn't use money to try to. That's why a gift is better than a loan. If Mom and Dad lend their kid money for a car, they are more likely to want a say in the choice and be angry when their child doesn't make a prudent purchase. And very importantly, parents shouldn't let their child try to control them with money or, more likely, his lack of it. Just because the job of his dreams hasn't come along does not mean that his parents should support him.

Finally, parents should be careful not to confuse love with money. Our love for our child should motivate us to help him become independent, which sometimes means that the best thing we can do for our kid is to not give him a cent.

~~~~~~

Save Me from My Son

Dear Gail and Susan,

I own a nice-sized furniture business that I inherited from my father. We sell good-quality merchandise, and I like that we have personal relationships with our customers in the community. My son Malcolm has an MBA and worked for a big company for a few years. Now he wants me to take him into my business. He thinks that we should expand, buy from cheaper Asian markets, and eventually have a chain of stores.

As his father, how can I refuse him? My father took me into the business; can I do any less for my son? It's not as if he isn't qualified. He has his MBA and business experience. I have been having sleepless nights and my ulcer is acting up since he proposed this idea. I don't like thinking that my life is going to change to the extent that it would. My wife tells me it's only my fear and Depression-era mentality that's creating a problem, and she says I owe it to my son.

Cyrus

Dear Ulcerated Cyrus,

Your father left you his business. In turn, you can leave it to your son. However, you don't have to let him mess it up while you are still alive. Right now the business seems to be doing fine. Malcolm might have an MBA, but he is not recognizing that bigger may not be better. While you may not have an advanced degree, you certainly know how to run your business, and you used to know how to sleep.

Keep it small. You and your son are at different stages of life. He's willing to take risks. You're not. That's normal. I love normal.

Self-employed, Gail

Gail, parents are obligated to raise their children until the children are legally allowed to be on their own. Parents are not even obligated to pay for college, although many do as an investment in their child's future. Parents are definitely not obligated to provide a business for their children, qualified or not. Likewise, though a parent might want a child to join the family business, the child is not obligated to do so.

What our parents did for us is not binding on what we do for our children. Every adult gets to decide for himself, because every situation is different.

If Cyrus does not want to change his life for his son's ambition, he shouldn't have to. Malcolm has other options and if he is that good a businessman, he will find a business to build on his own.

Susan

Big Daddy

Dear Gail and Susan,

My husband and I often go out for meals with my daughter and son-in-law and my husband always picks up the check. Neither my son-in-law nor my daughter ever offers. My husband says we can afford it so no harm, no foul, and that he enjoys playing Big Daddy. It makes me uncomfortable to be out with adults whom we treat like children. Who's right?

Robin

Robin, You're Right but So What?

Your husband wants to retain some sort of control and respect. But what are you going to do? Change the guy or fight with him? Big Daddy is Big Daddy and you've got him. In some families, the parents are "Santa Claus" to their children their whole lives. It's only really harmful when the kids expect more than a dinner out.

I feel I can't buy my kids' groceries all the time or pay their mortgages, but that I can treat them to dinner at a nice restaurant. I'm guilty of always picking up the check when I'm out with them.

Please write to me again and let me know what "no foul" really means. Does it mean no chicken or turkey?

Gail, who likes taking her kids out

Well, Gail, we don't agree on this one. When our children become adults, we should treat them like adults who are our equals now. We need to change the way we relate. Parents who routinely pick up the tab may feel good about it, but paying all the time does nothing for the adult child's self-esteem, nor for his sense of finally being an equal.

It's time for Big Daddy to step down from being Big Daddy and let his kids in on the feelings of adult power. Parents' personal power shouldn't come from having power over their children. Parents shouldn't think that they lose their personal power when they allow their grown children to have theirs.

That's not to say that a parent can't occasionally treat, but as a regular practice the adults can split the bill or take turns paying.

By the way, Gail, in basketball, if you hit a player's arm but he makes the basket anyway, a foul may not be called because it didn't do the shooter any harm. No harm, no foul.

Susan

Margaret's Mess

Dear Gail and Susan,

I'm very well-off financially. My forty-five-year-old daughter Patricia is a high earner with two children. Her soon-to-be-ex was a stay-at-home dad. Now that they are divorcing, he wants a large alimony settlement and custody of the children. Given their arrangement, he has a case.

My daughter's legal bills are enormous—more than she can really afford. I have offered her money, but she refuses to take it. She says that she would rather sell her house. I don't understand her. Any money I give her I would leave to her anyway.

She may as well have it now. How can I bring her to her senses?

                                                    Margaret

Margaret, You Crazy Mother You,

How can you bring *her* to *her* senses? How can I bring you to your senses? Your daughter is a grown-up and she knows it. That's why she is refusing to take money from you. If she sells her house and moves into an apartment, the time will come when she no longer has legal bills and she can buy another house since she's a big earner.

From the time I was twenty-one, I was embarrassed to take money from my parents. Your daughter is forty-five. She must be embarrassed, too. I like her. Let her have her pride.

               Gail, who didn't take money from her parents, but cried
                                             easily until she was fifty

Margaret's daughter is facing an increasingly common, stressful situation. Some women are now paying alimony. But that's because they earn more than their husbands do.

To Patricia's credit, she is not clinging to her old life at all costs and is willing to sell her house to pay her bills. A divorce means a change in life. Some people want to hang on to the house when it is not financially realistic to do so.

Margaret should not get in the way of Patricia's taking care of business, responsibly and independently. I hope that Margaret comes to understand that her daughter is handling her divorce, including the legal bills, very competently.

                                                    Susan

Rehab Repeat

Dear Gail and Susan,

My thirty-six-year-old son is a drug addict. I have paid for rehab twice. He stays clean for a while and then goes back to using. Should I pay for another rehab? I so want to see him have a normal life. What should I do?

William

William, Father of an Addict,

Right. Pay for another rehab. Then pay again and again. Hasn't reading the *National Enquirer* taught you anything? I know what happens to drug addicts if their fathers don't send them to endless rehabs. I know because I watch *Law and Order* and the reruns. Addicts commit a couple of crimes to get money to keep their habit going and are jailed for a couple of years where they can't get drugs. Incarceration may not be the best way to get over an addiction, but most of the time it works. At least it does on television. Have a nice day.

Your tell-it-like-it-is woman, Gail

In my opinion, rehab is a misnomer. Rehab should be called detox, because no one leaves rehab, which is usually one month long, recovered from his addiction. He may not be drinking or doing drugs, and he may have some better coping tools to take with him. But true rehabilitation takes a commitment to an ongoing treatment program and to never taking drugs.

A parent might consider paying for one rehab/detox to give his son or daughter the opportunity to begin to deal with his or her addiction. If the child does not pursue the path that rehab/detox sets out, then a parent should not pay again. To an addict, rehab repeatedly paid for by parents is just another fix. Getting over an addiction requires a whole new way of life. William's son has to do that work and he should pay the price.

William says that he wants his son to have a normal life. I certainly understand the pain a parent feels when a child is in the grips of a drug. Sadly, though, William cannot force his son into sobriety or pay his way there. His son has to want that for himself.

Susan

Jake, the Gigolo

Dear Gail and Susan,

My wife and I give our twenty-eight-year-old son Jake a tax-free gift of thirteen thousand dollars a year, which he uses for petty cash. His other money comes from older women he latches on to. He moves in with them. These women buy him expensive gifts and take him with them when they travel. There have been several of these "relationships." His mother and I are shocked. We didn't raise Jake to take advantage of people, much less to live the life of a gigolo. Is there anything we can do?

Sam

Dearest Sam,

The way I see it, there's only one thing you can do. Take away the thirteen-thousand-dollar yearly gift. Without that, Jake won't be able to take older women out to dinner or give them little gifts. I'm sure that's what he does when he meets them, so you have to take away his seduction power. Do this sooner rather than later. Without any money, he'll have to work. Like everyone else, gigolos have expenses. They need decent haircuts and good clothes, not to mention they have to smell good. You have to see to it that he has none of those things.

You might also drop a hint that he's out of your will.

Your sympathizer, Gail

Gail, I agree with you, although I would frame it differently. Jake has a financial system made up of his parents' funding and his ladies' "generosity." Sam and his wife can refuse to finance a system they don't approve of, just as parents might not give money to a child who uses it for heroin.

Susan

Josh, the Writer?

Dear Gail and Susan,

My son Josh is married with two children. He's been a successful dentist for years. Last week Josh told us that he is unhappy with his career choice. He feels that he has a creative side that isn't being given expression. Josh wants to take a year off and give himself the chance to see if he can make it as a writer.

The problem is that Josh and his wife Marcy have pretty much lived on their income and have little in savings, and Marcy doesn't work. Marcy said she would get a job. Even if she did, though, we know she could not earn enough to cover their expenses—big house, country club membership, nice cars, private school, etc. Josh has asked if we could either help support him or lend him the money. His argument is that it's money we would leave him anyway. In other words, could he have some of his inheritance now so he can have a chance at realizing his dream?

I thought you and Susan were the perfect people to advise me on what to do.

John

John, Father of Josh,

Yes, Josh can take the year off and focus on his writing. But he can't do it with your money. He's got to cut down his expenses, buy a smaller house, drop the country club, put the kids in public school, and get rid of the nice cars. Once he has enough money in the bank, he could take a year off to become a writer. His dream has got to be funded by him, or he could write on nights and weekends. That's the better choice. He won't have time to think about what he's missing at the country club.

Promise me, John, that you're going to stay out of this. Take it from someone who knows, writing isn't something you want to do. Writing is something you have to do.

Gail, who wrote in her spare time at the beginning

Gail, there are several red flags waving in this letter. First, if Josh just wanted to express his "creative side," he would take a painting or writing class at his local college. But that's not what he means, is it? What Josh really wants to do is "realize his dream" of being a successful writer. And he wants to do it in one year!

Building any career—and writing is harder than most—takes more than a year. Unless Josh writes a best-selling novel or a block-buster screenplay, he won't be making a sufficient income at the end of one year to support his lifestyle. Josh doesn't have a realistic career plan; he has a grandiose fantasy that he wants his family to buy into.

Second, ambition, any ambition—in this case to become a successful writer—requires personal sacrifice. In Josh's plan, his wife Marcy will sacrifice being a stay-at-home mom and go to work. His mother and father will sacrifice some of their money. Nowhere do we hear that Josh intends to make any sacrifice for his ambition.

If Josh wants to try his hand at writing, he can write before or after work or on weekends. He can join a writing group. He can find out if he has any talent. If he is ever able to support his lifestyle with his writing, he can quit his job.

John and his wife should put no money toward Josh's childish, unrealistic scheme.

Susan

Garry and Ginny

Dear Gail and Susan,

I am in a second marriage. I have two children, as does my wife Ginny. The problem is that she is much wealthier than I, and so her children live a much more privileged life than mine do. Her kids have gone to the best schools, drive fancy cars, and take luxury trips. Mine go to state schools, drive hand-me-down clunkers, and have never been out of the country. I feel depressed about my inability to give to my children what my wife can give to hers. I think my children feel like second-class citizens. I suppose I do, too. Any suggestions?

Gary

Dear Gary with the Inferiority Complex,

I do have a suggestion. Stop feeling depressed about your inability to give to your children. Children who aren't given everything make better adults. They are more appreciative of what they can do for themselves than what their parents handed them.

My answer is short but smart.

Gail, sometimes the mother of us all

That's not fair! Gail, that's what a young child says when his older sister gets a bigger bicycle than he does. When a child complains that something isn't fair, he really means that he doesn't get the same as someone else. Part of our job as parents is to help our young children understand that we don't all get the same. Gary seems not to have learned that concept. He is still caught up in childish rivalry and envy about material acquisitions and luxury experiences.

Blending families takes time and effort. Of primary importance is a strong marital bond. The parents need to work together to create a new family of individuals who develop relationships with each other and their own family history. Gary's letter suggests that this is not happening. His envy and rivalry are divisive. He sees himself aligned with his children against his wife and her children.

I would suggest to Gary that he concentrate on his marriage, that he make the relationship with his wife his focus. Then he and his wife can together tackle the tasks of relating to each other's children, working with their financial differences, and cultivating connections in the reconfigured family.

Sometimes the best way to help our children is to get help for ourselves. If Gary can't get over his envy, rivalry, and depression, then he may need professional help.

Susan

Terry Is Terrible

Dear Gail and Susan,

My husband Terry buys his daughter, my stepdaughter Milly, anything she wants—which means that, as a couple, we have less money. Milly's mother doesn't work. She lives on alimony. I work and contribute financially to our lifestyle. I don't want to be a wicked stepmother, but shouldn't Terry see that although it's technically his money to give to Milly, Milly is in a way getting money from me, too? I know neither one of them sees it that way. But don't you think that at the very least, she and Terry should be grateful to me?

Zoe

Zoe, Wife of Terry, Stepmother of Milly, and Provider of Terry's Ex-Wife,

Hah! Do you really expect your husband's daughter to be grateful to you? And if you talk to Terry, will he be more grateful? I don't think so. He might cut down on what he gives Milly, but I doubt it. (Sometimes fathers feel so guilty for leaving their child's mother, they try to make up for it by giving their children gifts. Sometimes they even give their ex-wives things. You would hate that, wouldn't you, Zoe?)

If you and your husband put your money into one pot, then you should have a say of what comes out of that pot. The problem is, Terry has established a pattern with his daughter that won't easily go away. Why don't you open up a charge account at Saks Fifth Avenue and every time your husband buys something for Milly, buy something for yourself? He'll start to worry about the bills and you can suggest that both you and your stepdaughter cut back. If he won't cut back on Milly, he doesn't love you enough.

Aren't you happy you wrote to us?

Gail, who actually wants you to have more

Gail, I love your idea of a shopping spree followed by mutual agreement to rein in the spending. Very creative! The only problem with the solution is that it exacerbates the already existing rivalry Zoe feels toward her stepdaughter.

I can understand Zoe's disappointment that she and Terry

aren't making all the financial decisions together, including gifts
to Milly. Parents should be the primary team.

However, sometimes with blended families, for many reasons,
that concept gets lost. As you suggest, Gail, Terry may feel guilty
for having left his child and is trying to buy absolution from her.
Terry may not know how to say no to his daughter. Perhaps Terry
does not know how to parent and hopes to buy his way through it.
Or Milly may want assurances that she will not be left the way her
mother was, and controlling her father's money may make her
think she's safe.

Zoe has let her feelings of rivalry take hold of her. She is measur-
ing her importance to her husband only in monetary terms. She
needs to remind herself that Terry chose her as his partner. That
she is his number one.

Zoe also needs to remember that Milly has suffered a big loss,
that Milly was sacrificed. I suggest that Zoe warmly include Milly
in the new family and help her feel loved and secure. If Milly believes that she belongs, that she has not lost her dad, perhaps her
need for things from him will abate.

Susan

Blackjack Loser

Dear Gail and Susan,

My daughter Jenny gambles. She started online and now goes
to casinos and plays blackjack. She's lost a lot of money, which
has put the family in debt. Her husband is on the verge of leaving
her. Should we lend her money to help pay her bills and maybe
save her marriage while she is trying to deal with her problem?

Liz

Dear Lending Liz,

Haven't you heard that throwing money at a problem
doesn't solve it? (Don't feel badly if you haven't heard it. Our
entire government apparently hasn't heard it, either.) Your

daughter's husband is on the verge of leaving her. However, true addicts don't care about things on the verge. They only do something when they hit bottom. And you, her mother, have got to let her hit hard. Stay away with your checkbook.

However, your daughter's husband can do something, and that is to close down all the credit cards, ATM cards, and bank accounts, making sure the whole family doesn't hit bottom. Also, you can try to get Jenny to a Gamblers Anonymous meeting if you can.

> Gail, who always thought it would be a good idea
> to look for a husband at Gamblers Anonymous
> (they earned enough money to lose it in the
> first place and now they're getting cured)

I love your husband-hunting logic, Gail.

Now to Liz's daughter and her gambling problem. Rule number one—never give addicts money! They will spend it on their addiction, guaranteed. Addicts in the grips of their problem do not make wise decisions. Addicts are secretive and they lie. So even if they say they will do the right thing with the money, they will spend it on their addiction.

Liz's daughter needs to be in a program for gambling addiction. Her husband should find himself a support group where he will learn how to protect himself and his finances from his wife. Liz and her husband could join a support group as well. They all need ongoing help to cope with Jenny and her gambling.

You are right, Gail. Jenny's access to money should be cut off if possible. Her credit cards and ATM cards should be confiscated. But in reality, addicts are very clever about meeting their needs for their "drug." Addicts are self-destructive, so going more into debt, mixing with unsavory people to get money, or the threat of losing their marriage usually won't deter them.

So, to best help her daughter, Liz should absolutely not give her money. As you say, Gail, she should take her to a Gamblers Anonymous meeting and hope that Jenny gets with the program.

Susan

Gone with the Inheritance

Dear Gail and Susan,

If I don't buy my daughter Roz something she wants, she goes to her grandmother, my mother, who gets it for her. My mother just bought Roz a new car. Not only do I think that Roz, at thirty-five, should have bought her own car, but I'm also annoyed that the money is coming out of my inheritance. It's two against me in my family. Neither Roz nor my mother listen to me.

Nancy Lynn

Nancy Lynn, Nancy Lynn,

Tell your mother that she's spoiling your daughter. That's all you can do. She might not mind having a diminishing bank account. Try to remember it's *her* money. It's not your inheritance while your mother is alive. So what are you going to do? The only thing you can do in a case like this is write to us. And I can't be helpful.

She's all yours, Susan.

Gail, who hates not coming up with the
perfect answer

Thanks, Gail. I'll give it a try. Here are three generations of women acting out an interesting drama. Nancy Lynn is vying with her daughter for Grandma's money. Grandma is vying with her own daughter, Nancy Lynn, for Roz. And Roz is playing her mother and grandmother against each other. So rivalry is passed down from one generation to the other. It's their way of life.

Nancy Lynn needs to extricate herself from the dynamic—to not care what her mother does for Roz. If one player opts out, the game will stop.

And you were right on an important issue, Gail. Nancy Lynn's inheritance isn't hers until her mother is dead and the will says she gets the money.

Susan

Bernie Is Frustrated

Dear Gail and Susan,

My son Bernie is an engineer and has worked for years at a job that doesn't pay well. When I talk to Bernie on the phone, all I hear is that he is overworked and frustrated and that he has very little time for a social life, let alone time to find a wife. He found one wife whom we all hated. My husband and I were so happy when she left. Bernie, who wanted her to go, still feels depressed that she left him. I feel that he should go on a vacation and have some fun. He says the divorce has left him broke. Bernie is in our will. I would like to pay for his vacation so I can see him enjoy our money while we're alive. My husband doesn't want to give Bernie a cent.

Clarice

Dear, Dear, Soft Clarice,

There seems to be a trend of giving offspring money when the parents are still alive so that the parents can see them enjoy it. In this case, Bernie has to spend the money the way you want him to. A trip might be nice, but he still has to face things when he gets home. He'll still be overworked and frustrated and have very little time for a social life. Nothing will change. Unless he goes to the South Pacific and marries a native and stays there like Gauguin did. You and your husband should take a vacation.

Gail, who has been to Gauguinland

Gail, Freud suggested that we should have satisfying work and personal lives to feel fulfilled and content. Bernie has neither. He left home and created an adult life, but it doesn't work: he doesn't like his job, and he didn't like his wife but doesn't like being without her.

Bernie's got a big *problem. His mother wants to fix it with a little fun vacation. Bernie tries to tell Clarice how unhappy he is, but she doesn't see the scope and the depth of his troubles. I would tell Clarice to hear Bernie's complaints not as a hustle for a free vacation, but as a cry for big-picture clarity and serious answers.*

Bernie needs professional help. I hope that Clarice can get some perspective on Bernie's life and advise therapy. She might even offer to help pay for it.

Susan

Susan, Darling,

I thought the person in therapy had to pay for it himself in order for the therapy to be effective.

Gail

Gail,

You are well-informed. The thought is that unless a patient pays for therapy himself, he will not seriously do the work. For the most part, I adhere to that rule. In some cases, though, and Bernie's is one of them, I suggest that a parent help *pay, if the adult child really can't afford the whole fee. However, the child should make some financial sacrifice for his own treatment.*

Susan

Diamonds Are Not a Girl's Best Friend

Dear Gail and Susan,

I was widowed ten years ago. It was hard on me for a few years, and I really leaned on my son Jeffrey. My problem is that since my husband died, Jeffrey has made a lot of money and insists on giving me gifts of expensive jewelry. And not understated expensive. I don't have the kind of life or circle of friends where I can wear these elaborate necklaces and rings. I've tried hinting that he should stop, but the diamonds and rubies keep coming. Should I just wear them, even though they make me uncomfortable? Should I talk to him and get him to take them back? I can't return them secretly, because I couldn't keep the money. Please help me out of my dilemma. I love Jeffrey.

Selma

Selma, Oh, Selma,

Wear the jewelry and tell everybody it's fake. As far as talking to Jeffrey about taking the jewels back, why spoil his pleasure just because you are miserable with diamonds and rubies? Here's the deal. You say the loss of your husband was hard on you. It was hard on Jeffrey, too. Not only did he lose a father, he lost one of his shoulders because you were leaning on it. He feels more comfortable giving you presents so that he can have that shoulder back. Pay him back by reveling in his gifts. If you have such a simple lifestyle, maybe you're living too small a life. Put on all your jewels and take yourself to a nice restaurant once in a while.

If you really don't want those precious gems, send them to me.

Your BFF, Gail

When children are young, parents receive their gifts with great pleasure. They hang their scribbles as if they were Picassos. They put the lopsided ashtrays on the coffee table. Children take delight in their parents' delight. The gifts represent what the child can do, who he is at the time.

Jeffrey still likes to give his mom presents. Now he can afford expensive jewelry. That is who he is as an adult, a man of means and expensive taste. Perhaps he wants his mother to accept and enjoy the man of means he has become.

Selma might question why she does not feel worthy of such lavishness. Rubies and diamonds are not usually a source of embarrassment, unless they are stolen.

However, that being said, we can't control our adult children, not even the gifts they give. We need to accept graciously what they offer. Selma should receive the gifts in the generous spirit in which they are given.

There is no mention in the letter that Jeffrey is married. If he marries, Selma's problem will be solved. Jeffrey will shower his wife with the jewels and both Selma and Gail will be out of luck.

Susan

From the Grave and Beyond

Dear Gail and Susan,

My wife and I are in our fifties and doing our estate planning. We are not super rich, but I guess you would say we are sort of rich, so we have a sizable estate to leave. We have three children. One *is* super rich; one is rich; and the third is a teacher, so has a modest income and lifestyle.

Our dilemma is how to divide up our estate. The teacher could use the money more than the others, but then again, they are all our children, and for that, each is equal in our esteem. Do we divide the money equally, or give more to the one who needs it more?

Raymond

Listen, Raymond,

If you have three million dollars, divide it by three. If you have twenty thousand, divide it by three. You mentioned that the teacher has a modest income and lifestyle. Well, that's the life the teacher chose. What you don't want is one of the kids contesting the will. It probably will be the super rich one because he can afford a good lawyer. And you really don't want your family not to have each other when you're gone. Good parents make it possible for the siblings to support each other and enjoy each other even when you're no longer there. You may be the glue that holds them together now, but, eventually, they'll have to stick together on their own. An unbalanced will is likely to separate them and then they won't have Christmas together when you've gone to heaven.

P.S. You can put me in your will for giving you this advice.

The fairest of them all, Gail

What you are talking about, Gail, is sibling rivalry. Parents sometimes think they can avoid this state of affairs in their family, but in reality they cannot. They can, however, make sure that sibling rivalry among their children is resolved satisfactorily.

Sibling rivalry is competition for parental love. A very young child believes that his parents' love is finite and that subsequent siblings take away love he has heretofore gotten. In reality, when a baby comes along, a mother does have to limit her time with the older children. To a child, this seems like proof he's lost Mommy's love.

In healthy families, parents help children develop strategies to assure affection without having to compete with each other. Parents facilitate each child's becoming his or her own individual person with unique strengths and talents.

In this family's case, sibling rivalry seems to have been dealt with appropriately. Each child has developed his own career. Each is successful in his own right, despite the differences in earning power, related to the field chosen, not to competence.

None of the children should be rewarded or penalized for his career choice. Gail, you are correct. It is not about the money, but about the parents' affection for each child and validation of them all as individuals. The estate should not be parceled out in terms of monetary need. It should indicate that the parents love each child equally and value and respect their life choices.

Susan

Married a Bum

Dear Gail and Susan,

My daughter Leila is divorced and has a little daughter Amy, who is one year old. They both live with my husband and me. We were unhappy when our daughter married the bum she did, and we were right. He left right after Amy was born and has not paid the child support the court told him to pay. At the moment, we are completely supporting Leila and Amy. Our finances are stretched, but we're doing it. Should we continue to support them indefinitely?

Reba

Dear Burdened Reba,

You should continue to let your daughter and granddaughter live with you. Little Amy deserves to have a male figure and a stable home in her life. But why can't Leila go out and work like the rest of us while Amy is napping or asleep at night? And why can't she report the deadbeat dad? It sounds as though Leila has become a child again. I feel bad for you. You were unhappy when she married a bum and it seems you're unhappy now. However, I doubt that kicking them out will make you any happier. Tell Leila she has to work to pay for her and her daughter's expenses. You and your husband should give Amy as much love and stability as possible.

Bleeding heart, Gail

Gail, I respectfully disagree. Let me tell you why. This letter is about an adult daughter, Leila, who seems to drift irresponsibly through life and her parents allow it. An easy problem to see, but not an easy one to fix.

Ideally, Reba should help Leila make a plan that includes the following: a trip to the district attorney's office to file charges against the deadbeat dad; a reasonable deadline for Leila to get a job and move out to a place of her own; enrollment for Amy at an inexpensive day-care center. Reba can offer a gift of first and last month's rent and/or pay for day care to help Leila get started.

As I said, easier said than done. These family patterns were probably established a long time ago. I would strongly recommend that they find a therapist to help them—either a family therapist or an individual therapist to help Leila grow up and take responsibility and/or a therapist for Reba to learn how to set limits and foster Leila's independence. Most communities have clinics with a sliding fee scale. The local phone book is a place to start.

Without professional help, there could very well be more "bum" marriages and more children Leila can't take care of.

Susan

Dealing Drugs

Dear Gail and Susan,

My twenty-four-year-old son Cal smokes pot. I don't like it, but his friends all do it and he has a job and an apartment, so I couldn't really say anything. But Cal, along with a friend, got arrested for dealing. Cal needs a lawyer and says he can't afford one. Do we pay for a good lawyer or let a public defender take his case?

Thelma

Thelma, Thelma, Thelma,

Your son should rot in jail. Smoking pot is not a good idea because it dulls the senses and ruins the brain. It's now known that the brain continues to develop until you're twenty-five. Smoking pot limits that development. Dealing drugs is disgusting. Picture this. Your son Cal buying the dope from some scumbag standing on a corner in a bad neighborhood where scumbags gather. (That's probably how he got caught.) Then picture him selling the drug to his friends. Finally, picture him waiting outside a schoolyard so that he can broaden his business by selling to children. How would you feel if you heard Cal saying things like, "The first one is free," to an eleven-year-old?

You've got to let this son of yours drown. Don't pay for a good lawyer. Public defenders with big stomachs and shiny suits are good enough and are used to representing dealers. Let your son have consequences for his behavior.

And by the way, you could have said something when you first saw him smoking, even though he had a job and an apartment. I can only imagine that the reason you didn't say a word was because you were getting a contact high.

Gail, a nonsmoker

Gail, Cal may have the trappings of independence, but true independence means that the consequences of your choices are your own. He has chosen to break the law, yet wants his mother to fix it for him. He wants his pot and his mommy, too. Cal has a job, so he should be able to afford to pay for his own lawyer, but if he can't, then I agree with you, Gail: he should put himself in the hands of a public defender.

Cal wants the easy fix, whether it is dealing dope or having

someone else pay. Thelma does her son no favor by helping him out.
It's time for Cal to "deal" with his serious problem of criminality.
Having to face the consequences of his actions is his only hope of
avoiding a lifetime of hard time.

Susan

And Everything Else

Dear Gail and Susan,

I have a problem that I am embarrassed to ask you about, but
my wife pushed me to do it, so here goes. My wife and I are in our
eighties and although I worked until I was seventy and have a
pension, with the price of medications and everything else, we
are struggling. Our son is a lawyer and makes a good living. He
is married to a nice woman. They have two children, one in college and one in high school. My wife and I would like to approach
my son and daughter-in-law and ask if they could help us out
financially. Whatever they could spare would take some of the
stress off us. Should we ask, and, if so, how should we do it?

Barton

My Dear Embarrassed Barton,

I feel for you. Have you done everything possible to lower
the costs of your medications and everything else? Have you
figured out Medicare? Walmart fills some prescriptions for
four or five dollars. Are you cutting coupons? Have you heard
about reverse mortgages and how they work? The bank pays
you, usually a hefty amount, and then they own your house,
but here's the good part: you can live there until the day you
die.

If you've done everything you can, it's all right to go to your
son and daughter-in-law. (It's very thoughtful and correct to
include her. It's *their* money.) Prepare for the meeting. Write
down every expenditure you have, and I mean down to chew-
ing gum. Since your son is a lawyer, he'll appreciate that. Start
by saying that you know they're at a point in life where their

expenses are high. Mention in your discussion that you're aware of what it costs to send children through college these days. The amount you ask for should be very modest, just enough for you to cover your basic expenses. Ask them if they have any ideas that you might have overlooked in trying to balance your budget.

Finally, make sure you tell them that they shouldn't make a decision right there on the spot. Give them time to talk about it when you're not around. It won't hurt to tell them you'll love them in any case. Good luck.

Practical, Gail

I like your answer, Gail. Barton and his wife should ask both their son and daughter-in-law to participate in a realistic money discussion. We need to remember that our adult married children have their own families. We are no longer their primary family, nor their primary concern. Any money that goes to Barton will affect Barton's son's own family.

Barton should assume that his son will make a responsible decision, which might be to not give Barton money. In other words, the goal should be for Barton to find a way to relieve his financial strain, not to manipulate his son into an obligation.

Susan

Medically Inept

Dear Gail and Susan,

My thirty-five-year-old son Michael lives at home. He has no job at the moment, although he says he is looking for one. Because he doesn't work, he can't afford medical insurance. Frankly, my husband and I aren't happy that he is unemployed and living off of us and we are not inclined to pay for anything more than we do. What if he is in a car accident and needs medical care? Would we be "enabling" him to pay for medical insurance?

Joan

Dear Mother of Uninsured Michael,

Yes on medical insurance. You don't seem to be the type of person that would let your kid suffer.

The question is: what kind of medical insurance? Everyone deserves the basics, which includes going to a county hospital when you're bleeding to death. But just get him a very simple policy. He shouldn't get to go to his pediatrician. (He's a thirty-five-year-old living at home and probably the only doctor he wants to see is a doctor from his childhood.) You don't have to pay for anything that enables him to get priority care. In other words, spend just enough to give yourself peace of mind. However, I would try to get a policy that pays something toward a psychiatrist. You and your son both need one. Good luck. And don't worry about car accidents. Sounds like your baby doesn't leave your couch.

Properly insured, Gail

Gail, a thirty-five-year-old is an adult! Adults should know and care about how the world works. The need for medical insurance is one of those facts of the adult world that Michael should care about. Apparently, he doesn't. But then he doesn't seem to care about living on his own and supporting himself, also adult tasks.

If Michael has a medical need, his parents will most likely pay for it, which could wipe them out financially. Therefore, Joan and her husband should purchase medical insurance for Michael until he can buy it for himself. Michael is an irresponsible adult. His parents need to protect their money from his recklessness.

The fact that Joan asks if buying medical insurance would be "enabling" gives us some insight into a problem in the family. Joan and her husband provide Michael's room and board, but Joan doesn't refer to that as "enabling." What Joan worries might be bad for her son is really in fact taking care of herself. She writes to ask for permission to think of what is good for her. Michael is not only pathologically dependent on his parents and refusing to grow up, but he has also scared his parents into going along with him.

Susan

Friends Again

Dear Gail and Susan,

I have two daughters—Ally and Tanya—who are close in age and were friends when they were growing up. Ally married a successful lawyer and they have a lot of money. Tanya married a struggling musician. Since the girls married they have been distant. They rarely see each other. Is there anything I can do? I would like them to be friends again.

Shirley

Dear Mother of Two,

Unfortunately, money does define a lot of things. The daughter who has money can go out to fancy restaurants, have expensive vacations, and probably lives in a different neighborhood than your daughter who's married to a musician. (Don't worry about Tanya. She might be having fun. Musicians are fun and their friends are fun.) Can't you invite both of them over to your home where it won't cost anybody any money except you? Or you can take them out to lunch. Treat them to manicures. Sisters should have time together away from their husbands because it reminds them of the times they spent together growing up.

Of course you can include their husbands for dinner at your place. Once the husbands get to know each other, things may change. Maybe the lawyer really enjoys music and maybe the musician needs a lawyer.

Don't be upset over this. You don't say if your daughters are newly married. If they are, they may not be ready to socialize with anyone.

Gail, who really tried hard on this one

Being friends as children doesn't mean that siblings will be friends as adults. The converse is also true. Sometimes kids who were not close when they were young become fast friends as adults. In this case Ally and Tanya have drifted apart. I agree that money can sometimes be what defines the differences, but not always.

Shirley's daughters have made very different lifestyle choices. Being the wife of a young lawyer is not the same as being the wife of a musician. Their activities and friends are probably very different, as may be their goals. Perhaps Ally and Tanya want to develop their individuality. The fact that Shirley is concerned enough about their not being close to write to us suggests that maybe they couldn't truly find themselves until they left home. Maybe when they fully develop their own lives, they will reconnect.

I agree with you, Gail, that Shirley can invite them all over or try to get the sisters together without their husbands. However, if the girls really prefer to go their separate ways, Shirley should respect their choices and concentrate on having her own relationship with each daughter and spouse.

Susan

Susan, I have two sisters. There's nothing in the world like getting manicures with them.

Gail

Foreclosed

Dear Gail and Susan,

My daughter and son-in-law just went through foreclosure on their house. It was a nightmare. My son-in-law lost his job and is looking for another one. They have a little girl. The three of them moved in with us. We want to help but don't want this to be a permanent arrangement. How should we handle it?

David

Dear Anxious,

I addressed you as "dear anxious" not because you're worried about your children's welfare but because you're anxious about when they're going to leave. Usually I don't recommend that parents take their children in, but, in this case, you had to. In past eras of economic crisis, families moved in together. Now they're doing it again. You have to help them out for as long as it takes. Your son-in-law is not sitting around the house. He's out trying to get a job. So be welcoming. Be generous and don't make them feel unwanted. I'm sure they're embarrassed enough. If you're really uncomfortable about having your family in your home, then put them up someplace else until they're on their feet again. They won't be insulted if you present that solution in a nice way. Offer them the alternative and let them decide.

Try to remember, David, that they don't know when they'll be on their feet again, so don't ask.

Gail, who would welcome her family if they needed her

I don't think that this situation is as simple as it might seem at first read. First of all, foreclosure doesn't happen suddenly. It's an involved process. Presumably, there was a period of many months when David's daughter and son-in-law didn't pay the mortgage. They had to have known for a while that they were in financial trouble. There is no mention in the letter that David's daughter works or that she is looking for a job. I know that there is a small child, but it's not a given in today's world that moms must stay at home. When the problem first arose, had the daughter gotten a job, David and his wife might have helped out with either babysitting or paying for child care. So I don't see evidence that this couple did everything they could.

That being said, since they are living with David and he understandably doesn't want to make the arrangement permanent, he shouldn't just wait until they are ready to move out. I recommend a three-phase plan. Phase one is already partly in operation—they moved in with Mom and Dad. But the daughter has to be looking for a job as well as the son-in-law. Phase two: When either or both get a job, they move out into an apartment. Mom and Dad may pay for child care or give them a stipend for a set period of time to get them back on their feet with the proviso that the young couple make a plan to save for the rough times. Phase three: Mom and Dad withdraw their financial help.

Parents should be careful that when they help out, they are not really bailing out. They should always think about how their decision can not only solve an immediate problem but also foster new and better ways of coping.

Susan

Giving a Gift

Dear Gail and Susan,

My son Ford is buying his first house. I know he doesn't have enough for a substantial down payment. My wife and I can afford to give or lend him some money to lower the mortgage payments. First, should we offer the money? And second, should we lend it or give it as a gift?

Art

Dear Wants to Be a Nice Guy,

If you and your wife can afford it, give your son and daughter-in-law a sum of money. I said *give*. Don't lend. Your son is going to be strapped with house payments and don't you remember your high school Shakespeare? Allow me to refresh your memory, "Neither a borrower nor a lender be . . ." So you shouldn't be a lender. You shouldn't make him a borrower. Give the kid the money.

Lending always causes trouble. When you lend your kids money, it never works out. They start thinking it's unfair of you to want it back. Aren't you the parent? "Why would you want your money back when I can't afford to buy a new car?" They'll end up resenting you.

Gail, who gave her kids money for down payments and wonders if they remember

I'm with you, Gail. If parents want to help financially with a home purchase, they should make a gift and let their children start off only owing the bank. A gift, unlike a loan, helps the children be separate and not be tied to Mom and Dad by owing them.

Worse is if Mom and Dad give the couple a loan that neither the couple nor the parents expect to be repaid. That's an ersatz agreement and adults should never enter into ersatz contracts. Contract obligations in the adult world, even between parents and children, should be scrupulously met. I recommend that Art give his son and daughter-in-law a gift and avoid the problems.

Susan

College Tuition

Dear Gail and Susan,

Our son and daughter-in-law have never saved for their kids' college education. We told them to, but they were busy getting a house and car, taking vacations, and buying the children things. Well, anyway, they never did save. The oldest grandchild will be ready for college next year. Should my wife and I offer to pay the tuition?

Brad

Dear Willing to Pay,

I really feel that it's not the responsibility of grandparents to pay for their grandchildren's education. Your children can take out loans and stop taking vacations and giving expensive presents to their spoiled-rotten children. If they refuse to do that, then your grandchildren are going to have to work their way through college and take out loans themselves.

What you can do is help. Provide things like books, clothing, and money they may need for computers or special projects. You can even slip them money for fun.

Gail, who believes in parents taking care of their own kids

Yes, parents should take care of their own kids. However, I have a slightly different perspective about this situation from yours, Gail. An issue that Brad brings up is that of a family who spends now and doesn't plan for the future, including their kids' education. Brad's kids haven't mastered the concept of delayed gratification. Because of that, I strongly advise against bailing this family out. If Brad were to give his son and daughter-in-law money for college tuition, he would be contributing to and perpetuating a value system he doesn't approve of.

However, if he believes in investing in a child's education, he has another option. He can deal directly with his grandchild and make a deal with him. He can offer to pay some or all of the tuition under the following conditions: his grandchild goes to a state school; he works during summers and perhaps during school; he also takes out college loans. And he needs to research colleges, loans, and jobs in order to make a reasonable budget for Brad to assess. If Brad's grandchild will do the work, then Brad can invest knowing that he is spending his money well, not compromising his value system and teaching his grandchild what his own child hasn't learned. If Brad's grandchild won't do the work and just wants it for nothing, then Brad should keep his money and hope that his grandchild learns the lessons of financial planning and delayed gratification, and sacrifice some other way.

Susan

Having a Say

Dear Gail and Susan,

I told my daughter and son-in-law that I would give them a down payment on their first house. They found a house they like, but I hate it. I don't like the neighborhood, nor do I think it's a good investment. If I am investing money in their property, do I have a say in the house choice?

George

George, Who Doesn't Get It,

If you give your daughter and son-in-law money to buy a house, it's not *your* investment. You've given it to them to pick the house they want. You don't have a say in their choice of house, even if you hate it. And it doesn't matter if you don't like the neighborhood. Don't go when they ask you over. Although once you express your hatred for their new home, you may never get that invitation.

Gail, who knows the difference between giving and forcing

Right, Gail, a gift is not an investment. If George, his daughter, and his son-in-law want to invest in property together, then they have to draw up a business agreement. There are legal issues to iron out about ownership and financial liability.

As an aside, I absolutely advise against parents investing in their children's house. A person's house should be his alone, his achievement and his responsibility. Otherwise, the boundaries between parent and child become blurred. If a parent invests, is it the child's house or the parent's? Does the parent have rights to remodel and sell? Can the child reroof without consulting Dad? The child can't feel separate and fully adult.

Back to George. I believe that George meant his offer as a generous gift to help the couple get started. Therefore, he has no control over what house they buy. He certainly can respectfully express his concerns, but at the end of the day, the house decision is his daughter's and son-in-law's to make.

Susan

Mo, the Executor

Dear Gail and Susan,

My oldest daughter Grace expects to be executor of my estate. But my wife and I have thought it through and feel that her younger brother Mo would do a better job. He's a man and more savvy about money. We just think he's a better choice. We don't want to start trouble with my daughter. Should we tell her now, or just put it in our will and say nothing?

Alex

Alex, Who Thinks Boys Are Better with Money Than Girls,

Just put it in your will and say nothing. Who knows if there's an afterlife and if you'll ever see these people again?

That was easy.

Love and all the other emotions, Gail

I am guessing that the reason Grace wants to be executor has nothing to do with wanting the task but everything to do with a rivalry with her brother. We know that Grace's one-of-a-kind status was usurped by her brother when he was born. Grace apparently has some unresolved sibling rivalry. In some cultures, boys are favored over girls. Maybe that is also operating here.

I generally advise that parents be up-front about their estate planning at least to the extent that the children know whom to contact and where the documents are in the event of death. If the children ask who is executor, I think the parents need to be honest. If not asked, Alex need not volunteer the information.

However, in this case Grace has solicited the job, so she is likely to ask. Alex and his wife should be prepared to answer it, explain their decision, and deal with Grace's rivalry and disappointment.

Susan

Tony's Friends

Dear Gail and Susan,

I'm uncomfortable around my son Tony's friends. I never went to college. I work in a day-care center as an aide. He invites me to his parties. Tony's social circle includes doctors and lawyers. I often don't know how to relate to them and their wives. I become awkward and at a loss for words. Plus the wives wear sophisticated clothes and I feel dowdy and out of place and can't afford to buy new clothes. Should I tell my boy that I don't want to come to his gatherings?

Carly

Dear Uncomfortable,

Obviously Tony is proud of you and wants you to be part of his circle of friends. You may feel awkward and at a loss for words, but nobody else realizes that, nor are they noticing your clothes. And guess what? Interesting people are also interested people. Do you smile? Do you say hello? There are times when I would much rather talk to a friendly woman than another college graduate. Your son seems like a nice guy. If you say something to him, he'll be considerate and not invite you again. I'd hate to know that you're sitting alone at home while he's entertaining.

Gail, who would hold your hand if she could

Clearly Tony and his friends enjoy having Carly at their parties, because they seem to regularly include her. However, Carly's self-consciousness and preoccupation with how people dress and their social status keep her from connecting with people on human terms. Carly is so self-absorbed that she isn't interested in what her son's friends do or think. The fact that Carly is considering excluding herself to protect her fragile self-esteem suggests that she needs professional help. Without it, when Tony marries and advances at work, the situation will only get worse—Carly will more and more alienate herself from her son.

Telling her son she is dropping out is not a good solution to her problem.

Susan

Ripped Off

Dear Gail and Susan,

My son and daughter-in-law are remodeling their first condo. They hired a designer and, from what they tell me, I am sure they are getting ripped off. I've redone enough houses to know what things cost and the kids are paying way too much. My son says my daughter-in-law likes the designer. Do I tell him/them what I think?

Louise

Dear Unnecessarily Worried,

You've already said something, haven't you, Louise?

Gail

I think you're right, Gail. You can just tell, can't you?

What we also know from this letter is that Louise, experienced with decorators and costs, is resentful that she was not consulted and included in the couple's decision.

The son and daughter-in-law have made their own decision about an adult task and are spending their own money. Bravo to

them. Louise should not tell them they are getting ripped off. She
should tell them how lovely their condo looks.

Susan

Trying to Get Pregnant

Dear Gail and Susan,

My daughter Uma and her husband Colin are financially strug-gling. Recently, Uma told me she is trying to get pregnant. I don't know how they are going to be able to manage the expense of a baby when they can barely support themselves. The money situ-ation is stressing them. A baby is just going to stress them more. Should I suggest that they wait until they are in a better financial position?

Bates

Dear Interferer,

I don't think you should say anything about whether Uma should have a baby or not. When couples are ready to con-ceive, it's because they have deep feelings about wanting to have a child. Even though your daughter confided in you, I wouldn't try to influence her. Deciding to have a baby is a very private thing between a husband and a wife. It's also one of life's biggest milestones. They're the ones who should de-cide. They're the ones who will have to provide for it. So don't think you're going to have any influence over their decisions. I never told my parents I was trying to get pregnant. I told them when I was pregnant. I had been married for two years and didn't want them to know I was having sex.

Gail, who didn't have much money
when her first baby was born

I understand why Bates is concerned. He knows that children are
an expense and can stress a marriage. However, there are other than
financial considerations when planning a baby. Timing, for instance.

Perhaps Uma and Colin want several children and need to get started. Perhaps they don't want to wait until they need fertility treatment and risk having multiple births. Maybe they want their children to be about the ages of their friends' kids.

In any case, the decision is Uma and Colin's to make. They didn't ask for advice and Bates should not interfere. He needs to accept that his daughter is an adult and gets to make her own decisions and deal with the consequences. Presumably she is prepared for the challenge.

If Bates wants to help out financially, he can offer a gift of a big-ticket baby item such as a crib, changing table, or stroller. He can offer to pay for two weeks of a baby nurse. Or he can set up a college fund for his new grandchild.

Susan

CHAPTER TWO

The College Years

As parents, we can become wrapped up in the pressure of our kids getting into college. One parent in Pacific Palisades, California, busted into a closed post office in hopes of finding his daughter's college acceptance letter. He found himself arrested instead. Then there are the emotions we don't want to feel when it comes to letting go and packing them off, which we really don't want to do. In the midst of all the stress and activity, it's hard to think about transforming our relationships with our now-becoming-adult children.

Leaving home for college should be viewed as a big step toward being a fully independent, self-supporting adult. Most college kids do not support themselves and are not necessarily thinking about being independent, except where it suits them—no curfew, no drinking prohibition, being able to have a messy room without compunction (unless they have a fastidious roommate, one of those kids you wish were yours). Nevertheless, the college years, from the very first day, should be seen as the bridge toward independence.

One issue is the college student's room in his parents' house. These words were chosen carefully. A college kid comes home for holidays and summers. He has gotten to the dorm or college apartment stage, but not to the "his own place" stage. Parents tend to keep the room exactly as it was when their kid left, like a shrine. Why not, before the young adult goes off to college, ask him to decide which of his childhood memorabilia he wants to keep and how he wants to store it, and make the room into one that an adult would feel comfortable staying in? The kid will probably rebel against this suggestion because it's work and he's lazy. Also he wants to hold on to his childhood. It's up to you to pry it away. If you change the room, when the young adult comes to "visit," he will not be returning to his high school (or junior high) milieu. That might help everyone—the college student and his parents—take steps toward separating from each other.

We can't wait until summer vacations for the family to be whole again. Then the kid shows up and we end up running a free hotel with an annoying guest. How about insisting before he gets home that he get a job to help pay for his education? Then summers provide another step toward growing up and growing away.

Which brings us to the issue of money. Parents sometimes get into the mode of overreacting when it comes to money. It is helpful for parents to come to some decisions early in the game, before college begins. What exactly will you pay for and how much? Do you want your child to have a job during college? Each family will have a different expectation, but whatever it is, it should be thought out ahead of time, shared with your child, and, except in extreme mitigating circumstances, stuck to. Most of us have a hard time doing that.

Another issue is loss. The empty-nest loss is real and needs to be mourned, not denied. Parents sometimes unconsciously spend the year, particularly the first, waiting for their son or daughter to come home and are ambivalent about the dance or skiing with friends that keeps the kid away. Sometimes parents want to seduce their college kid into coming home on weekends with promises of getting their laundry done or shopping trips.

The adult child who is not fully independent can easily regress. Parents should not encourage regression by trying to re-create the world the child left. Although things may look sort of the same, it really is a whole new world. Get used to it. Celebrate it. Raising children can be interesting, hectic, fun, and many other things. Watching them grow into responsible adults is extraordinarily rewarding.

So congratulations, they're going to college. And congratulations, one day soon you'll be able to convert their room into a den.

~~~~~~

Furious Randolph

Dear Gail and Susan,

Our son Randy Jr. earned exceptional grades in high school and got into a good college. My wife and I were thrilled and de-

cided to stretch ourselves financially to pay for his education.
He's been at college for two months and he sold his car to buy a
motorcycle! I am furious for several reasons. We bought him the
car. Shouldn't he have asked us before he sold it? And a motorcycle is dangerous. When I asked Randy why he did it, he said
it was more fun than a car. We didn't send him to college to look
for ways to have fun. What do we do about the motorcycle? And
how do we prevent him from spending money like this in the
future?

Randolph

All Right, Randolph,

Whose name was the car title in? If it was in your name,
he would have no right to sell it. So, in the future, you should
keep a major purchase in your name. Your money. Your name.
(I don't remember if I did this when I bought my kids' cars but
I should have.)

Good news. Since you're supporting him, you have the
right to give and to take away. Take away the damn motorcycle. He'll hate you for it, but not forever. You'll hate yourself
if Randy Jr. gets in an accident and you didn't do anything
about it.

I heard a story about a college kid and a motorcycle not long
ago. He's a man now and lucky to have lived. When he was in
school, he decided to visit someone, probably a girlfriend at
another school. He started out on his bike and it started to
snow. In his young mind, he decided to push ahead rather
than go back. (Obviously he was thinking with his body parts,
not his mind.) He ended up skidding into a snowbank and
spending the night packed in ice.

You also wrote that you didn't send him to college to look
for ways to have fun. I agree with you. You worked hard to
pay for his education and he owes it to you to work hard to get
it. Young college students away from home for the first time
feel their freedom and sometimes go overboard. Their brains
and reasoning powers haven't fully developed yet. Don't
worry. All the good lessons and morals you taught him while

he was growing up, he won't forget. I think you can count on him being a decent person.

Gail, who obviously despises motorcycles

First, the issue of whether Randy had the right to sell the car. Either the car is Randy's, in which case he can sell it, or the car is owned by Randolph, and Randy is the designated user of the vehicle and he may not sell it. It seems to me that Randy must have had the title documents, so I surmise that Randolph at least implied it was Randy's car.

When we give our kid a car, we should clarify who owns it, who maintains it, who pays for the registration and insurance, and who has the right to sell it. Kids sometimes want to leave the car ownership ambiguous because then they can believe they own it without taking full responsibility for its costs. Parents sometimes want to leave the car ownership ambiguous, because they can give a car but think they still have control over the driver. The ambiguity speaks to neither the parent nor the child wanting to fully separate.

In fact, we should clarify ownership of all the stuff we send our kids to college with—cars, microwaves, televisions, computers, etc. Are they on loan and do we have plans for them after college or are they gifts and so the property of the student?

Now, the issue of the motorcycle. My impression is that Randy, the exceptional student, wants to experiment with a new persona— less button-downed, wilder, perhaps; perhaps less like his father. This kind of identity experimentation is age appropriate for the college student.

Obviously, we don't want our college students to do anything potentially harmful to themselves, whether it's driving a car unsafely or drunk, doing drugs, or, as Randolph and Gail believe, riding a motorcycle.

What can Randolph do? Gail, I think Randy's over eighteen and therefore not a minor, which means that Randolph can't legally take the motorcycle. But he can go to his neighborhood police station, get information about motorcycle accidents, laws, and safety, and respectfully pass it on to Randy. He can also strongly voice his hopes that Randy ride safely and with good judgment. He can tell Randy his concerns without getting into a power struggle or being condescending or infantilizing. In other words, Randolph should treat Randy like an adult who made a personal choice, so the motorcycle doesn't become Randy's fight for independence. A few times of riding in the heat, the rain, and perhaps the snow and Randy may be ready to trade back to a more comfortable car.

As to the rest of Randolph's letter, I don't object to college students having fun, provided they fulfill the expectations for grades and career planning. As far as Randy's spending is concerned, Randolph and his son can make an expense budget and Randolph can send the money agreed upon. But he can't control how Randy spends the money he gets for selling his property.

Susan

Philosophy Major

Dear Gail and Susan,

My daughter Leeanne has decided to major in philosophy. When I asked her what she was planning to do with that major, meaning what kind of career she was thinking about, she said she wasn't. She just liked philosophy and would worry about a career after she graduated. When I told my husband, he hit the roof. Isn't Leeanne being cavalier with our money? Do we have a say in what she majors in?

Serena

Serena with a Husband Who Hit the Roof,

You don't have a say in what your daughter majors in. I imagine there was a time in the way distant past—and by the past I mean anything prior to 1967—when a parent might have been able to speak to a person connected to the university that they sent their child to. Those days are long gone.

Every parent I know whose kid majored in philosophy had a minor nervous breakdown about it. They saw what you saw, that their child wasn't prepared to have a career. Cheer up, Serena. Since your daughter is still in school, here's what you can do: Give Leeanne a reality check. Get the Help Wanted section from a major newspaper. Prove to your daughter that there are no jobs in what she's majoring in. I showed my adorable, college-bound children the Help Wanted section in the *New York Times* before they left for school. There they could easily see what jobs there were for college graduates. So in a way, it wasn't me telling them, it was the *Times* telling them. Then I told them they could be an artist if they did brain surgery as a hobby.

> Gail, who's pretty smart about these things

Gail, to my mind the problem isn't that Leeanne wants to major in philosophy. It's true that you can't get a job as a "philosopher," and that there are very few jobs teaching philosophy. However, philosophy is a good major for law school as well as other graduate programs. For me Leeanne's problem is her refusal to anticipate her future until after college. She wants to go along day to day like a young child.

Gail, back in our day, a liberal arts degree alone would get you a job. The world has changed a lot since we went to school. Now jobs require special preparation. Students need to plan ahead. Despite that reality, there are college students who drift through four years without appropriate career goals or a good plan for after graduation. These kids are more likely to move home, because they have resisted the next developmental step: choosing their adult work life.

I know that deciding on an occupation can be daunting for a college student. He can legitimately argue that with his limited experience, he can't know what he wants to do for the rest of his life. However, life often requires that we make decisions without knowing the future.

A college student should make the best choice he can about a career and adjust later if he has to. College is the time for learning to take on an adult way of thinking, which includes anticipating and planning for the future.

Serena and her husband should make the expectation of completing this task clear to Leeanne. After hearing what her parents have to say, Leeanne may think differently. But if she continues to have difficulty with this developmental step, they should suggest she see her academic adviser and/or a counselor at her school's student health services.

Susan

Probation Problem

Dear Gail and Susan,

I have a very short question. Cutting to the chase, my son Arlen's college grades are awful, and not because he couldn't do the work. He was put on probation. Should we penalize him in any way for goofing off? Do we continue to send him the same amount of spending money we used to?

Nelson

Please, Nelson,

You didn't have a very short question. You had two questions and they're complicated. However, I'm going to keep my answers short. When a college student goes on probation, it's a shock to him and his parents. You can punish a kid in high school by taking away privileges. Unless your son lives at home, it's impossible to do that. First, Nelson, I would write him a very serious letter explaining that he has to get on board and that if he flunks out you're not going to send him to another school and that he'll have to get a low-level job and move out. Make it a letter in an envelope with a stamp—not an e-mail. E-mails are too casual. Then I would warn him that you're going to send him less money. He should only receive money for necessities. The two of you can work out that budget. Scare him. That's what he needs.

Gail, who hates being scared

Gail, we don't know if this is Arlen's first semester and he is having trouble adjusting to the demands of college courses. If so, Nelson should advise him to see his academic adviser. If Arlen is further along in school and this is a sudden change, he may be struggling over picking a major or a breakup with his girlfriend, or he may have gotten into drugs, in which case he should see a counselor at his school's student health services.

That being said, probation is serious. It's a wake-up call. If Arlen doesn't heed it, he will be thrown out. Nelson should let the college system work and not add any penalties to the situation.

Regarding money: If Nelson is financing trips to Bermuda or online gambling, he should stop. But if he is sending Arlen reasonable spending money for food and books, then nothing should change.

However, I would certainly encourage Nelson to warn Arlen that if he is not in school, he is on his own financially. And Nelson should follow through with cutting Arlen off if he is kicked out.

Susan

Private Grades

Dear Gail and Susan,

My daughter's college won't tell us her grades and she won't, either. We have no idea how she's doing—if she's doing well or in danger of flunking out. Iris says that she's an adult and has the right to privacy about her grades. But my husband and I think that if we're paying, we have rights, too . . . to know if our money is being squandered. We are stymied and angry about this situation, but feel stuck.

Ethel

My Dearest Stuck,

The '60s (which were strange partially because they started in the late '60s and ended around 1977) brought many advancements and some aggravation. Colleges used to send grades to parents. Then thousands of students did sit-ins in the halls of administration buildings because they were fighting for student rights. One of the rights they got was privacy about grades. Personally I think when kids do well, they're proud to show their parents their grades.

Still, you're the parent and if you feel you should know your daughter's grades, insist upon it. I believe that when dealing with college kids, money not only talks, it screams. You can send more to reward her or less to deprive her. Child psychologists think the reward system is more effective than punishment. I disagree because some children, especially boys, especially one of mine, needed very little and never reacted to my taking things away. When I was in school, I would have been devastated to have my allowance cut.

Sorry, Gail

Iris makes an interesting argument about the right to privacy, but like all rationalizations, it sounds good but is simply wrong. Parents pay for their kid to go to college as an investment in their child's future. An investor is entitled to regular reports about the progress of his investment. Iris should therefore produce her grades. If she refuses, her parents have the right to withdraw their money and invest it elsewhere.

Susan

Bart's Assistant

Dear Gail and Susan,

My son is a freshman in college. His name is Bart. Bart feels a little in over his head. A lot of it is my fault. I used to help Bart with his school projects and papers. I actually liked doing it and it meant he got good grades. I knew that he could do the work, but because he was always a high-energy kid, he was somewhat disorganized and a real procrastinator. So I helped him focus and plan. Well, now he's in college with the same problems. He called me to ask if I would do some research for his paper in anthropology. The subject interests me, so I wouldn't mind. My husband says that I shouldn't, that Bart needs to learn to do his own work. But I got him used to my help. Can I just cut him off now that the stakes are higher? His grades matter even more now than they did before, if he wants to get into a good professional school or get a good job.

Corinne

Dear Bart's Assistant,

Who went to high school, you or Bart? Who's going to college, you or Bart? Who will go to graduate school, you or Bart? When our children are young, it's important to teach them good skills. Parents, by supervising homework, can teach their children how to focus, plan, and organize, and you did that. But finally it's important to let go so that our children can do these things on their own. Your husband is right. (I love when they are. It makes my job easier.) You, Corinne, have not let go, and Bart hasn't, either. However, if he has any ability or memory, he knows what he has to do. He's lazy.

About his grades mattering even more now than they did before, that's his problem. Get it? Either he does the work or he doesn't get into a good professional school. Maybe he's better off in a simple job, one where his mother does not have to come to work with him.

If you want to study anthropology, why don't you go back to school? I'll bet Bart won't help you.

Gail, who didn't like doing homework

There are three issues here. One is Bart's problem with disorganization and procrastination. Rather than do his work for him in high school, Corinne should have sent him to a class that taught him how to study and write papers. Rather than do Bart's research in college, Corinne should suggest that Bart talk to his academic adviser to locate a similar class at college.

The second issue comes up often with parents. Corrine says it's her fault and because she got Bart used to her help, she can't ever withdraw it. Nonsense! Whenever you realize that you've done the wrong thing with a kid, apologize and stop doing it. Of course Corinne can cut him off.

The third issue is Bart and Corinne's mutual delusion. Bart doesn't want to take responsibility and accept and deal with his limitations. Corinne doesn't want to let go and accept Bart's real capabilities. If they both don't stop mythologizing Bart's capacity, they are in for a rude awakening when Bart gets out into the real work world.

Susan

Finding Ira

Dear Gail and Susan,

My son Ira has completed two years of college. He did well, but now he has to declare a major and has no idea what he wants to do with his life after school. Ira thinks that taking a year off to travel will give him the time and opportunity to "find himself" so he can decide on a career path. Is that a good idea? And what about the finances of it? It's not as though it would substitute for a year of college. We would still have to pay for the remaining two years after he found himself.

Greta

Dear Ira's Mom,

Some children don't know what they want to do by the time they're required to declare a major and they're frightened by their inability to choose. They have to choose anyway. A friend of mine told her children to choose premed or prelaw and she very clearly stated they didn't have to become a doctor or a lawyer, but that one day they might want to. That tactic sounds good to me. They would at least have a good education.

Tell Ira that if he doesn't find himself, he should find himself a job or find himself in the military. Traveling won't make him focus on himself and I've seen that most children who leave school don't go back.

Most of us feel obligated to get our children educated, but we're not obligated to send them traveling. If you can afford it, send yourself to Europe, but wait until the dollar is more stable.

> Gail, who's right once again

"Finding himself"—Gail, what does that really mean? It implies that Ira is lost and confused about how to proceed. Okay, in other words, he doesn't know how (or want) to move on to the next stage of life, which is deciding what career college is going to prepare him for. Can a year of travel make a difference? Two months in Europe with his girlfriend and the next nine months hanging out on Greta's couch won't help Ira move on. Is the year off then just a delaying tactic?

My point is that at this stage of a young adult's life—Ira is at least twenty, maybe older—he should be thinking, investigating, and planning, not drifting and hoping for inspiration.

I would like to see the young adult who is uncertain about his career choice explore fields of study and work. Greta can suggest that Ira take some courses in subjects he might be interested in. Also, colleges have alumni internships whereby a student can spend a summer working in a field he is considering.

> *Susan*

Gerald, the Sloppy

Dear Gail and Susan,

It is summertime and I am tearing my hair out. My son Gerald is home from college. Actually, he isn't home, except sometimes to sleep (but not always), to eat when he's hungry and doesn't have an offer for a meal elsewhere, to get money when he needs it, and to mess up his room. When I ask him to tell me when he'll be home or to commit to being here for dinner, he gets very irritated. He says I'm treating him like a child.

I understand that he lives his own, independent life at college where he can come and go as he pleases, but we're not just a rooming house with kitchen privileges. Should I just let him do as he wants or does he have some responsibility to us? I told Gerald I was writing to you. He said something about your both being mothers, so not exactly credible, but you are to me. Please advise.

Georgia

Dear Summer-Aggravated Parent,

First of all, I want to thank you for finding me credible. It's the most wonderful compliment coming from a stranger.

Summertime is a fabulous time for college kids and a nightmare for their parents, unless you have any of those extraordinary offspring who come home, get a job, keep their room clean, and report about their whereabouts. That's very rare, if not completely nonexistent. It only happens when parents and their children have an understanding of what is going to happen over the summer, before the summer. You should have told him that he had to get a job, be clean, and show up. You'll tell him next year.

Your perception of why college students cause chaos on vacation is perfect. When they're independent, they can do whatever they want. They choose to be messy and irresponsible. My sons were in the same fraternity, and you can't believe what it was like. They cleaned it all up every September and messed it all up during the rest of the year. I had to repeat to myself over and over again that someday it would be their wives' problem and eventually it was.

As far as telling you when he'll be home, or committing to dinner, you're going to have to tell him that you're not running a boardinghouse, and when he screams and says you're treating him like a child, tell him it's because that's how he behaves. If you can sit him down long enough, explain that people who are living together have a responsibility to one another. If he balks at this, do an intervention. Have the whole family surprise him, preferably early on a Sunday morning when he's still in bed. Talk about how he's behaving and why it's important to be part of his family. Don't stop talking until he gets it.

Gail, who knows a lot of people who went
through this and lived to tell about it

If you invited an adult friend to visit and he hardly spoke to you, raided your refrigerator, scattered his clothes, didn't communicate where he was going or when he was coming back, and asked for money on top of it, you would never invite him again. But Gerald, who does all of the above, will be invited for every summer and holiday because it's his "family home."

The problem, it seems to me, comes from not clearly focusing on the college years, including summers, as a transitional time for the whole family. Gerald is transitioning from being financially dependent and living in the family home to supporting himself and living in his own abode. The family is transitioning from being fully responsible for its children to facing an empty nest and letting go. Both Georgia and Gerald need to accept that things will be different from the way they were before college began.

It's a myth that Gerald "lives his own, independent life" at college, because he does not pay the bills. True independence means you support yourself entirely. Georgia and Gerald need to recognize and accept that the kid is still dependent on his parents, and with that dependence comes responsibility. The areas Georgia should discuss and decide about with her son are curfew, family obligations, paying for personal expenses, maybe doing chores, and calling when he'll be late.

Likewise, Georgia can't expect family life to be exactly as it was; it needs to be redefined. Gerald does live a more independent life in college than he did when he was in high school. Parents should acknowledge the change and agree to more freedoms. Perhaps Gerald will not be required to attend daily family meals or all the family outings.

Before summer and the return home of the college student, the family should discuss requirements, expectations, responsibilities, and freedoms, including whether the student is expected to work and what he is financially responsible for.

If Gerald balks, Georgia might remind him that after he is eighteen, she is not legally required to provide him a home.

Susan

Homesick

Dear Gail and Susan,

My daughter Rita is in her freshman year at college and she's homesick. She calls every day, sometimes two or three times, often crying. She says she likes the other students and her classes, but she misses her dog, her room, her high school friends, and us. (We come last on her list.) My husband and I are so worried about her that if she doesn't call, I call her. I just can't wait to hear that she's okay. I've found that wherever I am and no matter what I am doing, I am listening for my phone to ring. I've even thought of telling her to drop out and come home and put us all out of our agony. But in my more rational and hopeful times, I'm not sure that's the right thing to do or that I am doing the right thing by calling. I'm so wrapped up in my mommy feelings that I'm not thinking straight. Can you straighten me out?

Meredith

Dear Mommy,

Yes, I can straighten you out. Unfortunately, I can't straighten your daughter out and she seems to be a mess. College freshmen who are away from home for the first time in their lives might have an adjustment problem, but they're old enough to survive.

If only there were no cell phones, like when I went to college, and one called home once a week because it was long distance and expensive, things would be different. Cell phones are one of the main reasons the ties don't get cut when kids go away. I know you're worried and I know nothing will take your mind off that worry. So here's the solution. Tell your daughter that you have heard her. Tell her you understand what she's feeling, but she has to stay where she is for at least another semester. Then if she wants, she can transfer to another school close to home. Tell her that there will be work involved because she'll have to apply to college again. She'll have to get her transcripts and write all those essays. That alone may discourage her. Make sure she knows that if she leaves school and doesn't transfer, she'll go to work and not live at home. She'll have to take her dog with her.

The best thing that you could do right now is try to wean her. Try accepting her calls three times a day; then, ten days later, just two times; and then, another ten days later, only once a day. Don't call her more than a couple times a week. You can't wait to hear if she's okay, but I'm here to tell you she is okay. Millions of freshman have survived college and she will, too.

By the way, Tracey Ullman and I wrote a sketch for her Showtime program, *State of the Union*, that was exactly this situation. A college student who chose to go to school in the Northeast, and then hated it, calls her mother in sunny San Diego constantly and her conversation always begins with, "Mom, I am sooooo cold." She wants to come home. You are not alone.

Gail, who survived NYU

Anxiety is catching. With each phone call, Meredith and Rita transmit separation anxiety back and forth. But Meredith has some insight into the situation. She is correct in assessing that the calling is making it worse. Both mother and daughter have to deal with the separation. Meredith needs to face her empty nest and begin to build a new life that's not dependent on her daughter. Rita needs to push herself to get over her homesickness by getting involved at school. Meredith should explain the problem and the solution to her daughter. They can set up a once-a-week check-in calling time when they talk about their new experiences. If Rita cannot manage without help, Meredith should suggest she make an appointment to see a counselor at her school's student health services.

Gail, personally I wouldn't mention to Rita that she can leave school. Of course it's always an option. But knowing she has that out will not help her tackle and master the task in front of her.

Susan

Nate's Money

Dear Gail and Susan,

My son Rex is a college junior. Lately he has been calling to say he's short of money. It happens once or twice a month. He didn't do this the first two years of school, so I'm wondering why his expenses have so dramatically increased. The first two times he asked, I just sent him a check, but now I'm not sure that I did the right thing. I don't want to compound the problem, whatever it is, by sending more money. I am told that you women know about adult children and money. I would appreciate your advice.

Nate

Dear Not Sure,

You've come to the right place. We do know about adult children and money and I'm glad you appreciate our advice. I entitled this "Nate's Money" because your money is yours, Nate. You have the right to know what all your son's purchases are about.

I hope my older son doesn't kill me for telling this story. When he was a college freshman, he got a new hobby . . . jumping out of planes. He didn't tell me about it. I found out from my friend's son, who squealed on him. I told my son that I had to know what he was writing checks for, and from that point on, he let me know how he was spending his money and there was no more jumping out of planes.

Before you send Rex another dime, you're going to have to insist that your son tell you what he's spending money on. Also, you're not going to take his word for it. You need receipts. I wasn't born to alarm you but you've got to realize that he may be spending money on drugs. It's not easy to hear this, but one of the signs that a child is doing drugs is his need for more money, especially if there's a dramatic increase.

I hope I'm wrong.

Gail, who's always looking at the worst possible scenario

Clearly Rex's expenses have increased. The question is why. Does he need money for lab equipment, a poker stake, or, as you suggest, Gail, drugs? As Nate realizes, he should not just send a check. The burden should be on Rex to provide a detailed accounting of his expenses with a clear explanation for the increase in need. Then Nate can decide whether the budget change is one he wants to pay for.

Remember, your children are not independent if they are relying on you for money. And if you're investing money, you have the right to know what it's being used for.

Susan

Pete's Payments

Dear Gail and Susan,

My son wrote me a letter. I knew when it arrived, he was in trouble. He never writes, at least not letters with fully spelled words. You probably guessed it. Pete ran his credit card bill up to ten thousand dollars! I can't believe it! I've been so proud that he hasn't asked me for money, but now I know why. And what dumb credit card company would give a twenty-year-old a ten-thousand-dollar credit limit? You don't have to answer that question. My real question is, do I pay off his credit card and then ask him to pay me back over time? The credit card company is charging astronomical interest, so Pete can only make the minimum payment, which means he'll never pay it off. This would be a one-time loan.

Stan

Dear I Can't Believe It,

First, I'm going to answer the question you told me I didn't have to answer. Credit card companies send credit cards to college students because they figure if their parents can afford to send them away to school, they can afford to pay their credit card bills. It's disgusting and harmful. Students have committed suicide over the bills they incurred.

Now to your real question. If you can afford to pay off his bill, do it. Then sit down with Pete and work out a very precise schedule of repayment. Tell him he's going to have to get a job during the school year as well as during the summer. Plus, he can cut down on his expenses, which will cut down on your expenses. He's just going to have to give up his lavish lifestyle, the one that got him into trouble in the first place. Ten thousand dollars has nothing to do with necessities. He must be into buying stereo equipment or worse.

I love that you said it would be a one-time loan, because it's not a good idea to lend money to your children. They somehow feel it's wrong of you to want the money back, especially if they have to sacrifice anything to pay you.

I almost forgot. Take the card back and cut it up in front of him. It'll feel good.

I'm sorry this happened to you, Stan—Gail

Gail, there are two serious issues here. One is Pete's inability to budget and delay gratification. The second is his not facing problems. He had a problem when he owed several hundred dollars he couldn't pay.

I urge Stan to either send Pete to a competent financial person for review of the charges and an assessment of the problem or to do the analysis himself. After Stan has a report, he will know how Pete got into trouble. In any case, Pete needs strong and detailed counseling on fiscal responsibility and budgeting.

Since Stan has not said he can't afford to bail his son out, I assume that he has the money to pay the bill. Generally, I do not recommend giving loans to financially reckless children. So, if Stan decides to retire the debt, I suggest he make it a gift. Then he can require that Pete work during school and summers to contribute to his education as a way of being responsible for his credit card fiasco.

Susan

Eric's E-mail Mama

Dear Gail and Susan,

My son Eric and I e-mail or text two or three times a day at least. It was fun until I realized that Eric is spending way too much time on e-mail. He should be going to class and paying attention, studying, getting to know his classmates. And maybe it's not just me he's e-mailing. Maybe he's e-mailing everyone he knows, which means . . . I don't even want to think what it means. What can I do? I'm not there. I can't police him.

Janice

Well, Janice,

Thank you. You answered your own question. You aren't there and you can't police him. Why don't you say in your next e-mail to him that you hope and pray that he's not spending all his time online and that he's going to class and studying like he's supposed to? Sometimes when children realize they've been found out, they clean up their act. Eric just might be one of those kids.

If you are the only one he's e-mailing, that's another story. Then he's just one more child who has to be close to home no matter where he is. Instead of sending a million short messages to him, send one long one and do that only every few days. It might be important to keep telling him you love him.

Gail, who didn't even know about computers in college

No, Janice can't police her son, but she can police herself. Janice should tell Eric that she will no longer instant-message and text with him because it is interfering with what Eric is at school for—to get an education, grow socially, and find a career path. She should make it clear that she expects him to meet those expectations.

It is true that Janice has no control over what Eric does with other texters. But when parents are seduced into behaving like adolescents, their children have no leadership to more mature behavior.

If Janice points Eric in a mature direction, Eric is more likely to go there.

Susan

Returning Zach

Dear Gail and Susan,

Almost every weekend, my son Zach comes home from college to do his laundry. Or, really, to have my wife do it, although she claims she's only helping. During the weekend Zach hangs out with a couple of high school buddies, then takes his clean laundry back to school. When I was in college, I didn't have whole weekends with no studying to do and I wanted to develop my college social life. What's up with Zach? Is this about laundry? And if it is, couldn't he be doing his laundry in the machines provided on campus? I did. I have a feeling my wife and I went wrong someplace.

Henry

Oh, Henry,

Your wife and you may have gone wrong, but the good thing is, you can immediately go right. If Zach absolutely needs to be home on the weekend, why don't you ask him if he'd like to go to a local college and live at home? He won't want to. He chose to go away to college in the first place.

I have an idea that would work, unless Zach has such an acute case of separation anxiety that he needs professional help. (I don't think that's the case, because he can stay away for most of the week. I think he has fear of doing laundry.) Next time he comes home, tie your wife to a chair and gag her. Give your son a roll of quarters and tell him to use the local laundromat.

I think it's important to mention that a lot of times, parents are afraid of losing their child's love or they're afraid of their child, period. They're scared to confront them. Your wife may feel that she could never tell her son that he isn't welcome at home whenever he wants to come. She might worry that he might feel abandoned and that he would choose not to ever come home again. (Then she will feel abandoned.) All these fears lead to parents keeping quiet. However, when problems are handled in the right way, firmly but sweetly, they can get very good results. In this case, it would be something like, "We love you very much, which is why we feel you should be spending more time at college. College is a great experience and we feel you might be missing a lot of it by coming home every weekend. Of course we're happy to see you, but we would also be happy if you were having a good time at school on the weekends. So we're asking you to stay there and see for yourself." Or you could turn his room into a den.

> Gail, who lived in a coed dorm and therefore
> wanted to stay at school on weekends

Zach is avoiding growing up by going back to his old home, his old friends, and his old dependency on his mother. Gail, if our kids are not moving forward, they are moving backward. Not a good thing.

Parents have to be careful not to collude with this developmental resistance. It's all too easy to let our kids come home on weekends without thinking about what it really means. Henry should make clear to Zach that he needs to stay in college and not come home whenever he wants to, that he has to master college life. Mastery takes time, commitment, and dealing with frustration. Zach needs to stay on campus, make new friends, try new recreational activities, and find a laundromat. If Zach cannot master his new life, Henry should suggest he find a counselor at his school's student health services to help him.

Susan

Facebook and Friends

Dear Gail and Susan,

My daughter dropped me from her Facebook "friends." I feel hurt and rejected. Even though I didn't always like what she posted, I never said a word to her, so why would she do this to me?

Alice

Open Your Eyes, Alice,

Do you think your daughter dropped you from her Facebook page because she decided she was spending too much time on the computer and she needed to study? Or . . . do you think your daughter is putting things on Facebook that she doesn't want you to see? I'm guessing it's the latter, but that's a good thing. She's becoming independent. Our children don't separate from us all at once. They do it little by little and, although you still feel a need to be attached electronically, she needs to feel free from those ties. The truth is, Facebook Friends means just that. There's no such thing as Facebook Friends and Mother.

You, Alice, feel hurt and rejected by your daughter. If you don't let go, your hurts and rejections are going to get worse. It feels as if she slammed the door in your face. She's going to close many more doors, some hard, some softly. You are going to have to accept all of these closings.

I love this question because this problem didn't even exist five years ago. I can't wait for the next electronic problem to come up. My daughter is twittering instead of studying.

Gail, whose sons one day will have to cut
the electronic cord with their kids

In my opinion, Gail, parents should be interested in but not involved in their children's college life. College should be the student's experience separate from the family.

Alice legitimately can expect her daughter to get an education, keep up her grades, develop herself socially, and plan a career. That's what Alice is paying for. Being a Facebook Friend is not Mom's right, nor should it be her expectation.

That being said, I agree with you, Gail. Alice's daughter has apparently matured since the time she invited her mother to be a friend. She has decided she has the right to a life unavailable to her mother. Alice should not feel rejected. She should feel pleased about her daughter's growth.

Susan

College and Condos

Dear Gail and Susan,

My son Tommy will be a college sophomore. He lived in the dorms his freshman year, but this year he has to live off-campus. Since his school is in an expensive city, renting an apartment will cost me a pretty penny.

One of my friends at work suggested that I buy Tommy a two-bedroom condo. He'll have a place to live, and he can rent one of the rooms to a buddy. I can have an investment that will hopefully appreciate. It seems to me a financially smart thing to do. Surprisingly, Tommy is lukewarm about the idea, although he said he would go along with it if that's what I decide, since it's my money. What do you think?

Kenny

Kenny, Sweetheart,

If you are still calling yourself Kenny and your son Tommy, there's something wrong with you. Could it be that you don't want either of you to grow up? You say renting will cost you a pretty penny; buying a two-bedroom condo won't? Let me tell you about owning a condo and expecting to rent one of the rooms. When you don't have a renter, you'll have a fifty percent vacancy to fill. And if you do, I am sure that your tenants—your son and another college student—are going to keep the place perfectly clean and neat so you can resell it. I'm sure they won't wreck anything and that you won't have any replacement costs, even when they have seventy of their friends over to watch the Super Bowl.

Why don't you ask your son why he is lukewarm about the idea? Maybe it's because he was just planning on having a place to stay rather than giving his father a big investment opportunity. Maybe he knows the fate of apartments that have college students for tenants. Maybe he is embarrassed by having a father who goes overboard. Maybe he wants to be called Tom.

It was lovely of you to write.

Gail, whose sons lived in a fraternity house

Gail, you are brilliant to have noted that Dad calls himself "Kenny" and his son "Tommy." You have also put your manicured finger on one of the important issues related to the time of life called "going to college."

Every stage of life has its developmental tasks. So what are the tasks of the college years? College students have to make good decisions about what courses to take. They have to decide what to major in. They have to make a plan that leads not only to a degree but also to the ability to support themselves. They have to figure out how to manage practical things like laundry, meals, and checking accounts; how to study amid myriad distractions, including homesickness and no parents around to nag them; and how to cope with unlimited freedom. That's a lot to master. Kenny should encourage Tommy to focus on these things and not burden him with being a landlord/property manager.

In addition, college is the time to complete the separation process. Parents and children both need to stop trying to control each other. They need to stop being dependent on one another. College should be solely Tommy's experience.

I know that in some circles parents buy their college kids condos and rationalize that it's a good investment. Paying for college is a good investment in a child's future. Buying a kid a condo may make Dad money, but it is not a good investment in his child's growth.

Cutting the ties is hard for both parents and kids. I think that Tommy is lukewarm about the condo idea because he senses that he needs to make the necessary snip. Kenny should help his son choose the grown-up path by getting out of Tommy's way. Perhaps if Kenny does his job, Tommy will call himself Tom.

Susan

My Son, the Degree Addict

Dear Gail and Susan,

Jerry, my son, got a BA in psychology, but by the time he graduated, he knew it was not the right field for him. He had minored in history, which he liked a lot, so he went on to get a PhD in history with the idea that he would teach at a university. However, there aren't many jobs out there and for the last two years he has only been able to get temporary posts. Jerry thinks that he should get an MBA, because with his history degree and a graduate business degree, he would be very marketable to a company. Needless to say, he can't afford to pay the tuition, so he has asked us to pay it. What do you think?

Bob

Bob, Who's Soon to Be a Poor Man,

Hear me loud and clear. Your son will never get out of school. Next he will think that he would really do well if he got a degree in women's studies.

He sounds smart. Why aren't you? (He must get his IQ from his mother.) Truthfully, it takes more than intelligence to be successful. You have to have drive and the ability to see things through. Your son lacks those qualities. (He probably got that from his mother, too. Maybe he isn't even your kid.)

Tell him you are finished paying tuition for him. Being an academic is like being on heroin. It's an expensive addiction. Write when he gets work.

Gail, who has a BS

We do not live in a utopia where Jerry can study whatever his heart desires and be rewarded with a job in the end. Before a college student chooses a field, he should make sure there are jobs to be had in it. Liking something is not reason enough to invest enormous sums of time and money, unless he calls it a hobby and has another source of income that comes from his real job.

Does Jerry really know that an MBA will make him more mar-ketable? For what?

But that is not really Jerry's issue, is it? Gail, did you know that you don't end adolescence until you close doors? Jerry and his parents haven't. Apparently they don't even know that they should. Jerry seems to want to remain a dependent adolescent.

Jerry's parents should close the door on supporting more school. If Jerry is serious about joining the adult world, he will get a job. There are jobs that offer training and don't require any more degrees than he already has. If, years down the road, Jerry discovers that an MBA would enhance his chances for promotion, he can at-tend at night on his own dime.

Susan

Rosalyn Is Dropping Out

Dear Gail and Susan,

I never thought I would have this problem, so I am totally un-prepared and don't know what to do. My eighteen-year-old daugh-ter Rosalyn wants to marry a twenty-eight-year-old man and drop out of college. To say I'm very upset is an understatement.

Should I try to talk her out of it—if I even could? Should I talk to the guy? I'm afraid Rozzie is setting herself up for tough times. What if the marriage doesn't last? She will have no edu-cation and be unable to support herself.

Annette

Dear Mother of a Possible Dropout,

Eighteen-year-old girls are very romantic and fall deeply in love. They can't picture themselves at thirty or forty. All they know is that it feels really good to have someone want you forever. They fantasize about the wedding and being the cen-ter of attention in a long white gown. They don't think drop-ping out of school is a terrible thing. So, Annette, you're facing a battle that you probably won't win.

There is a bright side. If your daughter gets married young, she'll have her children early, and then when they're in school, she can go back to school and get herself an education. I'm happy to report that when my son was twenty-two, he married a twenty-year-old woman who dropped out of school. Eighteen years and four children later, they're still married and my daughter-in-law just graduated from the University of Washington. Although statistics say otherwise, there are happy endings.

I think your husband should give you a nice piece of jewelry to wear to the wedding.

> Gail, who's very familiar with
> this problem

I assume Rosalyn's boyfriend is a good guy and that at twenty-eight has a job and can support her. Nothing in the letter makes me think otherwise.

Therefore, Annette can talk to the couple and offer her opinion that Rosalyn would be better served in the long run if she completed her degree. She can then ask why they have decided that Rosalyn should drop out, reminding them that it's possible to be in college and be married at the same time. Annette can even offer to continue paying for Rosalyn's education.

However, if they still don't agree that Rosalyn should stay in school, I hope that the young couple has an alternative plan that makes sense. Because Rosalyn is eighteen, Annette has no legal power to prevent her from marrying.

> *Susan*

Sorority Girl

Dear Gail and Susan,

My daughter wants to join a college sorority. I think it will adversely affect her grades. Do I have the right to forbid her to pledge?

> Leeza

Dear Wondering,

You cannot forbid your daughter to join a sorority. However, if it'll cost you extra, you can refuse to pay. Your daughter will be really pissed. You assume that a sorority will affect your daughter's grades. That's not necessarily true. Some sororities aim to have good grade-point averages. They even help each other study. She'll get a big sister who has already taken the courses she will be taking, and that can be helpful, too. Also, she'll have the feeling of belonging and the feeling of sisterhood.

Relax, Leeza. Sororities are not necessarily like the ones in stupid, disgusting movies.

Gail, who values sisterhood

Usually sororities have grade requirements and exert peer pressure on their sisters to meet them. Living in a sorority house with a house parent and rules can be less distracting than living in an apartment. So I believe that Leeza is unnecessarily worried about her daughter and a sorority. However, to reassure herself, she can talk to the house parents of the sororities her daughter is interested in.

And as you say, Gail, Leeza can refuse to pay the extra expense of a sorority and require that her daughter get a job on campus in order to make up the difference.

Susan

Leading Robbie Astray

Dear Gail and Susan,

I happily sent my son Robbie off to college. But since he's gone, I have been worried about the kind of friends he will make. My wife and I always knew the kids he hung out with. We even knew most of their parents. But now we don't know how to vet his friends. They could do drugs, be flakes, lead Robbie astray. Do you have any suggestions for making sure our son's friends are good for him?

Angus

Dear Father of Robbie,

Personally, I think you're assuming that Robbie is a flake already. Did you not raise him carefully? If you didn't, he could be led astray. When our children are little, we can choose their friends for them because we drive them to their friends' houses. We can try to keep them away from bullies. We can refuse to drive them to places where they'll be unsupervised. When they get to high school, we have a good idea of who they're hanging out with. And, as you said, we might know their friends' parents. So for eighteen years you supposedly trained them to be around decent people. If he can be led astray, he's a weak person.

> Gail, who trusted her
> kids' decisions

Presumably, before we send our children to college, they have had lots of experience in judging new people and being discriminating about the friends they make. That's why we should allow our children to have experiences outside the family circle, such as going to camp, working as a bagger in a supermarket, or selling in a department store. College shouldn't be the first time our children meet peers their parents don't know. Then, while our kids are still living with us, we have time and opportunity to judge how they make decisions and help them if they get misled. By the time our children reach college, we want them to be able to deal competently in the larger world of unknown people.

My sense is that in the past, Angus has overly controlled his son's social life, which may have limited Robbie's own development and his ability to make good choices in friends. Now that Angus has no control, he is very anxious. If that's the case, he might discuss the situation with his son, fill in what Robbie hasn't yet been taught, offer to be a sounding board if Robbie needs it, but then finally let Robbie develop himself and his own social life.

Susan

Concerned

Dear Gail and Susan,

My wife and I are concerned about our daughter Sammy, a college freshman. We have heard hair-raising stories about campus binge drinking and drugs. So far as we know, Sammy didn't do any of that in high school, but the stress and peer pressure in college can be great. Is there anything we can do to make sure our daughter doesn't get caught up in this kind of destructive behavior?

Francis

Dear Concerned,

Parents tend to be concerned about their kids getting into drugs and drinking when they go away to school. That's normal. You're overly concerned or else you wouldn't have written to us.

Parents have to have that drinking-and-drugs conversation with their kids by the time they're twelve. And those discussions should be an ongoing thing. A really serious sit-down talk about the dangers of drugs and alcohol should take place right before the child leaves for school. She'll say she's heard it before. You say, "And you'll hear it again."

There's nothing more you can do at this point. You can't be there with her, watching her every move. Just look out for certain signs, such as an increase in the amount of cash she's using, her grades, her speech pattern, and what she does when she comes home for vacation.

Drugstores have in-home drug kits. If you suspect anything, use one. Francis, this may be the first time your daughter is away from home, but she has taken the values of home with her.

Gail, who, thankfully, was needlessly concerned

If we never let our children make their own decisions, suffer the consequences of their mistakes, or cope with frustration when they are living with us, then our children might be inclined to disastrously submit to peer pressure or follow a charismatic leader down a druggie path.

But if our kids have a chance to establish their own identities and to think for themselves, they will be less likely to collapse and make self-destructive choices under the stress of college.

In addition, as you say, Gail, by this time Sammy should know a lot about the dangers of drugs and binge drinking. She should also have good ways of coping with stress and frustration.

In any case, Francis can't control his daughter's college environment and her choices. Dad will have to wait and see and take appropriate action if Sammy gets into trouble.

Susan

CHAPTER THREE

Young Adults: Living Arrangements

In order to move from adolescence to adulthood, a child must separate from his parents. He needs to get his own job, live on his own money, and live in his own home. Moving out can be exciting and challenging. And it can be fraught with anxiety for both parents and child. The child wonders if he can make it on his own. Parents feel bereft when their nest is empty. But, as with any developmental step, parents have to keep the child moving forward. Sometimes it takes a big push. Here's a true story. A twenty-two-year-old kept planning to move out of his parents' house. He found roommates. He rented apartments. He kept changing his mind and within a few days ran back home. One night he went to a show, not a traditional one. There was a psychiatrist onstage and people went up and got their problems solved, or so they thought. This young man went up and in front of a whole audience resolved his separation anxiety. Strangely, it worked. He moved out the next day. That was forty years ago and he never lived with his parents again. This is not a recommended method.

Whether parents mean it or not, inviting a child to move back home tells him that they don't approve of his leaving or at the very least that they are ambivalent about it. It's like keeping the baby bottle around when a child can drink from a glass. The growing child is tempted to go back to the bottle, because whether she says it or not, the mother is sending the message that it's okay to stay a baby. It works the same way when you invite your child to move home after college. (It can be temporary until the graduate can get settled . . . somewhere else.) The already independent kid will most likely resist the temptation, but the child who most needs help to move forward won't. And if he can't get his hands on a bottle, he'll reach for his pacifier.

So, Mom and Dad, you are going to have to keep your anxieties to yourself, be happy about his moving out, and give the move your stamp of approval. You might help him find an apartment or help him furnish it. You can offer some furniture or even a gift of first and last months' rent if he needs start-up funds. Most important, you should always send a clear message that you want him to live on his own. Then he can learn about budgeting, cleaning, repairs, rent increases, getting a mortgage, decorating, entertaining, loneliness.

There seems to be a trend today of adult children who, when there's a setback like a job loss or divorce, move in with their parents. These last words were chosen carefully because the phenomenon is more often misnamed "moving back home." The misnomer implies that the parents' home is still the kid's home, which it is not. Once a child is an adult, he does not get to call home a place he doesn't pay the mortgage on. If we agree that our goal is to facilitate our child's independence, then first we have to stop calling our home theirs. One fifty-six-year-old woman moved "back home" and her mother was in a retirement community. Better than a rest home, but not much.

Job loss is a reality. But if that's the case, why aren't more adults preparing for that possibility? The rule of thumb used to be that we needed three months' expenses in savings in case we ended up out of work. How many current parents teach their kids this rule? Sure, it's hard to save, but kids should be prepared to save for their rainy days. Young people don't think this way, because parents are all too ready to let them "move back home" as soon as the going gets rough out there.

Both parents and adult children would rather do the "move back home" thing than choose the "get any job you can to pay your rent" solution. Many young adults hold out a long time for a job commensurate with the one they lost. And they can do it because their parents have a "better" solution to offer—moving back home. Then the trouble begins. The adult child does not have the urgency to find a job. He can afford to wait for the "right" job—one that he likes, one that is narcissistically gratifying. For the child living with his parents, the right job is not defined as one that pays the bills, because his parents are financing him.

Only in an extreme emergency should you open your door. But how? Very carefully, with a carefully thought-out financial plan. Financial plan?

Yes. Let's face it, moving back home is your child's financial plan, and a financial plan needs to include specific numbers, a time frame, and periodic review. The plan should not be vague and open-ended. "I live at home until I get a job I like or until I save enough money" is not a financial plan.

An adult child should not be entitled to move into his parents' house whenever he wants to—even if he is in trouble. The "move into the parents' house" plan should not just be assumed. The adult child, after carefully going over his finances and options, should *ask* his parents if it's possible to *temporarily* move into their home. Parents should not suggest it. And if the child asks, the parents should require a financial plan that makes sense and demonstrates that the adult child is working toward getting out as soon as possible. However, if your child doesn't want to do that, suggest he join the military. In some countries it's compulsory, and after a couple of years of service, they're ready to be strong adults.

~~~~~~~~~~~~~~~~~~~~~~~~~~~~~~~~~~~~~~~

April's Day

Dear Gail and Susan,

My husband and I live in a small town. We raised our children here and have had a good life. My daughter April is graduating from college soon and I have thought about what it will be like for her to live here and I want to suggest that she move to a large city. She's young. There are more job opportunities, more people, more to do in a city, and I think she will benefit from the experience of being in a new environment. On the other hand, I worry that she won't make it on her own. Should I just keep my thoughts to myself or share them with April?

Amy

Dear "On the Other Hand" Amy,

I was so proud of the letter you sent until the very last sentence. I thought here's a mother who really cares about her daughter's life. I thought here's someone who understands that her child needs her own life. And then, at the very end, you caved. Whenever I read the words "on the other hand," I get worried. You're concerned that April won't make it on her own. Why? Is she infantile?

I know a mother who did it right. My friend grew up in a very small town in Georgia and her mother told her and her brother that they must move away after college. She wanted her children to have bigger lives than she had.

Props to you, Amy, on five-sixths of your letter. The rest? Not so much.

Gail, the truth teller

Gail, I think a little differently from the way you do about this situation. I certainly encourage a parent to make it clear to a child that she can choose where she wants to live as an adult, that it's okay to create a life that's different from her parents' life. And I hope that the parent has the conversation about life after college before graduation day arrives.

However, parents shouldn't push their child to live the life they may have wanted but never got. Our children are separate from us. Some of them authentically want to move away and some don't. Sharing knowledge is not the same as telling a child what to do. Amy can offer any information she has about living in a city with April; however, the final decision is her daughter's to make.

There's another point in this letter that I want to address. Like learning to walk, living in the adult world is a developmental step to be mastered. Just as parents encourage their children to walk— "Of course you can do it"—so should they encourage their adult children to take on living on their own. Parents should never express their anxieties about their child's ability to survive in the adult world. Therefore, Amy should not share her worries about April's making it on her own.

Susan

Apprehension Reigns

Dear Gail and Susan,

I am a single mom. For the past two years, my son Mike has lived at home with me. He's had a job but he couldn't afford to move out until now. He recently got a promotion and a raise and now makes enough money to enable him to move in with some buddies. Apartments are expensive in the city we live in. The place his friends have is in a dangerous part of the city. I can tell he's apprehensive because he's put off the move more than once. I'm apprehensive, too. Is there anything I can do or say to him?

Tina

Dear Single Tina,

You don't want your son to move out, do you, Tina? It's nice for you to have a husband substitute, isn't it, darling?

You, Tina, should get your ex or any decent father figure to talk to your son. You are too emotionally involved to do it. I believe in women's rights one hundred percent, but I also believe that men and women are different and this should be a father-son conversation, not a mother-son one. Men can get down to the cold, hard facts. Women want their sons to put on sweaters. In this case, the talk would be about how much Mike's new rent will be and if he can possibly get his buddies to move. Maybe now that Mike is joining his friends and contributing to the rent, they can live in a less dangerous part of the city. A man can have this conversation without pity, hesitation, or tears. You, however, would talk to Mike for much too long about his feelings and your feelings. If you do it, by the end of the talk both you and your son will be immobile.

I was a single mother of two boys and sometimes didn't call in the adult males in my life. I'm going to have to apologize about that. Maybe when they're around sixty.

Sorry, boys . . . and Tina—Gail

Gail, Tina implies in her letter that Mike has only two housing options: her house or living with buddies in a violent neighborhood. So I don't know if the apprehension is really about the potential danger in the city or about a single mother and her adult son separating after two years of living with each other.

The letter suggests that Mike has done no real apartment hunting. He's conveniently lived at home and now wants the convenience of moving in with guys he already knows who already have an apartment.

Tina can suggest that Mike make a realistic assessment of the danger by checking the crime rate with the police department. If the crime rate is extraordinarily high and Mike is serious about going out on his own, he has the option of finding another apartment with strangers who might become new buddies.

Susan

She's Ba-ack

Dear Gail and Susan,

My daughter Gale works in the buyers' training program at a department store and lives at home. Her father and I decided that it would make financial sense for her to live with us for a while until she can save some money. However, we decided that Gale should pay us rent. After all, she is an adult and she would have to pay a lot more if she lived in her own apartment.

We told Gale about the rent and she agreed, but so far she hasn't paid it. I know at the beginning she had clothing expenses, transforming her college wardrobe into a working one. She's been here four months. How long should we wait for her to start paying?

Sally

Dear Sally Who Doesn't Have a Clue,

Your letter tells me a lot. "Her father and I decided . . . ," and you "told Gale about the rent . . ." You sound like benevolent dictators. All three of you should have worked these things out together. Then she would have been part of the decision making and would have been more responsible.

I like that you acknowledge that your daughter is an adult. If you really believe that, have an adult conversation with her. Be specific. Decide on what day of the month rent should be paid.

P.S. Make the rent reasonable so she can pay it and buy all those clothes you can't fit into.

Don't let Gale get too comfortable—Gail

My preference is that children not find their way back to their parents' house after college. I know that it's tough, meaning expensive, in the outside world. However, that will be just as true a year from now as it is now.

Why do I think it a bad thing to move back home? Because it is all too easy for everyone to fall back into old patterns. That's what happened with Sally's family. Mom and Dad decided on the financial plan, and Gale said she agreed, but then family life kind of went back to the way it was before she left for college. If Gale were renting an apartment from a landlord, she would pay her rent on time, even if it meant forgoing the department store shopping spree. She doesn't have to when she's living at home. Mom and Dad will just wait.

I would prefer that parents give their children money to get started—for clothes, first and last months' rent, furniture, whatever—rather than a key to the front door and the kid's old room back.

However, what if, like Sally's Gale, your kid has moved home after college? If you reinstate things the way they were, your child will regress, guaranteed, as Gale has. She is behaving like a teenager, spending her money on clothes and depending on her parents for room and board.

Gale and her parents need to agree upon some clear rules and responsibilities, perhaps paying rent, paying for her own phone, etc., with a date specified for the end of the "lease." They might have a contract. In other words, set it up to look like the real adult world that Gale is headed for.

Parents think they are providing support and love when they offer a temporary free ride. However, the message the child gets is that she can't make it on her own, that the world is more than she can handle. If the family system continues to allow Gale to act like a teen, she will have less confidence that she can make it in the adult world and will find it harder and harder to move out.

Susan

Stop! Thief!

Dear Gail and Susan,

This is going to sound crazy, but my daughter Bethany stole furniture from me. Here's how it happened. When she was moving out to her own apartment, she asked if she could have the furniture from her room. I told her no, because I was planning to use her room as a guest room. When I got home, everything was gone. Should I report it to the police? What should I say to Bethany? Should I demand the furniture be returned?

Helene

Helene, the Pissed,

Forget the police. They have better things to do than listen to a mother and daughter arguing about a mattress and a lamp.

This is exactly the type of situation that can separate a mother and daughter for years, if not forever, especially if you call in the cops. Yes, I know. There was more stuff than a bed and a lamp, like a dresser and maybe even sheets, but don't you dare call 911.

Often when they're first going off on their own, kids need to have something from the room they grew up in. It's comforting. However, I don't think your daughter was right to take the furniture once you told her not to. You can demand that your furniture be returned. But since Bethany stole it in the first place, I doubt that she'll bring it back.

How about a negotiation? Can she keep the quilt and the bed if she brings back the rest? The quilt will remind her of home and you can feel you're giving her some warmth when she's out in the world.

I'm not saying that Bethany isn't a little bitch. But think about what you really need back. You may have the means to purchase some new items for your guest room. If this is possible, do it. Keep a relationship going with your daughter and be happy that she's out of the house, even though some of the house went with her.

Gail, whose kids have furniture of hers

It seems to me that Bethany is having a hard time separating. Although she moved out, she created a situation that will either sever the tie with her mother or start a long-term argument.

Gail, moving out is a big developmental event. It involves loss—of the dependent relationship, of a way of life. There is no indication that Helene is participating in the process. In fact, Helene is pretty cold to Bethany's leaving home.

What Bethany did is clearly wrong and, technically, a crime. But in this case, I wouldn't suggest reporting it to the police. Bethany is acting out. Her mother's coldness and seeming indifference felt like a bigger loss than just the loss of moving out of her family home and into her own apartment and life. Bethany wants something from her mother, so she takes something, making her mother a loser, too.

I'd go a step further than you did, Gail, and suggest that Helene offer some or all of the furniture as a going-away gift. And, more important, encourage Helene to show interest in Bethany's new apartment and new life. In other words, make this developmental step a pleasant milestone that doesn't mean that Helene or Bethany has to lose the relationship.

By the way, Gail, how do you think Bethany got the furniture moved out?

Susan

It's simple. She slept with some guy who has a truck.

Rock-and-Roll Blues

Dear Gail and Susan,

My son Darren had a brief (very brief) success with a rock band. If I told you the name of it you wouldn't recognize it. They made a CD, which they paid for themselves, but then everything

fizzled. Now Darren is depressed and doing nothing. I think he
feels that he can only pursue a career that makes him feel "special." An ordinary job, he thinks, makes him ordinary. Darren
sleeps on his friend's couch and his friend's mother feeds him.
How can I help him?

Ivy

You Know What, Ivy?

You can help him by thinking of a job that will make Darren
feel a little special. I once suggested to a friend who was having
a similar problem with her son that her son become a DJ. He
liked the idea; he started out very small but got a reputation
and got to DJ in bigger and better clubs.

Basically what I'm saying is you can only help him in a
practical way by suggesting something specific. If there are no
clubs where you live, you're going to have to think of an idea
as brilliant as the one I thought of.

At least his friend's mother is feeding him so you don't
have to.

Be brave—Gail

*How can Ivy help? In my opinion, by not rescuing Darren the
way his friend's mother has. By not giving him money. By expecting that he support himself.*

*Little children want to feel special, and they are, to their par-
ents. But adults know that they are also ordinary human beings
who need to be financially independent, responsible, and contribute
to society.*

*Ironically, Gail, adults who are afraid of being ordinary often
end up less successful than they could be. They are so caught up
with how the job looks and reflects on them that they do not focus on
developing their skills and building their careers. Like Darren, they
give up and become depressed when life doesn't go the way they fantasize it should.*

Being independent should be the goal. But Darren can't feel good about being independent unless Ivy makes it clear that independence is a value she believes in. Parents think that by rescuing their adult child, they are showing love. But what they are really communicating to their child is that Mom and Dad don't think he can do it alone and that they don't want him to be truly independent.

Susan

Moved Back Home

Dear Gail and Susan,

My son Eric was living with us for a little while after college. He finally got a good job and moved into his own apartment. That was two and a half years ago. He just lost that job and has moved back in with us. He's depressed. How can I help him?

Robin

Dear Supermom,

If you, Robin, can get Eric out of his depression, someone should hand you a psychology degree immediately. He needs therapy. But until you get him to a doctor's office, what you can do is help him get his work situation under control. I know he knows what to do but . . . remind him, gently. It means sending out résumés, networking at LinkedIn, and going on Yahoo!, HotJobs, and other job-search websites. Remind him it's not a one-time thing. It has to be done every day. At least he'll be proactive and not feel that he can't do anything about his situation.

We get depressed when our kids get depressed. Try to smile for his sake. Also, remind him that he's not alone and that this is a difficult time to find work and other kids are in the exact same situation he is. It's not easy, but nothing ever is.

Gail, who has told her sons that if they ever need to, they can move back in with her

Sometimes a safety net becomes a trap. Moving in with parents can sometimes make the problem for our child worse. Eric not only lost his job but he also lost his apartment, his independence, his adult identity. No wonder he's depressed. He thought he was launched and now he's right back where he started—at home with Mom and Dad. Moving in with parents should not be the only option if a kid gets in trouble. It's often not the best option.

But here Eric is home and depressed. I agree, Gail, that he should be looking for a job, every day in any way he can. However—and here's where parents have to take charge—Eric should not be allowed to give up his life and become a catered-to, dependent invalid who can do nothing but look for a job. There should be conditions for his room and board. For instance, he could be in charge of all the grocery shopping, the gardening, taking the younger kids to school—all of which get him into the world with people and making an adult contribution. The more his parents treat him like an invalid, the more helpless and depressed he will become.

I strongly recommend that parents and their children have a plan for dealing with losing a job that does not require that the kid move back home. How about keeping on hand three months' expenses in savings, getting unemployment insurance, trying to move in with roommates, and getting a temporary job to make ends meet? Life brings its challenges and we have to cope with them. Going back to Mom and Dad should not be a child's only coping tool.

Certainly, if Eric is too depressed to do any of the above, he should see a doctor for medication and therapy.

Susan

Living with Us

Dear Gail and Susan,

Our daughter Erin recently graduated from college and is living with us. Some nights she doesn't come home, which upsets my husband and me. We have tried to reason with her and get her to understand that we worry, but she insists that she's an adult and can do what she wants, and that our worrying is our problem. The situation is causing my husband and me stress. Can you tell us what to do?

Lori

Dear Mother of an Inconsiderate Child,

Your daughter claims she's an adult but she's not acting like one. Even if she were out of the house and had a roommate, it would be polite to tell that person when she won't be home. Which brings me to a difficult suggestion: kick her out. If she's the adult she thinks she is, she shouldn't be living with her mommy and daddy. You've already tried everything else. So give her a warning that if she doesn't comply with your rules, she has to be out of the house in a month. That'll give her time to find a place. And it also might scare her enough to be considerate to you and your husband. Once she's out, you'll have much less stress. It'll be much easier when you don't know about every minute of Erin's life.

Gail, who hates to tell you this because she doesn't want to upset you, but whose sons are perfect

No child of any age gets to make the rules in her parents' house—ever. Only parents have that prerogative. A twenty-one-year-old only gets to make the rules in her own house, the one she's paying for. If Mom and Dad have invited her to live with them temporarily to help her out financially, she needs to accede to any rules they set. Or she can find another solution to her problem. Adults accept rules and boundaries. A twenty-one-year-old in the military is an adult and she doesn't set the rules. Two-year-olds and adolescents erroneously think that rules and limits are negotiable. If Lori and her husband negotiate, they are colluding with keeping Erin an adolescent.

Susan

Bringing Girlfriends Home

Dear Gail and Susan,

My son Derek lives with us. He has a job, but he wants to save money. We charge him rent, but not as much as he would have to pay for an apartment. The problem is that he brings his girlfriends home to spend the night. He says he's paying rent, so he's entitled. Is he?

Forrest

Listen Up, Forrest,

If you were running a boardinghouse, you would have rules and people would have to comply, even though they were paying rent. In a way, you are running a boardinghouse, with one boarder who thinks he can do anything he wants. It's your roof and he's under it. Tell him that under the circumstances, if he wants to spend the night with his girlfriends, he should have his own place. By the way, if he's bringing more than one girl to your home, he can't call them girlfriends. He doesn't have one.

Gail, who would never be a girlfriend to somebody
who had another girlfriend at the same time

Forrest should read my answer to Lori, above. I reiterate—in Forrest's house, he makes the rules. Paying rent entitles Derek to whatever his parents decide the rent entitles him to. The people who own the house get to set the rules of the contract. If Derek doesn't like the deal, he can live elsewhere.

Susan

Fanny Speaks Up

Dear Gail and Susan,

My mother Fanny is ill and lives with us. She is constantly telling my twenty-two-year-old son Lee, who also lives with us, what to do. I am going crazy. Can you help me?

Vivian

Dear Going Crazy,

It seems your mother has to live with you. Your twenty-two-year-old son doesn't. One day, hopefully soon, he will move out. Grandma may even help the process. Who wants to live with nagging?

By the way, you're never going to get Fanny to keep quiet.

Gail, who hopes she doesn't talk too much

Here are three generations living under one roof who seem to have nothing to do but be involved with each other. If Fanny is capable enough to tell her grandson what to do, why isn't she seeing friends, going to the senior center, belonging to the garden club? And why is a twenty-two-year-old at home enough to drive his mother crazy? Why isn't he in school, doing homework, or working? And what does Vivian do all day? She should have a job, volunteer for a charity, or belong to a women's group.

Vivian is creating a problem she can complain about. She wants us to tell her how to control her mother and her son. She can't control them but she can have expectations of her mother and son to have appropriate adult lives. And Vivian should develop her own life and stop being a martyr.

Susan

Wow, Susan, you took care of the whole family. Bless you. Gail.

Miranda Is Responsible

Dear Gail and Susan,

Our daughter Miranda is a very responsible girl. She got a good job after college and moved into her own apartment. Unfortunately, she just lost her job. She came to us to discuss what she should do. Should she give up her apartment and move in with us until she gets another job? Should we lend her money to live on rather than have her move home? We would like your advice, because we all want to do the right thing.

Peyton

Dear Father Who Wants to Do the Right Thing,

I have an idea. Why don't you give your daughter three months' worth of living expenses? Give. Not lend. When a person loses her job, she's concerned enough about money without having to worry about paying it back. If after three months she doesn't have another job, she'll have to move back in with you. If she's as responsible a girl as you say she is, she'll be looking very hard for another job. If she does have to move in with you, you won't have her with you for long.

I like you, Peyton.

Gail, who is on a "family first campaign"

P.S. Susan, we both seem to be on a "three-month" kick. Do you know why?

My understanding, Gail, is that the waiting period for disability benefits to be paid is three months, so we were taught to always keep enough savings on hand to cover three months of expenses for a rainy day.

Now back to Miranda. I'm with you. I'm for a gift of three months' living expenses, unemployment insurance, taking in one or two roommates, and a temporary job just to make ends meet rather than suggesting that Miranda move in with Peyton and his wife. Adults need to learn other ways of coping with adversity than moving back in with their parents.

Susan

Absolute Silence

Dear Gail and Susan,

My husband and I have a problem I hope you can help us with. My son Bobby is in graduate school. We are paying the tuition but couldn't afford to pay room and board as well. So he moved back home. At night he has to study. We have a small house and he complains that the television his father and I like to watch is distracting. He says he needs absolute silence. We want to be supportive and expect Bobby to do well with his studies but we feel like unwanted guests in our own home. My husband even said the other day that maybe we should move out and let Bobby have the house. Do you have another solution? We can't afford to move.

Libby

Dear Can't Afford to Move,

Yes, I can help. I suggest that Bobby get a part-time job and move out. He may not want to work but he'll have to in order to bring peace to the family. Since he's spending all his time studying, it doesn't have to be an elaborate place. Then you and your husband can watch TV. I'm glad you do watch television because I've been a television writer for a long time now and I get residuals.

Gail, who enjoys watching television, too

Gail, I am sometimes amazed at the predicaments parents get themselves into and more amazed that they can't see the solutions. One solution for Libby's family would be for Bobby to use the library on campus to do his studying. College libraries have carrels for just that purpose. Another solution is the one you suggest. Working part-time while you are in school is not unheard of. Lots of kids have done it. So Bobby could get a job and his own place near campus.

But for me, the issue is not Bobby's graduate studies. Life does not arrange itself to accommodate unreasonable demands. And absolute silence in someone else's house is an unreasonable demand. Even if Bobby moved into his own apartment, there might be noise from the street or from other tenants. After he gets his degree and a job, will Bobby demand absolute silence from his employer?

Bobby may technically be a graduate student, but he is emotionally a tyrannical child who has not separated. Libby and her husband have capitulated to a hostile takeover. As I said, this is not about studying. This is about Bobby being a dictatorial little kid.

Being supportive does not require colluding with childish behav-

ior, yielding to unrealistic demands, or letting your child make the rules in your home. The thing about adult children is that they have options. Libby should suggest some of them to her son. Studying at the library or getting his own place are two possibilities. And then she should turn on the television and watch reruns of The Golden Girls.

Susan

Cottage on a Lake

Dear Gail and Susan,

We have a small vacation cottage on a lake. We let our son temporarily move into it while he was deciding what he wanted to do with his life. My wife and I figured he would be there for a few months, but it's been three years. We don't know how to get him out. By the way, our son did decide what he wanted to be—a poet. Are we just stuck with the situation?

Lawrence

Dear Father of a Poet,

Don't worry. Your son will make a lot of money selling poetry and then he can buy his own cottage. You're not happy with my answer, are you? Let me try again. You and your wife shouldn't have let your son be in your house for a few months. "Temporarily" should have been defined. But that boat has sailed. (You probably do have a sailboat that your son is using.)

Your son has an adult body but the brain of a seven-year-old. Children think they can be poets and artists and movie stars without knowing how they'll support themselves. The only thing he's good at is rhyming. I'm almost as angry at him as you are.

You're probably going to have to evict him. I know. You can't do that to your precious leech. So you are going to have to hide out in the woods until he leaves the cottage, pack all his things in boxes, and leave them on the front porch. And be sure to change the locks. When he comes crying to you, tell him that unless he becomes poet laureate of this country and can support himself, you're not going to be proud of him. Seven-year-olds worry about their parents being proud of them.

You're only stuck with a situation if you let yourself get stuck with a situation. This boy needs to grow up immediately. He's no Walt Whitman.

Gail, who supports artists but only
when they deserve it

I love your answer, Gail. What is it with some parents today? They seem to have such a hard time setting limits and saying no. And then they wonder why they end up with entitled, immature, unrealistic, poorly coping, dependent children.

Lawrence and his wife should put their son on notice ASAP: he needs to get his own place. If he refuses to move, then I'm with you, Gail. Pack him up and change the locks. This is not a kid who even remotely sees himself or the world realistically. He would stay forever and dream. But of course he can, because his parents are letting him.

Limits—"temporarily" is not a limit; three months is.

Boundaries—"my house is not your house" is a boundary.

No—means separateness. "I have a vacation house I pay for; you do not have a vacation house. We are separate."

Susan

The Last Hurrah

Dear Gail and Susan,

George is living with us so he can save up to get married. But in the meantime, he's having guys over every night. It's like a bachelor party around here all the time. George calls it his last hurrah before he settles down. My wife and I think we're being used. Is there anything we can do?

Patrick

Dear Being Used,

You think you're being used because you *are* being used. Your son is immature and not ready to get married. Is he going to have his buddies over every night when he does? He'll soon be divorced and wanting to live with you again. You don't say if this is a very temporary situation and if he has definite plans to move out. Does he have a date for the wedding? If he's not going to move out next week, move him out. Tell him to pick up the dirty underwear in his room before he leaves. (I'm only guessing his underwear is on the floor, but it's a really good guess.) Since he's not ready to get married, he can save up for his own place, slowly. The bum needs to be on his own for a while.

Gail, who's sorry your son is smelling up your place

Gail, this is a letter that makes me want to scream. It's from a family where the child is running the show. He's taken over his parents' house with a con. George is pretending to be a responsible man (saving to get married). Hooey! And he talked his parents into believing his charade. George is behaving like an adolescent in a fraternity house.

Patrick and his wife should see their son realistically, as an emotionally immature, entitled user. They should explain to him that there is something more important for him to do now than save money—grow up and really be responsible. They should inform him that he needs to move out and fend for himself.

Susan

CHAPTER FOUR

Work

How a child plays has a lot to do with how he works as an adult. Our generation played checkers and chess and pickup sticks, built tree houses, and put together baseball games with a group of friends on a vacant lot. We walked or rode our bikes everywhere—to school, friends' houses, or the movies. Our play forced us to take initiative, be patient, strategize, and socialize without the benefit of an organization or our parents. Our children's generation played computer games, watched television, and played soccer, baseball, and basketball—all organized and chauffeured to by adults—and they got trophies for just showing up. Their play was instantly gratifying, less autonomous, and more dependent on parental involvement and approval than ours was. Ours was way better.

Work requires giving up the pleasure principle—doing what feels good, avoiding what doesn't—for the reality principle. Work demands the ability to tolerate frustration, to solve problems, and to take pleasure in finishing projects. It also takes the ability to listen to the boss. There are very few Americans who don't have to report to a higher-up. Some of our adult children do brilliantly. They are, after all, our children. Others have difficulty. They don't want to start at the bottom, they don't respect the authority of the boss, they give up when frustrated, and they don't persist until a problem is solved. The adult who leaves a job because he's not having any fun has not given up the infantile pleasure principle. Not that work shouldn't be fun; it should be. But to work maturely, we have to get our pleasure from problem solving, completing tasks, and reaching the end game, and we shouldn't need kudos to make work meaningful.

Adolescence isn't over until we de-idealize ourselves. Young children can imagine doing anything for a career—they want to be firemen or princesses—but by the time a kid really has to choose one, he needs to know what he can and can't do, what is a realistic goal. He has to close doors on impossible or improbable careers. He needs to be specific and have a plan. "I want to be rich and famous" is not a specific plan. Wanting and needing money to support oneself is a good goal. But it isn't a plan, either.

Getting a job, keeping a job, getting a better job, getting a new job—all require being very realistic and persistent, having an ability to get along with people, being able to tolerate frustration. We adults know how hard that is. We get it, because we played pickup sticks.

Parents have to be careful not to misread the difficulty a child is having at work. Perhaps the problem is not the stupid, unreasonable boss or the economy. Before parents jump in to the rescue by agreeing that it's someone else's fault, by supporting the kid if he loses his job, by giving him a job, by scrambling to get a friend to give him a job, or by moving him back home, we need to truly understand the situation. In other words, we should not just knee-jerk react. However, having said that, there's nothing wrong with reminding your child to wear a sweater to work because the air-conditioning is up too high. We leave you with some brilliant words from Robert Frost:

> *My object in living is to unite*
> *My avocation and my vocation*
> *As my two eyes make one in sight.*

Tell your kids.

~~~~~~

New York or Bust

Dear Gail and Susan,

Maybe this isn't really a problem, but it is to me. My son Jerry, who will be twenty-four on his next birthday, got two good job offers, one in New York City and one in Atlanta. The out-of-state job in Manhattan pays a little more, but I believe that money isn't everything and shouldn't be the deciding factor.

Jerry has asked me what I think. I know what I think . . . that he should take the job near us. He's an only child. He's all we have. We're all he has. If he stays here, we could see him more often. If he got sick, we'd be around to help. It just seems like the better choice all around. The only reason I haven't said anything yet is that my husband thinks that in this case I shouldn't weigh in, even though Jerry asked me to, because what if he follows my advice and the job doesn't work out? Should I speak or not?

Ellen

Oh, No, Ellen,

Not only should you not speak about this, you should not speak ever again. Let me tell you a story about old traditional Tahitian families. They have many children, and the youngest son is dressed like a girl from birth and grows all the way to adulthood dressed as a girl, then as a woman. The reason is the youngest son is the child designated to take care of the parents when the parents get old. I believe the thinking goes, if a boy is dressed as a girl, he will have no place to go and must stay near his family. To this day, there are bars where these men go to congregate so they have a bit of a social life. Now, why would this tradition remind me of you and your son? Allow me to quote you: "He's all we have. We're all he has."

It's time for Jerry to fly. Let him make his own decisions. I have big, alarming news for you, Ellen. This is his life.

If your baby gets sick, you can go to him and take his temperature.

Gail, who's been to Tahiti

What an interesting tradition you bring up, Gail, and to the point. Let me add my perspective. First, Jerry's being an only child should have nothing to do with his career decision. Unless he and his parents live on a deserted island (Tahiti doesn't qualify . . . I've been there, too), he is not all they have.

Second, Jerry didn't ask his mother for advice, only what thoughts she had, presumably about his career and lifestyle options.

Parents may have useful information and insights about assessing a career move or life in other parts of the country. If Ellen has such input, she can offer it. But she should not burden her son with her anxieties and dependency needs.

And finally, Ellen wants to control not only her son Jerry but also the outcome of her advice to him. A parent should always make it clear that whatever thoughts she shares, the decision and its consequences are entirely the adult child's.

Susan

Moving On

Dear Gail and Susan,

I have a family moving business and four sons. Each of my boys worked for the company during summers and holidays when they were still in school. When it came time for a full-time job, each came to work for me. The oldest worked his way up to partner. The problem I'm writing to you about is that the next-to-the-oldest, Seth, who has worked for me for three years, doesn't want to be a partner. He wants to start his own moving business in another town. I guess I can understand wanting to try it yourself, but I'm here to tell you, it's not easy starting from scratch. I know first-hand how hard it is. I imagined that eventually all the boys would be partners and I would retire knowing they were carrying on the family business. Should I try to talk Seth out of going it alone?

Tim

Dear Almost Really Cool Dad,

Remember when you were a young lad starting out? Could somebody have talked you out of going it alone? Unlike Susan, who knows what she's talking about, I'm going to guess about the psychology on this one. Seth is one of your middle children and needs to pull away in order to distinguish himself. He obviously doesn't want to be a carbon copy of his older brother, who might even be a carbon copy of you.

I think it's admirable when a father brings his children into his business and I've always thought that brothers who work together have a very strong bond and that can lead to success. However, you don't want to force the issue. What you do want to do is encourage your boy. Because of you, Seth isn't starting from scratch. During summers, holidays, and the three years he worked for you, he learned about the business and he will probably continue needing you. I would be proud of him.

Don't feel rejected, Tim. Seth isn't leaving you. He needs you.

I wanted my children to become writers and they were good at it, or at least I thought so. But they defied me and became scientists. What's a mother to do?

Gail

Gail, once more I agree with you. Tim thought he could control his adult children and realize a dream of having his sons carry on the family business. I can certainly understand a father's desire for family togetherness. But a father's aspiration is not a realistic career plan for his children, nor should it be binding on them.

Seth wants to separate from the family and distinguish himself by being his own boss. The developmental thrust toward individuation and independence is healthy. Of course, starting a business is hard and nothing is guaranteed. But, given his experience, with a sound business plan, hard work, and some good luck, Seth has a shot at making it. So my advice to Tim is to let Seth go and mourn the loss—of his vision for his family and his company.

Seth's brothers have chosen differently. Working for a family business and starting your own are both independent choices so long as you are not complying but are choosing for yourself.

Susan

Abby's Drunken Plan

Dear Gail and Susan,

My daughter Abby has come up with an idea for an e-business. She wants to develop a software program to help alcoholics online. It's a fantastic idea and could make a fortune! I'm not the only one who thinks so.

Abby needs start-up money and gave us first dibs at buying in. My husband George and I don't have that kind of money, but we discussed mortgaging our house to raise it. Our house has appreciated a lot, so we could get what Abby needs. It seems like such a great opportunity for all of us.

Melissa

Dear Idiot,

Here's what could and will happen if you don't listen to me. You'll mortgage your house, putting pressure on yourself and your husband because you'll have those monthly payments. Then you'll give Abby the money and your real heartache will begin. Start-up businesses never run smoothly and a start-up company that has to do with alcoholics . . . not so good. They may be in too big of a drunken stupor to realize they need help. They may not have a computer because they've spent all their money on booze. Chances are, Abby will need more cash than she originally anticipated. You might as well sell your jewelry, too. And don't forget to get a second job.

Your daughter, feeling guilty about the burden she's put on you, won't want to come home. Ever. Even the sight of your house will cause her pain and grief. That is, if you still have your house.

Can't you see that your daughter is a lousy businesswoman? If she were any good, she would go to a bank, not to her parents. Don't give Abby a cent. You could lose your house and your daughter, too.

Sober Gail

Gail, Abby has an idea, not a business plan, yet her mother is ready to mortgage her house to finance it. What's up here? Do we have an enmeshed family? "Gave us first dibs" and "opportunity for all of us" make me think that.

Members of enmeshed families don't develop their own individ-

ual, autonomous functioning. Rather, each member has a role to play. From what I read, Abby's role is to come up with a money-making scheme; Mom and Dad's is to supply the financing. The enmeshed family always sticks together, in this case probably all the way to bankruptcy.

I agree with you, Gail: Melissa should not invest. She should advise Abby to draw up a realistic business plan and take it to a bank. If the bank turns her down, then she needs to rethink her plan or scrap it.

Susan

Help Me! My Son Wants Our Money

Dear Gail and Susan,

My husband Bill and I are fairly well off, and we have money put away for our retirement. Our son Steven is an investment broker. Morgan Stanley took him on right out of college. He's worked for them for three years and has done pretty well. Recently he asked his father and me if we would turn over our money to him to manage.

To our present adviser, we're just another client. Steven would certainly take a personal interest in us and want to make sure that our future is secure. In other words, it would be a win-win for all of us, wouldn't it?

My husband insisted that I include some background on Steven. Although I think it's irrelevant, it happened a few years ago. When he went away to college, we found copies of IOUs in his room. It wasn't any big deal and it wasn't to bookies or anything—just a few hundred dollars he owed to girlfriends.

Marge

Dear Insane Woman,

Steven is way too inexperienced to do financial planning for retirement. Retirement to him is in a distant galaxy.

Would you give your entire retirement fund to a stranger—even the valedictorian of the Harvard Business School—who only has a few years of work experience? No? Then why give it to Steven, who I'm sure didn't go to a school in that league? (Why am I so sure? Because you didn't mention where he graduated from, even though you bragged about how well he is doing.) Ask your son if he is willing for you to come live in his apartment if he loses your money.

I think the most interesting part of your letter is about the IOUs. You say he didn't owe much, but to a high school kid, a few hundred dollars is a lot. Your husband wanted you to mention it because he really doesn't want to give your son your hard-earned money. He thought I would grab on to that information and remind you that your son is financially irresponsible. Obviously, your husband was right. I would call Steven and say, "Mommy and Daddy love you very much, but we have decided we love our money, too."

Fortunately not one of your son's girlfriends, Gail

Let's say the scenario ran something like this: A son has been a successful and responsible stockbroker for twenty-five years. His parents are aging and having trouble managing their money. Dad approaches his son and asks if he will help out. That would be a whole different story, wouldn't it, Gail?

But here an inexperienced son has gone to his parents to try to snare a big account. Sounds a lot like the same Steven who hustled money from his girlfriends in high school. Marge calls an important piece of Steven's history "irrelevant" rather than a potential red flag about his character.

Marge and her husband need to tell Steven that they will not entrust their money to an inexperienced stockbroker, even if he's their son.

Susan

Foisting Richard

Dear Gail and Susan,

My son Richard has just graduated from college. We moved him out of his fraternity house and he is now living with us. He says that he tried to get a job, but couldn't. So far, Rich has been sleeping late and watching television. My wife is nagging me to ask some friends, call in some favors if you will, to try to get him a job. But I am reluctant. Given what I see of his motivation and work habits, I couldn't recommend him. I wouldn't hire him, so how can I foist him on a friend who might hire him for my sake? My wife Dolores is sure that Rich will rise to the occasion, that he just needs the right chance. I'm not so sure. I am interested in hearing your take on our situation.

Mac

Mac, Listen,

I love your name. You seem like a go-to kind of guy. Boy, are you in trouble. If you can't foist him off the couch, how can you foist him onto a friend? You've got to talk to Richard, and I mean sternly. You won't have a hard time finding him, since he's just in the living room. Tell him he has a month to get off your couch and out of the house, which will force him to get a job. Then you'll be able to see his motivation and work habits. To give him hope, tell him that if he does well in the job he gets, you will try to get him a better job with one of your contacts.

Throwing a child out is a really difficult thing for parents to do, but it's really necessary. I've known too many twenty-five-year-olds who are still living at home. Their parents claim that it is too hard for their kids to get jobs or places to live because of the economy. Or there is some other excuse. It's always been difficult for graduates to get that first job unless they're in a field that has plenty of openings.

Thanks for writing. It gave me a chance to get some anger (having nothing to do with your question) out.

Your friend in troubled times, Gail

A responsible adult doesn't wait for the "right chance" to behave like . . . a responsible adult. According to Dolores, Rich should be sure of being rewarded before behaving well. Has she been rescuing her son? Excusing his bad behavior? Overlooking his poor work ethic and sense of entitlement? Maybe that's why they are all in this predicament.

I agree with you and Mac, Gail. Mac would not hire a deadbeat and cannot ask his friends to. But Gail, I respectfully disagree that Mac should entice Rich with the assurance of a better job if he performs. That just supports the notion that Rich should be guaranteed a special reward for being responsible. Mac should turn him down and promise nothing.

Richard is developmentally stuck. He is resisting moving on to the next stage of life. He needs clear expectations and guidelines from his parents, like a deadline for getting a job and moving out.

Susan

My Dear Coauthor Susan,

I respectfully disagree with you. I believe in bribing. That's how one parent I know got her daughter thin and another friend's son got an MD—because he was bribed all the way through school. They bought him Jaguars and paid for skiing vacations. He's forty-two now and very happy with his profession. Last year he bought his mother a really great birthday present.

Your friend Gail, who thinks she knows it all

Gail,

Your friend got a great present and an MD in the family. Did she get a grown-up son?

Susan

No, but so what? He lives in another city.

Laugh, Janie, Laugh!

Dear Gail and Susan,

I wasn't exactly happy when my son Rod dropped out of college after his sophomore year to be a comic. But I got on board and have been supportive and encouraging. I must say that in the last two years, he's done pretty well, but now he tells stories about me in his act. He gets big laughs at my expense and it embarrasses me. I'm a private person and feel used, humiliated, and betrayed. A lot of what he says about me isn't even true, but how would anyone know? It's hard for me to be happy for his success when I feel the way I do. What should I do?

Janie

Dear Used, Humiliated, and Betrayed,

I hate to tell you this, Janie, but I'm laughing at you, too. You say you're a private person. Are you also so private with your friends that they don't know anything about your life? If you are, get help.

You are the only one who's ever written to us who isn't happy about her kid's success. You say you've been supportive and encouraging. Was that just at the very beginning? Where did your son get his sense of humor? I only ask because you don't seem to have any.

I've been a comedy writer for decades. Not once did it embarrass my mother, even though I wrote about her all the time. Every writer that I worked with on *The Golden Girls* got the chance to use stories about their mothers and none of their mothers ever complained. They liked it.

Funny Gail

Humor is a good coping mechanism. When you can see the funny or ironic side of an issue, you have an easier time managing a problem. In Rod's case, he's also making a living at it. But as you say, Gail, Janie does not use humor to cope.

I am certainly an advocate of the right to privacy. However, I don't think it applies to our children's experience of their relationship with us. That belongs to them and they can do with it what they want.

That being said, a professional comedian is an entertainer. He bases his comedy on reality but embellishes and twists it to make it universal and funny. Rod creates stories about Janie for his act.

Janie is so preoccupied with how people see her that she can't see it as an act; she can't enjoy her son's ironic look at mothers, nor feel pleasure and pride in his accomplishments.

What should Janie do? If our answers don't change her perspective and help her override her self-absorption, in my view she has two options: never see her son perform, which would be a loss for both of them, or get professional help to deal with her narcissistic vulnerability.

Susan

Dan's Accomplishments

Dear Gail and Susan,

My thirty-two-year-old son Dan simply won't tell us about his accomplishments. I had to hear from my nephew that Dan got a promotion and a big raise. My son knows that I love hearing about his successes. It gives me a high to know he's doing well and when I get together with my friends I can do a little bragging. Why does Dan deprive me of this pleasure?

Sylvia

Sylvia,

Dan is really pissed at you.

Too bad—Gail

Children of all ages want their parents to be proud of them. But they don't want to be used as the ace in a bragging contest with Mom's friends. Now that Dan is an adult living on his own, he can keep his mother from using him by withholding information from her. Sylvia may not like being cut off from a source of narcissistic pleasure—her son's accomplishments—but Dan has the right not to be used. Sylvia should find narcissistic supplies in her own life. If she doesn't use her son's success, Dan may relent and share.

Susan

Beside Myself

Dear Gail and Susan,

I am beside myself. My daughter Judy stole money from her boss. Judy works for a small company as the secretary/bookkeeper. I know my daughter is stealing because she bragged to the daughter of a friend of mine that she wrote herself a check for three hundred dollars and put it in the company books as a telephone expense. My dilemma is whether to turn my daughter in and prevent this criminal behavior before it goes any further. Or should I pretend I know nothing and let my daughter live her life and take the consequences if they arise? After all, she is an adult. I have tried not thinking about it but can't make the thoughts go away. Please help me decide what to do. Thank you.

Arabella

Dear Tortured Arabella,

You heard information about your daughter's stealing from a third party. The first thing you should do is speak to your friend's daughter directly and let her tell you what she heard from your daughter. Then, if you think the story is true, which it very well might be, confront your daughter straight on. Hopefully she'll feel safe enough to confess to you. If she does, tell her that she has got to go to her boss, pay back the money, promise never to do anything like that again, and beg him to let her keep her job. (I doubt the boss will let her do that, or that he will give her a good recommendation so she can get a new job.)

When kids are little and they take things from a store or a friend, a good parent always insists that they return it and apologize. Because of this humiliation, they don't forget what it feels like to take something that's not theirs. However, decent adults don't steal. I know you realize this. If they do, it's usually not about the money or the things they take, but about the thrill of taking it and getting away with it. Or they're hoping to get caught. Sometimes it's both reasons.

If Judy didn't learn about stealing as a child, therapy is a must. You're right. The criminal behavior has got to stop or she will one day end up in jail.

By the way, do you have any idea how the expression "beside myself" started? How can anyone be beside himself?

Let me know—Gail

This is a tricky situation. I agree, Gail: Arabella has no evidence other than hearsay that her daughter committed a crime. Therefore, turning her in shouldn't be an option.

Arabella can try to talk to Judy, ask her whether the story is true. If Judy admits that she stole the money, Arabella can talk about the criminality of the act. Perhaps she can determine the motivation for the theft. Does Judy have a drug habit? Arabella can suggest an addiction program. Is Judy dealing with credit card debt? Arabella can recommend a financial planner. Is Judy acting out self-destructively? Arabella can encourage therapy.

However, if Judy denies that she did it, then Arabella needs to let it go, at least for now.

By the way, Gail, the phrase "beside myself" refers to a mental state or condition, meaning being out of one's wits or out of one's senses. Therefore, beside oneself.

Susan

Drinks and Parties

Dear Gail and Susan,

My son Rafe has had three jobs in the last three and a half years. He's been fired from two of them. I'm concerned that he will be fired from the one he has now, too. I think that he's lost his jobs because he drinks and parties and just isn't a good worker. His irresponsibility makes me mad. Is there anything I can do to get him to shape up or should I just let him live with the consequences of his actions?

Julius

Too bad, Julius,

Who told you that your son lost his job because he drinks and parties? I believe it's true; I'm just wondering who told you. I just can't imagine that a drunken and overly partied kid would tell his father what he does at night.

You sound astute. I think you know that the only way Rafe is going to learn is (and I'm about to quote you) if he has to "live with the consequences of his actions." So let's forget the kid. I'm more worried about you. His actions are making you a candidate for high blood pressure. Tell him not to tell you about his work anymore and that you're willing to talk about anything else. Go to ball games, talk about ball games, watch ball games, and then talk about the ball games some more when the ball games are over. Or talk about flowers. I don't care. Just don't let that person who's not a good worker make you unhealthy. Someday he'll learn and you'll be on Lotrel.

Gail, who invites you not to be concerned

Drinking, partying, fired from two jobs, and one firing away from not being able to get another job is a pretty self-destructive lifestyle. As hard as it may be, Julius should give nothing to this system—no money, no promise of a safety net, and, harder yet, no worrying.

In general I am against telling a child that if he gets into trouble, you'll help out (the proverbial safety net) for the following reason. Parents think that telling their child "you can always count on me" gives him confidence, but it does not. It offers the child the option of dependence and promotes ambivalence about being totally and seriously on his own. In other words, if the child believes that he doesn't absolutely have to, he might choose not to, even if it's not entirely conscious.

Rafe is one of these kids who is not being serious and responsible about his life. As much as Julius would like to control the situation and get Rafe in line, he is going to have to let life teach his son the lessons Rafe needs to learn.

I like your idea, Gail, that Rafe's work life be off the table for

discussion. Let Rafe deal with it all by himself. Adolescent Rafe is
now able to live his life and let his dad do the worrying. In not talk-
ing about Rafe's work, Julius will give the worry back to his son,
where it belongs.

Susan

Job Interviews

Dear Gail and Susan,

Our daughter Callie goes on job interviews but never lands
the job. Is there anything I can do to figure out what's going
wrong and help her?

Deborah

Dear Trying to Figure Out What's Wrong,

You can't, but maybe one of your friends can. (You can't
because you're too emotionally involved. She doesn't need her
mother's advice right now. She needs a legitimate opinion
from someone.) Do you know anybody who interviews for a
company or someone at an employment agency or someone
who has been in the business world forever and knows what
it takes to get a job? I would ask that person if they would
get together with your daughter for lunch. Then Callie can
get dressed and go out to a professional business lunch to get
the information she needs. Tell her not to order the most expensive thing on the menu.

If you don't know anybody who will do this for you, make
sure your daughter is well-groomed, has the proper attire, and
has her résumé in order, and yes, you can tell her to picture
the interviewer naked.

Gail, who has always tried to solicit outside help

Gail, your answer is right on the money. Knowing when and
where to get professional advice is part of being an adult. A busi-
ness problem needs to be brought to a business professional. An

*adult child has to de-idealize herself and her parents. Parents of
an adult child need to know when the child's problem is not for them
to solve and they should point her in the direction of an expert.*

*Parents should expect their adult child to have her own resources—
plumber, financial planner, doctor, psychotherapist, lawyer—and not
rely on Mom and Dad to answer or fix everything.*

Susan

Affair at Work

Dear Gail and Susan,

My daughter Chloe had an affair with someone at work.
They broke up but have to see each other every day, which is
upsetting to Chloe. So she's thinking of quitting her job. It won't
be that easy for her to find another one as good. I think she
should get over him and not let this ruin her career. What do
you think?

Kari

Dear Mother of Upset Chloe,

I, too, think Chloe should get over him and not let this ruin
her career. The problem is, it's not easy to get over someone
who's around all day. The best way to get over someone is to
never see them again, but that's impossible when you're working with someone. So here are some tricks. Tell Chloe to wear
a rubber band around her wrist and to snap it every time she
thinks of him. Then, hopefully, she'll associate him with pain.
If that doesn't work, make sure she knows that she's torturing
him as much as he's torturing her. Maybe that will cheer
her up.

Your daughter has got to get back on the dating scene as
soon as possible. Nothing cures a broken heart faster than
meeting someone new. She may not be ready to do that, but
she should be busy after work with friends and during lunch
with associates. Advise her to go to the gym. At the very least,
she'll be in shape to move on. Tell her I said she's a wimp if

she quits a good job. Dating always ends in disaster unless it ends in a wedding. Good jobs are worth more than one horrible man.

I think she's learned that dating coworkers puts you in a dangerous situation.

> Gail, who dated a cowriter once and lived to regret it

You're right, Gail. There's a reason that many businesses have a "no dating" rule. Dating at work can lead to obsessed, angry, distracted, or ambivalent employees.

I also agree that Chloe should not quit her job. If she did, then she'd have no boyfriend and no source of income. Quitting her job, which in essence is running away, would be an adolescent, self-destructive response to one of life's bumps in the road. Chloe needs to mourn her loss and move on. The process of mourning is denial, anger, bargaining, depression, acceptance. Since Chloe is considering a self-destructive action, I guess that she is still in denial and not able to get angry at the betrayer of her trust.

Kari should tell her daughter that leaving her job would be self-destructive and encourage Chloe to get therapy if she can't deal with her anger and disappointment in a healthier way.

> *Susan*

A Lousy Job

Dear Gail and Susan,

My son Justin works for me and is doing a lousy job. I want to fire him. His mother wants me to give him yet another chance. She's afraid he won't be able to get as good a job on his own and thinks that I should keep him on because he's our son. Can you settle this disagreement?

> Al

Father and Boss of Justin,

Your wife is afraid your son isn't going to be able to get as good a job as he has with you. Is she also afraid that he might ruin your business and that she won't be able to go shopping at Macy's anymore and will have to buy all her clothes at Costco? She's not taking into consideration that a poor worker is hard on a company or that when the job is filled with the right person, somebody who can help the company, everybody, especially you, will be happier. Maybe if you'll explain those things to her, she'll choose her husband over her son.

Have I settled this disagreement or am I too late? Has your wife left you and has your son burned down the building your business is in?

Let me know—Gail

Mom is one of Justin's problems. First, she does not want to think about the adult world and adult needs. As you note, Gail, she doesn't care about what a bad employee will do to her husband's business.

Second, she coddles her son. She treats his job like an unimportant game with no real stakes. According to Mom, keeping a job should be an entitlement and not dependent on performance. Her coddling is probably why Justin lacks an adult work ethic. Mom is right about one thing, though. Justin won't get as good a job elsewhere. Nor should he. No employer except Dad would put up with him.

Al really has two roles to play here. As his son's employer, he should treat Justin like any adult employee—hold him to standards and fire him if he doesn't meet them. As Justin's father, Al should set his son free to do some growing up in the world outside the family.

Our job as parents is not to prop our kids up. It's to prepare them for the real world they are going to have to live in.

Susan

Holding Himself Back

Dear Gail and Susan,

My son Eduardo and his girlfriend work for the same company. They like working together. The problem for me is that, as I see it, Eduardo has maxed out there. He can't advance at all. I think he would do well to move on to another company where there is opportunity for him to move up the ladder. He says that he is frustrated with his job, but that he won't leave his girl-friend, and my sense is that his girlfriend is not as marketable as he is. It pains me to think that Eduardo is holding himself back and that he will one day regret it. Should I try to persuade him to reconsider or just let him be?

Saul

Dear It Pains You to Think,

I think you should try to persuade Eduardo to take a new job. How persuasive are you? I try to persuade. It only works sometimes.

There may be another reason why Eduardo won't get on that ladder to success. Yes, he doesn't want to leave his girl-friend, but he also may not want to try to get another job be-cause he's afraid of failing. In my opinion people who are frustrated with their jobs will usually try to find something else. Since Eduardo isn't moving, I think you should do some things to make him feel confident. You know, the patting-him-on-the-back kind of thing. Brag about him to others in front of him. Reward him in small ways, like taking him to dinner because you think he's great company. If you do enough of these things, his confidence will grow. He may leave his job and he may even leave the girl. Wouldn't that be a nice future for him . . . and you?

Gail, who loves complimenting as much as
she loves being complimented

Gail, you give good, practical advice. Let me add something I suspect is going on with Eduardo. The letter says that although he's frustrated with his job, he won't look for a new one because he doesn't want to leave his girlfriend.

One of the challenges in a relationship is how to be separate without feeling abandoned and how to be together without giving yourself up. At the moment, Eduardo appears to be giving up his own career path to be with his girlfriend. He may be afraid that if he leaves his job, she will break up the relationship—abandon him.

So what can Saul do? He might suggest to his son that although a relationship requires compromise, it should not totally annihilate one's ambitions. He might suggest that his son talk to his girlfriend about his frustration and desire to get another job. Dealing with his relationship will at least clarify the issues. Maybe Eduardo's fears are unwarranted. However, if his girlfriend cannot accept his separateness, then maybe he needs to find another girlfriend as well as another job.

Susan

A Tough Business

Dear Gail and Susan,

My daughter Hannah wants to be a pop singer, but I don't think she's that good. Not only don't I think she has the talent, but I'm not sure she has what it takes to make it in such a tough business. Should I express my opinion? Should I try to guide her toward some other career?

Logan

Dear Logan, Who Wants to Guide,

What if Billy Ray Cyrus wanted to guide his daughter Miley away from music? There never would have been a Hannah Montana. Not that the world wouldn't have gone on, but he would have stopped her before she became such an icon to young girls.

I'm guessing that your daughter is in her twenties and, in her mind, she has to be a singer. When I started out, of course I wasn't as good as I am today. Fortunately, my parents encouraged me, didn't stand in my way, and applauded my very small successes. I was in my twenties, too. When I gave my mother a copy of my first book. I worried because it was a bit scatological. My mother said, "I love it! It has to be dirty to sell."

This is the time for Hannah to follow her dreams. If not now, when? She won't be able to when she has responsibilities like a husband and children.

Let her try. Her audiences will let her know whether she's good or not.

Gail, who can't carry a tune

When children are very young, they believe that their parents are omniscient and omnipotent. And parents feel they're supposed to be. They have to know how to comfort and protect their vulnerable children. As children get older, they no longer think their parents know everything or are all-powerful. Parents don't have to be.

Gail, I understand that Logan wants to guide his daughter away from what he considers she can't succeed at. But he really doesn't know that she can't. He thinks he knows, but he is only guessing or predicting, which doesn't determine any outcome. Does Hannah have enough talent? Will she develop her potential? Can she toughen up and stay with it? Hannah will or won't make it as a singer. Both she and her father will know when the reality becomes clear.

Logan can and should decide that Hannah has to support herself with a job to pay the bills. Logan does not have the power to know the future, but he does have power over his own resources.

Susan

CHAPTER FIVE

Dating

Dating is an activity important to developing independence and an adult life. Dating provides companionship, someone to explore the world with, pleasure, an opportunity to learn more about oneself and others, and a way to find a marriage partner. Some people like it. Some don't.

Why we are attracted to someone or fall in love is mysterious. Poets and psychologists have tried to account for what we still don't understand. Practically all songs are about love. How wonderful it is when two people fall in love with each other. How painful when one falls and the love is not reciprocated. Dating, like any other growing-up activity, can bring exhilaration, a boost in self-esteem, confusion, self-doubt, and emotional heartache. It can make you cry or give you a high that you've never felt before.

As with any other developmental challenge our children face—from walking to leaving home—parents need to be supportive of their children's mastery and independence. We can be listeners. We can sometimes give advice, but we always have to remember that dating is part of the learning experience of life and that we want to foster independence.

What if our child has a dating problem? Remember, we are talking about an adult over whom we have no control. We should give our child space to experiment, make mistakes, and learn. We have to guard against wanting to be heroes and rescue or protect our children from the pains of growing up. We shouldn't try to solve their problems; we shouldn't want to prove that we are right; we shouldn't get caught up in our kids' dating dramas; and we shouldn't become seduced by our children needing us the way they used to.

We have to watch out not to let our children triangle us into their relationships. Being "triangled in" means that someone—a parent—is brought into a relationship in a way that relieves the child's tension, and the child then feels he or she doesn't have to address and resolve the conflict or problem in the relationship. So if a daughter in a yo-yo relationship calls her mother after every breakup and her mother distracts her every time by paying for a mother-daughter spa day, the daughter may never fully feel her pain, confront her boyfriend, and/or leave him.

This is the one chapter where we disagree most. Gail usually wants to lend a shoulder. Susan usually wants parents to let their children deal with their pain. We decided that we're both right.

And what if the mother or father is dating? It's understandable that parents would like their children to approve of their dating choices. Some children easily accept a new companion in their single parent's life. Some may find their parents' dating discomforting and protest. Children can be jealous, rivalrous, or envious. But the bottom line is that parents need to make their own decisions and help their grown children adjust to them.

~~~~~~

Online

Dear Gail and Susan,

My daughter Kathy is doing online dating. I'm afraid that meeting on the Internet is potentially dangerous. You can't know if what they say is real. A guy could be a murderer. I don't think Kathy should meet men this way. What do you think?

Sarah

Dear Nervous,

Try not to worry about your daughter's online dating. Kathy is probably a smart girl and hopefully knows how to take care of herself. Millions of people use dating services in order to find someone and the big dating services do some screening themselves. (It's good business. They want their clients alive.) Another way of meeting men is in bars and I bet you wouldn't be too thrilled about that, either.

What you can suggest to Kathy is that she should meet the men in public places and not give them her home address. And she should drive her own car there and back. Another way to protect herself would be to introduce him, in a public place, to friends and get their input. A person who is not involved emotionally with someone is a better judge. If you talk to Kathy about my suggestions, she'll say, "Oh, Mom. Don't you think I know that?" But it'll make you feel better knowing that she's being careful. My job is to make you feel better.

Gail, who's known lots of people who have
done online dating and all survived

Daters have to take precautions no matter how they meet a date. Any stranger a dater meets—in the supermarket, elevator, doctor's office, church, or online—is a potential sociopath, jerk, nice guy, or husband material. True, we have more information when we meet someone in person, but sociopaths are expert con men. Good sense should always prevail. Gail, you have provided lots of safety measures to take. Sarah should discuss them with her daughter.

Online dating has the advantage of providing a large database. A young woman has many more opportunities to find a date than if she relies on friends' recommendations or chance encounters.

As much as we would like to control and protect our children, they have to live their own lives. Sarah should accept online dating as a tool of modern culture.

Susan

Men in Bars

Dear Gail and Susan,

Please help before something terrible happens. I just found out that my daughter picks up men in bars. I'm scared she's going to get a disease. My husband is furious, but I told him we should get your advice before we talk to her, since we really don't know what to say.

Louisa

Dear Scared,

Does your daughter go to bars with girlfriends and give men her telephone number or does she take them back to her place and have sex with them? There's a big difference. A lot of young people meet in bars. It's one of the ways that people get together these days. Hopefully, they take the time to get to know each other before letting them into their homes or having sex. Because you're worried about disease, I'm thinking you think that your daughter is having sex with these men. Nobody ever got a disease by talking with a nice man who buys her a beer.

I don't want to scare you, but there are worse things than getting diseases when picking up men in bars. You and your husband should sit down with your daughter and watch a movie called *Looking for Mr. Goodbar*. It was made in the '70s when singles bars first became popular. If it doesn't frighten your daughter about picking up men and taking them home, I'd be surprised. After the three of you watch that movie together, you won't have to think of what to say. It will be very clear why she shouldn't take home men that she just picked up.

Gail, who hardly has a drink

Gail, if Louisa's daughter goes to bars to meet men to date, then Louisa is overreacting to a style of modern dating. But if we are talking about a preoccupation with one-night stands with strangers, then Louisa's daughter is not only in potential danger, but also in the grips of a compulsion. In that case, Louisa and her husband should strongly advise her daughter to participate in therapy or a sex addiction program and go with her if necessary to get her problem under control.

Susan

Brendan Is Angry

Dear Gail and Susan,

I was pretty depressed when I was married. I know that my son Brendan suffered because of it. Now that I am on my own and dating, I'm a new person. I am livelier and more fun. Brendan is very angry with me because now I'm having a good time. He is not happy with how much I have changed since I left his father. How can I get Brendan to stop being angry with me?

Kirsten

Dear Pretty Depressed,

I would be angry with you, too. What you were going through with your husband shouldn't have affected your relationship with your child. A lot of women have bad marriages, but they protect their children from them.

Obviously you weren't chemically depressed, since you're happy now. You may be a new person to yourself and you might be a lot more fun. Brendan didn't have that person growing up. No wonder he's pissed. I don't think you can get Brendan to stop being mad at you. He'll probably need years of therapy. It's going to take time.

My mother always said when she knew someone was having psychological problems and going into therapy, "They always blame it on the mother." In this case, it's absolutely true.

Gail, who didn't blame it on her mother

You're right, Gail. Brendan had a depressed mother when he was growing up, which was probably very painful and confusing. He wondered if he caused the sadness and why he couldn't alleviate it. Now he realizes that his mother's depression wasn't about him. But neither is her happiness. In fact, Brendan's mother's emotional life has little to do with her son and she seems to have no insight into the situation. Notice, Gail, that she didn't ask how she could help her son, only how to stop his anger toward her.

If Kirsten understands what we are saying, she will be able to see things from her son's point of view. She should apologize to him for her self-absorption, empathize with his reality, and accept his anger as valid. However, I am not optimistic that Kirsten will. Sadly,

Brendan is most likely not going to get validation and support from his mother. Hopefully he will come to see that he was cheated, that his mother is self-centered, and then he will be able to get on with his life.

Susan

Going for It

Dear Gail and Susan,

I am forty-five and divorced. My eighteen-year-old daughter's friend Sierra keeps coming on to me. I try to ignore her, but she's hot. Would it be terribly wrong of me to give in to temptation? We're all adults, after all.

Jerry

Dear Stupid,

Don't you know hot sex is overrated? (Just kidding, but I'm totally serious from this point on.) You have to ask yourself, what does she want from you? She can have sex with any boy in her high school, if she's that hot. Does she need a father or a sugar daddy? She might just want a one-night stand with an older man to see what it's like. Can you think with your head? Would your daughter like you sleeping with her friend? Someone's gonna cry over this and it might be you.

Let's suppose you invite her over and she arrives in a coat with nothing on under it. How's your heart, Jerry? Do you think you could withstand her attack? Would it be at all embarrassing to you if she giggles when she sees you naked? Don't forget, if you do go through with this, you'll be using a forty-five-year-old penis. And you know she's going to want to take naked pictures of you with her cell phone when you fall asleep—and you will fall asleep, because she will exhaust you.

Have I said enough to turn you off?

Gail, who would rather you sleep with Diane Keaton

There are several issues here, Gail. Sierra's sexualizing the relationship with her friend's father is a symptom of emotional disturbance. If Jerry acted on his impulse, he as the father in the house would be taking advantage of a very troubled young woman.

He would also be betraying his daughter, who should be able to bring girlfriends to the house and not end up a madam.

Forty-five-year-old men with a conscience can resist temptation. Jerry can and should set boundaries with Sierra, making it clear to her that she is his daughter's friend and nothing more.

Susan

Lanie Is Dating Her Boss

Dear Gail and Susan,

I'm kind of disgusted with my daughter Lanie. She is dating her boss for the sole purpose of getting ahead at her job. She's open about the fact that she is using him and I don't approve. I haven't said anything to her yet, but I want to. What would you both advise?

Damon

Dear Father of a Liar,

In Hollywood, where I live, the casting couch has supposedly been a way for young starlets to get ahead. I have been in show business for decades now and I've never heard of anybody who slept with a producer or director getting anything but a bit part. Nobody sleeps with writers because they know it doesn't get them anywhere. Nobody I know who played their hand that way ever became a star. Women with talent, however, got in the door without needing to sleep around.

I don't know if your daughter is talented in her field or not. She says she's using her boss, but you don't mention if it's worked. Here's what's probably going to happen. If he's married he'll stay married, and if she causes any problems in his relationship, he'll fire her. Underline the last sentence and give her this book. She's selling her body and it doesn't seem to be working. Where's her promotion? Underline those sentences, too.

Gail, who's seen it all

Aside from Lanie's behavior being manipulative, it is potentially dangerous for her. Lanie thinks she's in control of the situation, but she's not. Bosses don't get to be bosses without knowing how to manage people. Her boss knows what's going on and has more expertise and power in this matter than Lanie does.

Office romances more often than not end badly for the employee, unless she has a legitimate sexual harassment suit, which, since Lanie is bragging about sleeping with her boss to get ahead, she doesn't have.

Damon should inform his daughter about the ways of the world. Lanie may believe her father and stop what she's doing or she may have to go further down the path she has started on and learn the lesson the harder way.

Susan

Marny Is Hooked

Dear Gail and Susan,

My thirty-three-year-old daughter Marny is dating a friend of mine I play golf with. His name is Ted and he is fifty. Marny thinks it would be fun for us all to double-date. At first I thought she was kidding, but I've come to believe that she isn't. The whole situation makes me very uncomfortable. I don't want to play golf with Ted and hear about his dates, knowing that one of them is my daughter. Marny is pretty hooked on him. I am afraid—no, I'm pretty certain—she is going to be hurt, because Ted isn't interested in settling down. Is there anything I can do?

Chase

Dear Fearful of Double-Dating,

There are so many issues here that I'm dizzy from reading your letter. First of all, these two are in different stages of life.

Usually, thirty-three-year-old women are thinking of settling down and having children. They're hearing that clock ticking. A fifty-year-old man who is not married and is having fun, as your friend Ted is, is in a different place altogether. It's not a good match.

You're right. It wouldn't be fun for a father and daughter to double-date. You don't want to see them flirting or, worse, touching each other, kissing each other, going home together. Tell Marny it's not something you want to do and tell her why. Because you'd be uncomfortable should be enough of an explanation.

Then you mention that you don't want to play golf with Ted and hear about his dates. Talk about being uncomfortable! Knowing that your daughter likes him and that he's dating other women must make those eighteen holes, which should be pleasurable except for those shots you missed, into a miserable time for you. Stop playing golf with him while he's dating your daughter. Maybe he'll give her up so that you'll join him again.

You're afraid your daughter is going to get hurt. Why don't you tell her the truth about Ted's attitude? She may not believe you, but you'd be doing her a great favor. It may get her to ask him if they have a future.

Chase, fathers used to ask men who went out with their daughters what their intentions were. And they didn't approve if the young men's intentions weren't honorable. Next time your daughter falls for someone, you should bring the good old days back.

Gail, who wants to know what everyone's
intentions are

Chase needs to deal with both Ted and his daughter Marny.

Let's start with Ted. How outrageous that he dates the daughter and brags to the father about his womanizing. Not a nice guy. But what about Chase? He's been listening to this. His silence has given Ted tacit approval.

Chase should immediately tell Ted to stop dating Marny. If Ted has any conscience, he will end the affair, which admittedly will break Marny's heart—temporarily. If Ted refuses, I would advise Chase to end the friendship.

Then Chase needs to talk to Marny and clearly explain Ted's MO.

Neither Ted nor Marny may listen. Marny may be angry for a while. However, eventually the relationship with Ted will run its course to its inevitable end. Marny will be hurt, but hopefully she will also learn a lesson about "players," and I don't mean the golf kind.

Susan

Gerard Had an Affair

Dear Gail and Susan,

My son Gerard had an affair with a woman at work. Her marriage broke up over it. Now Marguerite wants him to marry her. Gerard wasn't planning on that. He was just having a fling. I feel sorry for this woman and am angry at my son, but I also don't think he should marry someone he doesn't want to. What should I say to him?

Louis

Dear Angry at Your Son,

You're a smart man, Louis. A lot of fathers wouldn't be angry at their sons because they feel, well, "that's what boys do." It's very dangerous for a man to date a married woman, because once he sleeps with her, the woman often falls in love. It's a law of nature, one that has been established since the beginning of man. Before people used birth control, women had to know who the father of her child was, so she became focused on the male who had sex with her. The primal instinct is still there. Obviously Marguerite became focused on Gerard.

Also, an affair is romantic and exciting, and compared with that, marriage can seem dull. That's why married women have affairs in the first place. Your son should know that it's dangerous to sleep with a married woman, because it can break up the marriage, even if she says it won't.

Of course your son shouldn't marry someone he doesn't want to marry. Those marriages last about twenty-five minutes. So tell him what you really want to tell him, Louis: not to marry her.

Gail, who has always married someone she wanted to

I hope that Gerard has learned some life lessons—that he can't control another person and that actions have consequences. Just because he was having "a fling" doesn't mean his partner was, too.

However, that being said, no, he shouldn't marry Marguerite. I understand Louis's anger with his son and his empathy for Marguerite, but she is an adult who took a chance and lost. Hopefully, she learned a lesson, too.

Louis should tell his son that he is not obliged to marry Marguerite and that he shouldn't if he doesn't want to.

Susan

Dating a Married Man

Dear Gail and Susan,

We have an age-old situation. My daughter Celine has been dating a married man for a year and a half. He keeps telling her he's going to ask his wife for a divorce, but there's always a reason it's not the right time. Sound familiar? I've seen this in the movies. In two hours, the problem is resolved one way or another.

But this is real life and I absolutely don't know what to do. Celine spends a lot of time at my house crying. Can you help us?

Estelle

Dear Upset Mother,

I'm sure you've already told Celine that dating a married man is not a good idea. Since she comes to your house to cry, you can tell her over and over again. Maybe eventually she'll get the message.

You could also show her a couple of those movies you're talking about. Get a hold of the old ones where the woman has to live in some lousy apartment and spend holidays alone. Those movies are tragedies and end really badly. The woman never gets the married man and is marked for life. The two of you will need plenty of Kleenex to get through those. At the very least, your daughter will see that she's not unique.

You know, Estelle, it's really hard on us when our children are unhappy. But you have to realize that once you do your best to keep them out of a tragic situation, there's nothing left to do. You know that one day this will all be over and your daughter's pain will go away, so why not smile now?

Unless.

Sometimes women date married men because they really don't want to have a full-blown relationship. If she does this again, she needs help.

Gail, whose mother always said, "This, too, will pass"

Celine does not want to accept the reality that this man is irresponsible, manipulative, and self-centered. Dating a married man is always risky. Sometimes they leave their wives, but most times they don't. However, in my opinion, Estelle is ultimately not helping her daughter by providing her a shoulder to cry on. A mother should empathize with her daughter's understandable disappointment, but she should not let the situation become a romantic drama, with teary Celine the pitied, tragic victim rewarded in the end for her sacrifice. Estelle should point out to Celine that life and men sometimes disappoint and that married men usually stay with their wives. Estelle should encourage her daughter to acknowledge that she was misled and betrayed, to learn from her experience, and to move on.

Susan

The Good Child

Dear Gail and Susan,

Everyone tells me I am lucky to have such a good daughter. She takes me out for dinner at least once a week. She is good to her sisters and their children and is very involved in their lives. But Tracy doesn't have her own personal life and I'm afraid she'll never have children. She's forty-three, unmarried, and just dating. How can I help her?

Fran

Dear Mother of Just Dating,

This may sound shocking, but Tracy may be having a hell of a time in life. Maybe being an aunt is a good job for her. And maybe it's what she wants. Think about this. Tracy may like dating. She may not want to be tied down to a man. Your question is, How can I help her? My question to you is, Why do you think she needs help?

Gail, who knows a happily dating woman in her forties

I can understand that Fran might be baffled and disappointed that her daughter has chosen to be an involved aunt rather than a mother and to date rather than marry. However, there is no indication in the letter that Tracy is unhappy with her choices. And unless she is, I agree, Gail, nothing needs to be fixed.

Susan

Keeps Breaking Up

Dear Gail and Susan,

Kelly, my twenty-eight-year-old daughter, keeps breaking up with her boyfriend Dusty. They go out for a few months, have a fight, break up for a while, and then get back together again. Kelly is always in a state of anxiety. How can I get my daughter to see that this isn't the way a relationship should be and that she should get rid of Dusty once and for all?

                                                                    Fern

Dear Wanting to Get Rid of Dusty,

Fern, do you realize that nobody is really named Dusty and that men who use nicknames are usually immature? I made up that last part, but it sounds sort of right, doesn't it? You want to know how you can get Kelly to see that this isn't the way a relationship should be.

Mothers teach their daughters how to love. Has she grown up watching you love someone? That doesn't have to mean you have never been divorced, but she will have picked up on whether your life with men has been calm and loving or anxiety-ridden. Fathers also have a lesson to give daughters about relationships. They teach their daughters how to be loved. This, hopefully, is a lesson your daughter learned since birth.

You can help your daughter by giving her your shoulder to lean on.

Unless.

Some couples enjoy a back-and-forth relationship. It's horrible when they break up but when they get back together, it's very passionate. Let's hope Kelly isn't addicted to that.

                    Gail, who's been supportive to her family and friends
                         when their relationships aren't going well

Gail, I understand why you advise Fern to give her daughter a shoulder to lean on. But sometimes in an effort to be supportive of our distraught children, we exacerbate their problems. I suspect that this is just such a case. Kelly isn't suffering from a sad breakup. She is caught up in the high drama of a yo-yo relationship.

Fern obviously knows all about the Dusty breakups and reconciliations, so that means Kelly tells her about them. Therefore, I think that Kelly is using Fern. By getting her mother to help her cope with her pain, Kelly can continue doing what she is doing.

Fern can tell her daughter that, in her opinion, this isn't a healthy relationship and her advice is to get rid of Dusty once and for all. But she should also say that it is Kelly's decision to make. As difficult as it may be, Fern should let Kelly cope with her anguish and not be so available for counsel or support. Sometimes parents can be most helpful by stating their opinion, then nicely backing off.

Susan

A Threatening Niece

Dear Gail and Susan,

I have been secretly dating Matt, my ex-husband's brother. My niece Gina found out and is threatening to expose us. My children will be devastated because they always thought my brother-in-law and I were having an affair when I was married to their father. It's true that Matt and I always liked each other and that there was chemistry between us, but nothing happened until after the divorce. By the way, Matt is still married to Gina's mother. I need quick advice before my niece tells all.

Alma

Dear Unfaithful,

It didn't matter that you and Matt weren't having an affair when you were married. You lusted after each other and that's what your kids picked up on. And now you're in real trouble. Gina will expose you one of these days. She's mad that you may break up her parents' marriage. Your children will be devastated and so will Matt's wife. So, Alma, you have done, and continue to do, everything wrong. Stop the affair immediately. My advice is to move as far away as possible or fall off the face of the earth. Don't forget to be ashamed.

Gail, who has morals

What a mess, Gail. Alma is having an affair with a married man, made more complicated by the fact that her lover is her for-

mer brother-in-law. However, she doesn't seem dismayed by her behavior; she's just worried that there'll be trouble if her kids find out. She's not even worried about breaking up Matt's marriage. And she wants our answer quick. Well, I can give her quick advice: stop the affair ASAP, distance herself from Matt, and mean it. Perhaps her niece will let her off the hook and not tell in order to preserve her own family.

In the future if Alma doesn't want her kids to be devastated, then she shouldn't do something that will devastate them.

Susan

Girlfriends and Daughters

Dear Gail and Susan,

I'm forty-eight. My daughter Bess is twenty-eight. My girlfriend Liv is twenty-eight. I bet you already know what the problem is. My daughter thinks my relationship is very inappropriate. She says I embarrass her. She refuses to get together with me if Liv is along. In my judgment, Liv is mature for her age and she makes me happy. Shouldn't Beth just want me to be happy? Shouldn't she accept my choices? What can I say to her to get us over this impasse?

William

William, You Must Be Kidding,

I don't even know you and I think your relationship is inappropriate. I'm sure any woman over forty would agree with me. Ask yourself the following: Do you see a future with this young woman? Do you want to have more children? She will want your child and maybe even steal your sperm. Don't leave the protection up to her. Here's another thing I bet you don't know. A twenty-eight-year-old is very serious about love. She will fall deeply in love with you and unless you take her down the aisle, I predict there will be anger, lots of it.

Now, to answer your question. Your daughter should want you to be happy. And she should be able to accept your choices, even if you're acting like an idiot, which you are. I think it will be valuable to tell your daughter exactly where you stand with Liv. If you tell her you're just having fun, I think she'll understand. If you tell her you're in a very serious relationship, she'll react differently. She may be angry for quite a while. Eventually, if she wants to have you in her life, she'll have to come to terms with it. Good luck, William. Liv is in the sperm-stealing business.

> Gail, who knows what women
> are thinking

Gail, don't you think it disingenuous of William to be surprised that his daughter is uncomfortable with his young girlfriend? Or maybe he's just self-centered and immature. That's not to say that these relationships don't sometimes lead to marriage or that such a marriage can't work. But all his friends, not just his daughter, will notice the age difference and wonder about it.

Accepting her father's choices doesn't mean that Bess has to get involved with his dates. She has the right not to. But if William and Liv were to marry, then Bess would have to accept her new stepmother.

> *Susan*

Brenda's Partner

Dear Gail and Susan,

My daughter Brenda dated boys all through high school and college but recently announced that she is a lesbian. After the shock wore off, her mother and I accepted her sexual orientation as part of who she is. Brenda is bringing her partner Lucy to visit for the weekend. We always let Brenda and her boyfriends share a room when they came to stay, but the idea of Brenda in bed with a woman makes me want to throw up. I don't want to offend my daughter or Lucy, but I don't think I am ready to let them sleep together under my roof. What should I do?

> Ralph

I Have to Tell You, Ralph . . . You've Got a Problem,

You are going to offend Brenda if you don't let her share her room with Lucy under your heterosexual roof. Lucy may be in your life for a very long time, if not forever. If you hadn't let Brenda share a room with her boyfriends, you could easily say one of those manly sentences like, "No daughter of mine is going to sleep with anybody under my watch." Obviously it's too late for that. You might someday be planning a wedding for these two, so don't alienate them now. Tell your wife that she doesn't have to dye her shoes yet, but it might come to that. Be welcoming. Be the strong, liberal people that you think you are.

Don't be too nauseated—Gail

Some parents have a rule that in their home, unmarried children can't sleep with their boyfriends or girlfriends. Ralph clearly doesn't. Despite what he says, he has not fully accepted his daughter's sexual orientation. Ralph needs to find a way to deal with his feelings of unease. Perhaps he is disappointed, confused, or even ashamed. If he can face his feelings, he will more likely be able to get beyond them. I would encourage him to talk to Brenda about his discomfort and get to know Lucy better.

Susan

Only a Month

Dear Gail and Susan,

My thirty-year-old son Dirk wants to marry a girl he's known for only a month. I don't think it's a good idea and have told him he should know someone longer than a month before making a lifetime commitment. But since his father and I are divorced, he says I'm not very credible when it comes to picking a mate. He said he might listen to you ladies.

Hallie

Dear Mother of a Potential Groom,

First of all, your marriage has nothing to do with his marriage and he shouldn't compare the two. That's just an excuse for him.

Knowing someone for only a month is really not knowing him or her at all. There's a state called limerence that can last for at least six months. It's that time when a relationship is brand-new and each of the participants have shined such a bright light upon each other that they're not really seeing what the other person is like. They're projecting qualities that they want the other person to have. . . . And then reality sets in. People start to reveal themselves. Sometimes they only have minor flaws, as everyone does, and the relationship blossoms. Sometimes they have big flaws, and that's why no one should marry after only a month. Your son and the woman should go through the seasons together. They should vomit in front of each other. Then they'll really know if they want to stay together.

Hopefully, he will listen to us. He needs to slow down.

Gail, who believes in long engagements

Once more we agree, Gail. Some short courtships lead to successful marriages, but not because the courtship was brief. I, like you, advise him to slow down. He can't know in a month his girlfriend's character, how she'll handle adversity, or how mature she is.

The beginning of a relationship, ironically called the "honeymoon period," is characterized by an initial time of harmony. Each person is on good behavior, projects onto the other the qualities he or she wants, and ignores qualities he or she doesn't like.

Dirk and his girlfriend need to get past the honeymoon period before they make plans for a real honeymoon. Hallie should show Dirk our answers. He said he'd listen to us, Gail. I hope he does.

Susan

Not Using Birth Control

Dear Gail and Susan,

Last week, my son Ned's girlfriend told him she is pregnant. Ned says he isn't sure he's the father because he and Kimberly were separated for a while. I'm angry at them both for being irresponsible and not using birth control. Ned is only twenty-five, just getting started as a lawyer and not ready to get married. He certainly wouldn't consider it if he isn't the father. One of my questions is, Should Ned do anything or just wait until Kimberly asks something of him? And if he's the father, then what do I advise him to do?

Bradley

Dear Angry at Them Both,

Bradley, did you ever have that talk with your son about using protection? You can be angry at both Kimberly and Ned, but it's not going to do any good. This is complicated and I know you know it. Your son can't know if Kimberly's child is his until the child is born and a DNA test can be done. So let's put that possibility aside for the moment.

I don't think Ned should make any big moves until Kimberly gets him involved. If he truly loves her, maybe he'll stay with her whether or not the child is his. If he doesn't love her and it turns out that he's the father, hopefully he'll be a good one whether he marries Kimberly or not.

Don't worry so much, Bradley. These things sort themselves out.

Gail, who secretly hopes the baby is not Ned's

Whew! Let's sort this out. First, Kimberly needs to decide what she wants to do—have an abortion, have the baby, have paternity tests, marry someone. Until Kimberly clarifies her thoughts and feelings, Ned will have to wait.

If Kimberly chooses to have the child and she wants to marry Ned, then Ned will have to decide whether to marry her. Bradley might suggest some professional counseling to help his son make this decision.

If Ned is actually the father and he and Kimberly decide not to marry, they will have to work out child support and child custody with a mediator or lawyer.

I suggest that Bradley advise his son to take one step at a time. And remind him to use birth control until he is ready to have children.

Susan

Hiding Out

Dear Gail and Susan,

I have been trying to get in touch with my twenty-five-year-old son Ralph by phone and by e-mail, but he doesn't answer either. He got a girl pregnant and is hiding out. Should I just let him sort this situation out for himself or push harder to get him to talk to me?

Jordan

Dear Wanting to Push Harder,

If your son isn't answering his phone, that's one thing. He doesn't want to hear from the woman. If he isn't answering his e-mail, he doesn't want to hear from you, either. He probably thinks you're going to let him have it.

Yours is a silly letter, Jordan, because you have no choice. You *have* to let him sort the situation out for himself. I don't know how you can push harder other than going to his residence and pushing his door in. Or showing up at his work and embarrassing him. Let it go. He'll emerge someday, probably to ask you to lend him money for child support.

Gail, who told her sons to be careful

Ralph at twenty-five is very immature and irresponsible with potentially two lives—a young woman's and a baby's. He is hoping that by hiding out, the problem will go away. Maybe he'll luck out and the girl will decide that he is not worth finding. Or the girl and the law will eventually track him down.

    In any case, Jordan will have to wait until his son is ferreted out or thinks he's in the clear and reappears. When Ralph surfaces, Jordan should advise therapy. His son has a lot of growing up to do.

Susan

My Son Warren

Dear Gail and Susan,

    My son Warren is dating a very strong woman who pushes him around. Warren used to exude an air of confidence, but now he seems indecisive and insecure. I'm afraid Nina will talk him into marrying her and that he will live the life of a broken man.

Hildegarde

Dear Possible Mother-in-Law of a Very Strong Woman,

    Since your son is in an indecisive and insecure state because of Nina, you can move in and, while she's talking him into marrying her, try to convince him that he will live the life of a broken man if he does. It's going to be a battle between you and Nina for your son, Hildegarde. If you become as strong as she is, you have a really good chance of winning. Can I place a bet?

    By the way, your letter sounds as if it comes from a different century, and I'm not talking about the last one. I'm talking about the one before that, the one before people wrote letters to get advice.

Gail, who tries to exude an air of confidence

    Clearly Warren exuded an air of confidence he really didn't have. Ergo, he was attracted to a woman he could rely on to tell him what to do. Young adults often experiment with different kinds of relationships to learn more about themselves and to help them grow up. That's the value of dating.

Our children must learn a lot about life from trial and error. Warren is trying out being with a strong woman. He may decide he likes turning decisions over to someone else. He may learn from Nina and develop real confidence himself. He may stay with her. Or this experiment may run its course and he'll move on.

Warren needs to learn and grow from this relationship. If Hildegarde gets into a power struggle with Nina, she will not be furthering her son's independence.

Susan

Uncomfortable around Harlan

Dear Gail and Susan,

My daughter Rachel is dating a man, Harlan, who is of mixed race—his father is white and his mother is black. In addition, Harlan and his family are Christian and we are Jewish. Rachel is thinking of converting. I'm very confused and disappointed. I feel very uncomfortable around Harlan. There are so many problems facing young couples these days, and I think taking on race and religion doesn't seem like a good idea. What do you think?

Myra

Dear Confused and Disappointed,

Let me start out by saying I believe love is more important than race and religion. Forgive your daughter for converting, if she does, and forgive yourself for feeling uncomfortable around Harlan. You're not a racist. You're just not used to having a brown man around. In the future, we're all going to be light brown because there are so many mixed marriages and more of them on the way. If President Obama's parents hadn't met, we wouldn't have him. (I believe a true mixed marriage is between Democrats and Republicans.)

It's very confusing when kids convert. But it's best in the long run, because if they have children, both parents practice the same religion. They'll have harmony. Look at it this way: you'll only be heartbroken until you die.

Gail, who really hopes it all turns out well

I want to make three points here. First, mixed marriages of any sort are not uncommon and are much more accepted than they used to be. Differences of religion and ethnicity may bring stress to a relationship, but differences of all kinds must be dealt with in any relationship if it is to thrive.

Two, because of technology and the media, our children's generation, no matter what their religious or ethnic background, grew up with many shared experiences—television shows, video games, Internet sites, Starbucks. Black and white, Christians, Muslims, and Jews have had a lot of common experiences. To that point, the couple met in some shared place—college, work, or maybe the gym.

Third, Myra's discomfort is understandable. She comes from a generation with much less racial and ethnic interaction than her child's generation. I advise Myra not to discount her feelings—they are real—but also not to be paralyzed by them. She would do well to share her discomfort and confusion with Harlan and her daughter and ask them to help her develop new ways of thinking and feeling as she gets to know someone from a different ethnic and religious background from hers.

Susan

Missy's Arrangement

Dear Gail and Susan,

I know that my problem isn't unique, but for me it is a *big* problem. My twenty-one-year-old daughter Missy graduated from college and got a job. Her mother and I were very proud of her for that. We offered her the opportunity to live with us while she got started. She's our youngest, so we didn't mind postponing our empty nest. But Missy announced that she was moving in with her boyfriend, which is what she did. My wife said I would get used to the idea, but I haven't. Not only does the arrangement not fit in with my old-fashioned ideas, but I read recently that kids who live together before marriage are more likely to get a divorce. That didn't help my state of mind. Can you?

Dominick

Dear Old-Fashioned Dominick,

Here's what I know. Missy at twenty-one knows very little about life. She's playing house. Unless she and her boyfriend are very mature, they're not going to make it. She's going to pull into your driveway one night crying. Her mascara will be down to her lips because she and her boyfriend had a fight, and you're going to be relieved that she's home, refilling your empty nest. She'll be sobbing and happy to be a little girl in her own bed, in her own room, especially since her mother will bring her soup. The next day, the boyfriend will apologize and tell her how much he loves her. And she'll go back home. Yes, home to her is where she and her boyfriend live, not your house. She may eventually break up with him. She may marry him. And there's nothing you can do or say that will make her change her mind.

Love is a strange force, and when parents try to separate their child from the person they love, it never works. Ask Romeo and Juliet . . . oops, you can't ask them. They're dead— because their parents meddled in their lives. You want to say to your daughter, "Don't you know you're ruining your life?" but she doesn't think so and won't believe you.

Dominick, enjoy your empty nest.

Gail, who at least tried to help

Dominick and his wife tried to bribe and lure Missy back home. They were willing to sacrifice her launching to postpone their empty nest. Missy turned them down. Brava to her! Now that Missy has graduated from college and gotten a job, she wants to live her life independent of her parents, which is an age-appropriate choice. One way to do that is to move in with her boyfriend.

Dominick is correct that couples who live together before marriage are more likely to get divorced, but I don't get the impression that Missy and her boyfriend are focusing on marriage. I think, more to the point, they can be independent of their parents but not be alone. They can support each other as they begin their adult work lives.

Another issue that Dominick raises is that of his old-fashioned values, which don't include unmarried couples living together. However, when our children leave adolescence and become adults, they take on their own value system, which may or may not be like ours.

Dominick has a lot to mourn . . . his child's having left the "nest," the loss of his vision of how Missy's adult path would be, the loss of his power to control his now-grown daughter.

Susan

A Broken Engagement

Dear Gail and Susan,

My son Eddie was dating a woman named Nadia. They were engaged, but Eddie changed his mind and broke up with her. Now Nadia keeps calling me wanting me to use my influence with Eddie. She thinks that because they broke up after a fight, he should give their relationship another chance. I like Nadia a lot and feel sorry for her. Should I talk to Eddie?

Wynne

Dear Mother of Eddie,

I addressed this letter to you as "Mother of Eddie" because that's what you are, and your loyalty has to be with your son. His perception of why they broke up and her perception of why they did might be quite different. Sometimes one person in a relationship causes a fight in order to break up with the other, and that might have happened in this case. Your son might have been okay with dating this woman, but not okay with being engaged. So stay out of it, Mom, and tell Nadia that you're very sorry, that you like her, but that there's nothing you can do. She may keep calling for a while. Be polite. Don't stay on the phone with her for very long and she'll probably stop calling once there's another man in her life.

Gail, who may have interfered too much

Eddie made a decision not to marry Nadia. Nadia doesn't like what he decided and is trying to coerce him back via his mother. We can have sympathy for the victim of a broken engagement, but that happens in life.

I concur, Gail. Wynne should not meddle in her son's love life. She should politely tell Nadia not to call anymore and wish her well in finding someone who wants her.

Susan

A Guy Named Christopher

Dear Gail and Susan,

My older daughter Terri used to date a guy named Christopher. They broke up about a year ago. Now my younger daughter Dorrie is dating him. Seeing Christopher again made Terri think she made a mistake in ending the relationship and now she wants him back. Christopher seems to like the attention from my two girls. Is there anything I can do? I have a feeling this is not going to end well.

Betsy

Dear Mother of Girls,

It would be much easier to be Christopher's mother than you right now. I'm sure you're right about this guy enjoying the attention from your daughters. I've heard more than once that men like to date sisters and that they like twins even better. I think your feeling that this is not going to end well is correct.

You ask what you can do. I, who pride myself on coming up with solutions, can think of only one thing. You and your girls should move to another state and don't leave a forwarding address.

> Gail, who has two sisters and we have
> never dated the same man

Gail, your solutions are always so creative! Expensive, but ingenious.

Love triangles, sibling rivalry, and adolescent drama! That's what I think when I read this letter.

Terri and Dorrie both have some growing up to do. My advice to Betsy is to tell her daughters that, in her opinion, they are participating in a high-schoolish, melodramatic situation and that they should get rid of Christopher. And Mom doesn't want to hear about it anymore. If they don't have Mom to talk to, the excitement of the rivalry will abate and the daughters will more likely move on.

Susan

CHAPTER SIX

Family Rituals

Family rituals—holiday parties, weddings, special birthdays, reunions— are a way for a family to establish bonds and continuity. Rituals provide a group of individuals an opportunity for shared experiences and a celebration history. They can also be annoying, stressful, and exhausting. Family members may spend too much time talking about the stock market or, worse, politics. Fights can occur. You have to make everyone check their weapons at the door and remove the knife that cuts the turkey immediately. Most of the time, family parties are cherished moments, except for the person who has to wash the pots.

Parents shouldn't forget that the family is constantly changing—more children, children getting older, divorce, people marrying in, family members dying. If we don't pay attention to and accommodate these changes in the family structure and dynamics, the rituals can become rigid prescriptions. Prescriptions can become obligations. Obligation can breed resentment—the children attend only because they are afraid not to. It's important that we and our children adapt to the inevitable changes. We know a woman in Los Angeles who leaves her Christmas decorations up all year as a constant reminder to her children where they are supposed to be on December 25 . . . and she's Jewish.

Things can change when our kid is in college. He may ask to invite a friend to our Thanksgiving dinner. Or he may be invited to his girlfriend's family's ski lodge for Christmas. We want our child to become independent. Independence means that his world expands beyond us. If we deny him these new experiences for the sake of a rigid ritual, we are in effect negating our kid's thrust toward independence. You might find yourself envious of your child's new life, if while he's skiing you're staying home and eating a twenty-pound turkey on your own. So you're going to have to fill your life with new traditions. You can finally make that stuffing recipe with the snails in it that made your son vomit. You can also inject the turkey with vodka and really enjoy the holiday.

When our adult child marries, his family expands. He now has in-laws to take into account. We should respect the decisions he makes to deal with them. As parents, we have to guard against becoming rivals with the in-laws for who gets the marrieds for the holidays. And be sure not to make a big deal over our adult child choosing to go to our ex's house. At eighteen, it's his choice. One mother got very upset when her daughter decided to go to her father's for Christmas and demanded to know if it was the ex's turn. The daughter was forty-three.

Another issue is where the rituals are held. Typically, Grandma and Grandpa or Mom and Dad host the holiday parties year after year. But when our children become adults, they should host some of the parties some of the time. They need the practice. They need to experience the achievement and the responsibility of being hosts. In addition, adult children need to become invested in perpetuating the rituals themselves and not be dependent on their parents to do it for them. If the scepter isn't shared or passed to the next generation, the rituals may come to an end once the older generation gets tired or dies, or both.

Independence means being creative, taking initiative, being open and flexible, having choice, showing respect, and solving problems. Parents need to foster independence, not inhibit it. If rituals evolve, they will remain alive and nurturing and promote adult independence. If we insist on everything staying the same no matter what, the ritual will at best become musty; at worst it will be stifling, and independence will be thwarted.

Think back to your own mother-in-law and the holidays. Annoying, wasn't she? She insisted that everyone show up. If you didn't, she was annoyed at you for the rest of the year. Didn't you once promise yourself that you'd never be like her?

If you're upset with change, here's a way to get over it. Look at your old holiday family albums. Have a good cry and then think about it. The pictures show that your family members were different people back then. Your children have grown into the adults you wanted them to be. Nobody even looks the same . . . except you, of course.

And then there's the wedding. Weddings can be fraught with all sorts of angst. The cliché that it's the bride's day is just that, a cliché. Mom does most of the planning and Dad pays. Should the daughter have whatever she wants, because it's her day? Shouldn't we as parents have a realistic budget and stick to it so we can teach our soon-to-be-married child fiscal responsibility? Vera Wang wouldn't want to hear this, but the dress can be borrowed. Invitations can be simple, flowers can be wild, the drinks can just be wine, forget the champagne, it'll look the same in the photographs, which can be taken by Uncle Jack, who has been an amateur photographer his whole life. The cake doesn't have to be majestic and the bottom layer can be fake. Better yet, get the young couple to elope and you won't have to take out your checkbook at all.

A Real Turkey

Dear Gail and Susan,

My husband Dave and I divorced five years ago. My nineteen-year-old son Mark is away at college most of the time. When he comes home, he stays with me in the home we all lived in when Dave and I were married.

The problem is that my ex and his new wife want Mark to have Thanksgiving dinner at their condo this year. Since Mark was born, I have made a lovely Thanksgiving dinner for family and friends. It just wouldn't be the same without him there. My heart wouldn't be in it.

It seems to me that since I am his mother, my wishes come first. Dave can see Mark another day of the weekend, so we can continue the tradition we began years ago that Mark grew up with. What do you think?

Karen

Listen, Conceited Karen,

Since your son is nineteen, he is legally an adult and the courts can't tell him where to go for the holidays. It's up to him. You write, "It seems to me that since I am his mother, my wishes come first." Wrong! Your son Mark's wishes should come first. And don't burden him with your tears. In an effort to please everyone, some kids eat two complete Thanksgiving meals and then want to throw up.

Mark is old enough to decide whether the tradition you began years ago should continue every year or maybe every other year. My guess is that he will stick with you because turkey doesn't taste as good in a condo. Should he choose to go to his father's, continue making your lovely meal for the rest of your family and friends and get used to being without him sometimes. Either learn to have some Thanksgivings without Mark or take a cruise in November.

And you're not going to believe this. Someday you're going to have to share him with his wife's parents.

Happy holidays to you, Gail

Gail, you immediately picked up on the two issues here. The first has to do with rituals. Rituals can provide continuity, stability, comfort, and fun. But rituals need to change, to evolve, if you will, with the inevitable changes in the family. An open family system is flexible and adaptive and responds to changes in relevant ways. A closed family system is rigid and unresponsive and, consequently, crippling. In a closed system, rituals become obligations.

Despite a divorce and her son's becoming an adult, Karen wants the old rituals to continue unchanged. Karen is so rigid about her Thanksgiving ritual that without her son Mark, her "heart wouldn't be in it."

The second issue Karen's letter brings up is Mark's autonomy or, rather, Karen's denial of it. When children are young, we tell them where they will be for Thanksgiving. With a divorce, where young children will spend their holidays is often written into the custody agreement. However, Mark is nineteen and therefore considered an adult. No parent can tell him where he spends his Thanksgiving. Both parents can issue him an invitation. Mark is old enough to deal with this problem and decide how he is going to divide his time between parents. Or if he will.

Susan

The Wonderful World of Disney

Dear Gail and Susan,

I come from a large family, seven brothers and sisters, and every year we, our spouses, kids, and grandkids get together for a summer reunion. This year we are going to the beach, where we have rented several houses. Everyone always has a great time.

I'm writing because my daughter Marie told us that she and her husband Larry and their three children will not be at the reunion this year. Marie and Larry want to take their kids to Disney World. My wife Dee says it's their prerogative. I say they are insensitive and selfish. They can take their kids to Disney World another time that doesn't conflict with this special family event.

I want to write Marie and Larry and tell them how I feel. Dee doesn't want me to. Who is right?

Sy

Dear Insensitive Himself,

How do you know that Marie and Larry can take their kids to Disney World another time? You sound retired, Sy, but I assume Marie and her husband aren't, since they have three children who want to go to Disney World. When you have a job, you have a limited amount of time off. Not everybody can be at a family reunion and go someplace else in the same year. You want to write to Marie and Larry to tell them how you feel. Don't make them feel guilty. They probably already bought tickets.

I am thrilled to tell you that your wife Dee is right. Put down your pen, Sy. Put down your pen.

Another right woman, Gail

This letter gives me an opportunity to discuss a pet peeve of mine. It raises my hackles when adults expect that they will never be deprived of what they want. And if you are the one to deprive them, they call you "selfish."

Sy's grown daughter and her husband are deciding how to spend their family vacation time and money. It is their right and responsibility to do so. Good for them! Rather than seeing their decision as evidence of maturity and independence, Sy sees it as depriving him of what he thinks he's entitled to. We are not entitled to determine how our adult children spend their time and money. Two-year-olds can be told no. Adult children should be able to say no to their parents.

In addition, as I answered Karen in the previous letter, family rituals are not binding forever.

Susan

Finding Neutral Ground

Dear Gail and Susan,

My husband and I are very religious. We go to church regularly, don't drink or smoke, and don't believe in people living together before marriage.

My thirty-year-old son Chris is living with an atheist who drinks. I have refused to visit them or have them in our home, because I don't want them to think we condone their choices. My husband is willing to see them on neutral ground. He asked me to write to you since this situation that my son has created is causing tension in our marriage.

Olivia

Dear Saint Olivia,

First of all, you can't force your children to be like you. You gave your son the foundation you wanted him to have. You taught him your beliefs. He learned them and rejected them. I know how that can hurt, especially if you feel Chris is going to go to hell when he dies. Your son isn't turning his back on you. You're turning your back on him. The bigger problem is . . . once you refuse to have contact with Chris, it could lead to a permanent separation. You won't see him or your future grandchildren. This is exactly the type of thing that separates families.

I have a solution, like I always do. Your husband sees them on neutral ground. You don't. At least he'll be keeping the family lines of communication open. And by the way, your son didn't create the stress in your marriage . . . you did.

Gail, who will see Chris if you don't

Chris is thirty years old—an adult. Not only is he allowed to make personal choices about all kinds of things, religion included, he is supposed to. Olivia rigidly wants to control her son. She thinks that on this subject she has the right to.

Olivia says she is standing for principles, but in reality she is creating a childish power struggle with her son. And, like a child, when she doesn't get her way, she withholds, hoping that by doing so her son will give in.

Chris doesn't want to be in a power struggle with his mother; he is beyond that. He is living his own independent life with his own values. Because Olivia is deluding herself about her power, she is more likely to lose her family than win the battle.

Olivia can ask that the children not drink or smoke in front of her. Chris and his girlfriend can graciously honor that request. They can all agree to keep religion out of the conversation.

They can be a family of individuals who don't agree about some issues. Or Olivia can dig in her heels, withhold her love, and think she's won. But in truth, as you say, Gail, she will lose her son.

Susan

Happy Birthday, Thelma

Dear Gail and Susan,

It's my ninetieth birthday this year. My daughter and son-in-law have talked me into having a big party. When I told my son the date, he said that he had a business conference planned for that weekend and asked if I could pick another evening. My daughter is angry and thinks that my son should sacrifice his conference for my birthday. Personally, I don't mind changing the date, but now with the dissension, I'm thinking of going on a cruise instead. What do you think I should do?

Thelma

Thelma, You Birthday Girl, You,

Your daughter is a bitch. Your son isn't merely going to a meeting or having a business dinner. It's a conference, which was likely set up two years ago. And he may not get a chance to go to another one in God knows how long. I think it's a wonderful idea that you go on a cruise.

By the way, Thelma, this has nothing to do with your question, but did you know that some adult children are putting their parents on cruises, especially if they're physically or mentally challenged, because it's cheaper than putting them in a rest home? It reminds me of the Eskimos who put their elderly on a block of ice and pushed them out to sea when they were ready to die. Susan, does this sound familiar?

Bon voyage, Gail

Actually, Gail, I prefer warm weather cruises, maybe to Southeast Asia. In any case, according to my sources, the Eskimos haven't done that in centuries.

Back to Thelma's dilemma. First, Gail, when a child is young, his birthday day is important. Celebrating it on another day would be confusing to him. But as we get older, the celebration doesn't have to be on the exact date. We can understand that our birthday and the party day may be different. We don't get confused.

Second, we can't expect our grown children to drop their lives because we're giving a birthday party, no matter how old we are. Thelma's son had a conflict with the date and appropriately asked if it could be changed.

In a rigid, closed family system, the individuals' needs are not considered. The ritual event rules everybody and all conform to its requirements. In an open, flexible system, the individuals weigh in and rituals adapt to accommodate everybody.

I would encourage Thelma to explain to her rigid daughter how to be open and flexible. Then, no matter what her daughter says, Thelma should make her own decision—either change the date or take a cruise.

Susan

Sol, the Cook?

Dear Gail and Susan,

My wife and I have always had the family over for the Thanksgiving and Christmas holidays. We have our five children and their spouses and children, a total of at least twenty-six people, more if anyone brings a friend. My wife and I are in our seventies and I don't think we should do it anymore. My wife prepares for days before and is exhausted for days after. Even though everyone pitches in, it's a lot of work. We've gotten our kids so used to our doing it that the out-of-towners get their plane tickets a year in advance. I think that the children should take over the responsibility for maintaining our family traditions. My wife says that the kids will be so disappointed, she can't do that to them. I said I would. How do I do it?

Sol

Dear You Make Me Laugh, Sol,

I can't tell you how to make Thanksgiving dinner. I've never made a turkey. Hopefully, Susan has. Men make good chefs, but I don't think you have to be one. Thanksgiving can still be at your house, but the kids have to do more than just pitch in. They have to do whatever people do to a turkey. They have to prepare the stuffing, sweet potatoes, etc., etc., etc. You'll then be having the same tradition that you've had over the years and in the same place without your wife getting exhausted and without you having to do it by yourself. What you can do is the shopping. Then, when your family arrives, they'll have the ingredients they need to cook.

Kids want their parents to be strong and healthy and they would like us to live forever and to do all the holidays. It's up to you as the parent to hand over the reins so that they can perform perfectly without you, when you're no longer here on earth. When they're entering adulthood, you have to make sure they have the ability to live on their own. And when you yourself are entering your golden years, you have to make sure that they can live without you.

Thanks a lot, Sol, now you've gotten me depressed.

Gail, who will snap out of it

Gail, unlike the president, I have not pardoned the Thanksgiving turkey. Over the years, I've tried all kinds of recipes, and I'm here to tell you they're all a lot of work.

Now, let me address the ritual of the family Thanksgiving dinner, or any ritual get-together. Often, even after the children are grown and married, Mom and Dad continue to host the ritual dinner. Having it in the childhood home feels comforting and provides continuity.

However, the absolute predictability of the ritual has downsides as well. First, if traditions aren't turned over to the next generation when Mom and Dad are alive, they can disappear when Mom and Dad die. The family can become so dependent on the ritual as it was that they can devise no other plan.

That's why I encourage families not to let their rituals become unquestionably rigid. For instance, Mom and Dad can suggest that they and the children take turns hosting the dinner, a plan that can survive the parents. The children get practice and experience with Mom to advise them as they master what she knows. Each child can even add his own unique twist—maybe pecan pie instead of pumpkin now that a southerner has married into the family, so the ritual evolves as the family changes.

Second, it's good for adult children and their children to be the hosts, not always the guests. The host role brings with it responsibil-

ity and pride of accomplishment, important for adult children and grandchildren to experience.

So Sol's family can start out by following Gail's advice—same location, different roles for the family members—for this year. I'd add that Sol can get a ready-made turkey from a market to make it easier for his wife. I also recommend that Sol discuss with his children the concept of rituals and their need to evolve, and then make a plan to change the venue in years to come.

Susan

The Kids Don't Get Along

Dear Gail and Susan,

I have four grown children, ages thirty-four, thirty-two, twenty-eight, and twenty-six. They don't get along with each other. I'm very close with my three siblings; in fact, we are each other's best friends. I want that for my children. I suggest lots of family get-togethers but am often turned down. How can I get my children to be more like me and my siblings?

Anne

Oh My God, Anne,

You may never get your children to be more like you and your siblings, and that's too bad. I would have suggested that you gather them all together and get them to talk about why they don't get along, but I have the feeling that they won't come to such a gathering. It's sad when families fall apart, and I can't begin to guess the reason why yours did.

You're going to have to enjoy your children individually. And maybe if you start with one child, you can build up the family again. It's going to be difficult, but try. Take your eldest to lunch and try to have a conversation about why he or she can't stand his or her brothers and sisters. Ask if he or she would mind including one other sibling next time you get together. It's possible that he or she would agree to that—if he or she gets to pick the sibling. Someday, if you add them one at a time, you might get to have lunch with all four of them.

Anne, if you write again, tell me the names of your children so I don't have to do that awkward "he or she" stuff.

I feel for you—Gail

Gail, I'm going to hypothesize that one of the reasons Anne's children don't get along is that she has an agenda for them. She wants to make her children into a mirror image of her family. She wants them to be best friends. She hasn't acknowledged their individuality nor allowed them to form their own relationships with each other. Children get angry when they are forced into relationships. Now that they are adults, they don't have to be with each other.

It may be too late to change things, but perhaps if Anne stops trying to make her family conform to her wishes and sees them as individuals, she will make different choices, and therefore effect changes in the system. If the get-togethers are based on individuals' true interests—for instance, inviting two children who like the theater to the theater with her—she may be able to help forge some real connections that her children enjoy.

Susan

Family Reunion

Dear Gail and Susan,

My daughter has been dating a guy for about six months. Our whole family is going to a family reunion next month and my daughter wants to invite her boyfriend along. They are not engaged or even talking about a long-term relationship. Should we include him at the reunion? He might be gone by next year. The family will all have met him and connected with him and I might have to explain that my daughter and he broke up. Wouldn't it be simpler just to not include him?

Paula

Dear Paula with a Problem,

What's the big deal? Your daughter has a boyfriend. She feels close to him. She'll have a better time at the reunion if he's there with her. End of story.

Paula, you go too far. You're imagining that your family will have connected with your daughter's boyfriend. Are you kidding? At a family reunion, a once-a-year thing? It's most likely they'll be too busy connecting with each other. The boyfriend will be an insignificant part of the whole get-together. I can assure you that if he's gone by next year, you won't have to explain anything about how and why he and your daughter broke up. They might not remember him.

Go to the reunion. Have a good time. And let your daughter have a good time, too. Stop being so self-centered.

Gail, who always included her sons'
girlfriends

Paula believes that if her daughter brings a date, she will cause difficulties within the family. Is that because the family is a closed system? When you marry into a closed system, you have a legitimate identity. You are instructed about the rules and are entitled to attend the rituals. However, until you marry in, you have no acceptable position. A date does not have a sanctioned role.

Paula's daughter's adult identity includes the fact that she is dating someone. Without a date, she may feel like her mother's child.

The family may be curious about how serious the young couple is and may ask questions or speculate among themselves. But so what? If Paula can let go of her desire to keep the system closed, she will enjoy her daughter's new stage of life and make no apologies to the family now or next year.

Susan

A New Thanksgiving

Dear Gail and Susan,

My son just got married and he and his wife want to have
Thanksgiving dinner at their apartment. It's nice of them to
want to take on the work, but they will be inviting friends we
don't know in addition to our family. I know that I would rather
spend the holiday with just family. Also, since the kids don't
have enough dishes and silver yet, they want me to lend them
mine. I would like to tell them to just let me do Thanksgiving at
our house. My husband doesn't agree with me and has told me
to go along with what my son and daughter-in-law have planned.
I guess my question is, can't I get them to do it my way without
hurting their feelings?

                                                                Felice

Dear Felice, Owner of Dishes and Silver,

Your husband is right and my answer is no. You can't do it
your way.

When adult children marry, they might want to have new
traditions and do holidays their way. You're lucky they invited
you. They may have just wanted to have their friends there.
Get used to it, Felice. Your son and daughter-in-law might do
a lot of things differently than you do. They might even raise
their children differently than you did. They might even
understand that when their adult children get married,
they'll be bringing their dishes and silverware to their kid's
apartment.

The important thing is that the family stay together. It's
not important where they stay together.

Grow up, Felice. Your kid has.

        Gail, who still has holidays on her mother's dishes

*Gail, did you notice how Felice's letter is organized? She starts
out by acknowledging the change in her family. She even compli-
ments the newlyweds for their offer to host Thanksgiving. But then*

those pesky friends intrude and Felice ends by asking how she can keep things the way they were—Thanksgiving at her house, no friends.

So here's another example of a parent unwilling to change the family ritual when the family changes. Unlike Felice, I am heartened to know that young adults want to host family rituals even if they have to borrow from Mom to do it. And of course they get to add their own touch, in this case, friends.

If rituals become rigid, they become obligations. If rituals don't naturally alter as the family grows and changes, then the family gets stuck. And being stuck means going backward.

Susan

A Family Tradition

Dear Gail and Susan,

For years I've hosted a big family party at Christmas. Our immediate family and our extended family—grandparents, aunts, uncles, and cousins—are always invited. However, in the last few years, the grandparents (my mom and dad) and one of the aunts (my sister) have died and some of the cousins have moved away. I want to stop the tradition. I think its time has passed. But when I told everyone that I wasn't doing Christmas this year, my grown son and daughter and a couple of the others expressed their disappointment. Do I have to continue a tradition I've lost interest in?

Bernice

Dear Bernice, Maker of Christmas,

Your issue here should be with your adult children. Obviously they need to have the Christmas of their childhood, or as close to it as possible. You should be flattered that they care so much. It's nice that you gave your children a tradition that they want to continue.

That doesn't mean that everything has to be exactly the same and that it all has to be on your shoulders. Why don't you sit down with your son and daughter and plan this year's Christmas? They might want to add new things that will become traditions or take away the things they really don't care about. And get them to help.

What really concerns me is that you sound depressed about Christmas. You are concentrating on the losses you have experienced. Making plans with your children could lift your spirits. And don't forget there's a whole new generation to come. One day, in the not so distant future, your grandchildren will be joining the celebration.

Christmas is not a thing of the past.

                    Gail, who throws a holiday party every year

Gail, here is what happens if the family rituals don't change. When the older generation either dies or no longer wants to continue the ritual, the younger generation's only options are to disband the tradition or coerce the parents into keeping it alive when they don't want to. That's why I encourage parents to prepare their children for the time when they will have to take over.

Bernice is thinking only about herself in relation to her family of origin. Since she has suffered the loss of those very people, the tradition no longer has meaning to her. In her grief over the loss of her childhood family, she has forgotten that there is another generation for whom family rituals may be important.

What I suggest is that Bernice talk to her son and daughter about one or both of them taking on the job of continuing the family Christmas. The celebration doesn't have to be the same as it was. In fact, it should be conceived anew to reflect the way the family is now. So perhaps the first year under the new leadership, it will be smaller.

                                                          Susan

Ex-Husbands and New Wives

Dear Gail and Susan,

My twenty-six-year-old daughter Cherry and her husband have decided to have a big Christmas party and invite me and my second wife as well as her mother and her new husband. My ex-wife and I don't get along and my daughter knows that. Yes, it would be nice if after a divorce everybody liked each other, but that's not the case here. Sure, we could be civil for an evening, but I don't understand why my daughter is doing this. She's not a little kid anymore and should be able to accept that we are not one big happy family.

I think that my daughter is being provocative and insensitive. I don't want to go, I don't want this to become a big drama, but I also think that my daughter needs to accept that her parents are divorced. It's not as though this is her wedding when of course she would want both her parents there. Any advice on how to handle this?

                                                                    Glen

Dear Provocative and Insensitive Glen,

You are so wrong. Your daughter is throwing a big Christmas party. That means you and her mother will hardly have to see each other. You say Cherry is not a little kid anymore. Right. She's the one that's being mature. You're the one who's behaving like a child. She knows you're divorced. She doesn't expect you to be a big happy family. If she did, she would just be inviting you, her unreasonable father, your wife, her mother, and her husband to a small intimate dinner, hoping that everybody would get along.

I suggest you don't go. You're the one who would create the big drama. My advice on how to handle this? Tell her you don't want to be in a room with her mother and that you'd rather forgo a nice Christmas party than be civil. If you express yourself that way, you won't have to worry that she'll invite you to anything again.

I don't like you. I wouldn't invite you anywhere.

                                        Gail, who likes everyone else

Well, Gail, I don't agree with you here. True, the party is big and therefore not intimate. But it is just a party. I wonder why

Glen's daughter didn't talk to her father (and mother) before sending the invitations. Why didn't she inform each of them of her party plans and assure them that she would understand if either of her parents chose to decline. That would have been the mature and polite thing to do.

If we have a choice, we do not invite a divorced couple to the same party if we know they will be uncomfortable—or at least we give them a choice of attending or not. No obligation; no shame. It's not gracious or thoughtful to do otherwise, even if they are one's parents. As I sometimes say, parents have feelings, too. Adult children need to give up their idealizing and self-centeredness and think about their parents' feelings.

What can Glen do? He can opt to go to the party and get through the evening. Or he can respectfully decline. Perhaps as his daughter matures, she will develop empathy and be less egocentric.

Susan

Christmas Deprivation

Dear Gail and Susan,

My husband's family and my family spend Christmas together. My adult children Mel and Maureen always bring presents for everyone. My sister Jean's adult children do not. Consequently, my sister's grandkids get gifts from their aunt and uncle, but my grandchildren don't. Should I tell Mel and Maureen to stop buying presents?

Bethany

Dear Bethany, Who Should Keep Her Mouth Shut,

Why is it your problem that your sister's grandchildren get more gifts than your grandchildren? Obviously Mel and Maureen are generous people who enjoy giving. Why try to stop them? Do you want to stop Santa Claus, too?

What I really don't get is your basic attitude. You ask if you should tell your adult children to stop buying gifts. Why do you feel that you have the authority to tell them what to do? Remember this: When you tell kids who are taller than you what to do, they'll do one of two things. They'll either not listen or they'll argue with you.

> Gail, a woman who knows when to be
> quiet . . . sometimes

Children want everything to be equal. They call it being fair. Bethany resents that her sister's grandchildren get more than hers do. Bethany, like a child, wants things to be identical for her and her sister.

Over time, children learn that we don't all get the same. Bethany's grandchildren are learning that lesson. They are also learning the lesson of altruism.

Bethany would respect and admire Maureen's and Mel's family values were she not dealing with her own childish issues. She should definitely not tell her daughter and son to stop buying presents.

> *Susan*

The Floridians

Dear Gail and Susan,

My daughter Caroline has been married to Aaron for three years. So far, every Thanksgiving and Christmas they have gone to Aaron's family, who live in Florida. When I complained to Caroline, she said that since Aaron's folks don't see them very often, Aaron wants to at least spend the holidays with them. It's true that because Aaron and Caroline live near us, we can see them anytime during the year, but I still think that the holidays are special and that we should get our turn. What do you think?

> Carita

Dear Carita, the Concerned,

When our children are adults, they make their own decisions about where to go for holidays. However, I understand
your frustration. In some families both sets of in-laws join
their children. Suggest to your daughter that you would like
to go to Florida next Thanksgiving or Christmas, and that
way the whole extended family can be together (hopefully,
that'll work). If your in-laws have you over for, let's say,
Christmas, you could reciprocate by having them over to your
hotel for Christmas Eve. That's right: "hotel." Don't expect to
stay with them. Get in, have the holiday, and get out.

Another way to blend the family is to invite Aaron's parents to you for a holiday. I assume you live north of them.
When you live in very warm weather, it's nice to travel to
somewhere where there's hope for a white Christmas. If all
else fails, have your holidays with Caroline and Aaron before
they leave for Florida or after they get back. Once your daughter has a lot of children, I bet they'll stay home for the
holidays.

I hate to admit it, but when I was growing up, we always
had Thanksgiving on Friday because our housekeeper, our
beloved Minerva Elizabeth Taylor, was off on Thursday for
her own Thanksgiving. It never bothered any of us.

Gail, the holiday problem solver

*Gail, to paraphrase Shakespeare, Thanksgiving on any other
day still means turkey and giving thanks.*

*What caught my attention in this letter is the word "com-
plained." To complain means to express censure, to protest, to fault-
find, or to beg in a mean-spirited way. Why does Carita have to
complain to her daughter about her in-laws? Why doesn't she just
suggest an alternative plan—yours, for instance?*

*When our adult children marry, the family expands, sometimes
by a lot. Our child brings not only a spouse, but a mother-in-law,
father-in-law, brother- or sister-in-law, and on and on. A lot of
change. Change can be stressful. Stress can cause regression . . . yes,
even in parents.*

Like a child who thinks she's powerless, Carita protests and finds fault. She should instead creatively look for solutions.

Did you know, Gail, that the opposite of "to complain" is "to rejoice"?

Susan

No, Susan, I did not. It's certainly appropriate here.

Gail

Better Late Than Never

Dear Gail and Susan,

My forty-year-old daughter is getting married for the first time. She wants a big wedding and wants us to pay for it; as she says, "better late than never." She is right that if she were twenty, we probably would have given her the wedding she wanted without question. But now my husband and I are both retired. We do not have the kind of income we had twenty years ago, nor the belief in the big wedding we used to have. My daughter says we are penalizing her just because it took her so long to find someone to marry, and is angry and depressed.

We don't want to ruin our relationship with our daughter. This should be a happy time for us all. Maybe we should just give in and pay for the wedding.

Barbara

Dear Barbara, What's Wrong with You?

Aren't you seeing the most important point here? Your daughter is angry and depressed! She doesn't sound very bridal to me. You write that it took her a long time to find someone to marry. Personally, I don't think she's found him yet. Trust me, when true love is found, depression isn't hanging around so close to a wedding.

As you well know, she's forty years old. Please. She should be thinking about the marriage, not the wedding. If you decide to pay for the event, you'll be wasting your retirement money, since I'm sure your daughter will be divorced within a year. Are you going to pay for her second wedding when she finds someone at fifty?

Your wedding planner, Gail

Gail, do you know what constitutes an essential part of our identity? Age! In other words, we don't expect a six-year-old to behave the way an eleven-year-old does. A twenty-year-old bride is not a forty-year-old bride.

Barbara and her husband are retired. They have less income than they had when they were younger. Their daughter presumably has a larger income than she had when she was twenty. Age makes a difference. Barbara's daughter is unreasonably expecting to be treated as if she and her parents were younger. Barbara's fiancé is presumably Barbara's age. Does a forty-year-old man expect his retired in-laws to give him a free wedding ride?

Barbara and her husband need to be very realistic about what they can afford and want to spend and make that number clear to their daughter and her prospective husband. If being realistic "ruins" Barbara's relationship with her daughter, then they didn't have a real relationship before. Has the daughter been ruling the roost with her temper tantrums? Are her parents afraid of her? If Barbara's daughter cannot accept the reality of her situation and she continues to believe that her parents are penalizing her, I don't hold out much hope for this long-sought-after marriage working out.

Susan

The Big Event

Dear Gail and Susan,

My twenty-five-year-old daughter Susie is getting married. My ex-wife always wanted to plan the "big event." Okay, I understand that, but she wants to be in charge of the wedding and have me pay for it. I don't mind paying, but it seems to me that if I pay, I should get to plan it. After all, I should decide where my money is going. I don't want to cause my daughter distress, but I don't want to be taken advantage of, either. Help!

Brian

Oh, Boy, Brian,

You have written to the wrong people. This is more of an ex-husband–ex-wife dispute. However, it intrigued me to know that you, as a man, wanted to plan a wedding. I guess you want to deal with the centerpieces, pick out the color for the bridesmaids' dresses, and decide whether the dresses should match the flowers. It's not going to happen and it will distress your daughter if you try. Just set a budget and hope your daughter and ex-wife don't cry.

Fathers of the bride never decide where their money is going. They're lucky to get invited.

Gail, mother of grooms

I agree, Gail, this letter smacks of ex incompatibility. Nevertheless, I want to address a parent–adult child issue that is raised.

Brian can solve his problem by talking to his twenty-five-year-old daughter about money. Sometimes brides don't want hard cash to be part of their fantasy day, but it is. And I always say that if you are not old enough to have a realistic money conversation about the wedding, then you are not old enough to get married.

That being said, Brian can tell Susie exactly how much he will spend. Susie and her mother will have to make decisions to meet that bottom line. Brian can also ask that before Susie and her mother commit to an expense, he be consulted for approval. This will not only protect Brian from being taken advantage of, but it will also help Susie learn to make and stay within a budget, a good skill to master.

Susan

Enjoying Cocktails

Dear Gail and Susan,

My daughter is getting married. She and her fiancé are recovering alcoholics. They met in Alcoholics Anonymous. They have asked us not to serve liquor at the reception, since they are inviting friends from AA. Our problem is that many of the guests are our friends, who expect drinking at a wedding. My wife and I enjoy a cocktail or some wine at a party or event. I sympathize with the alcoholics' challenges, but don't they have to learn to live in the real world? Should they make the world over to keep themselves from temptation? Isn't it up to them to learn to discipline themselves and not have everyone cater to them? So should we serve liquor for the many, or acquiesce to the few?

Lester

Dear Lester,

It's not your wedding. It's your daughter's. While it's true that recovering alcoholics have to learn to live in the real world, your daughter doesn't have to learn that lesson on her wedding day.

You seem to be very angry at people who are in AA. Have a drink and calm down.

Gail, who needs a martini after dealing with this letter

Actually, Gail, I don't quite agree with you. True, it's the bride's wedding, but presumably the guests are not being invited just to worship her and bring gifts. There should be some concern for the guests' comfort and pleasure, since they will dress up, drive or fly some distance to attend, and bring presents.

What bothers me about the bride and groom's demand is that it is just that, a demand. Had they said to the parents, "We have a problem—how do we help our friends stay sober and also be gracious to the other guests," I would have deemed the soon-to-be married couple mature, thoughtful, and considerate. As presented, I would say that they are self-centered and ill-mannered.

That being said, the problem of accommodation is entirely up to Lester and his wife. They are not only paying, but they are also the hosts who have to consider all their guests. Remember, the invitation will read "Mr. and Mrs. Lester . . . cordially invite. . . ." Perhaps they want to avoid having wine on the tables but have liquor available on request. Or have a special nonalcoholic bar and tables for the bride and groom's AA friends.

Susan

Down to Rio

Dear Gail and Susan,

My daughter is getting married. As father of the bride I am of course paying for the wedding. My daughter and her fiancé want the wedding in Rio! They met there on a tour and want to say their vows in "the city that brought them together." I know that destination weddings are "in" now. But how can we ask people to go that distance for a wedding? It's a big trip and a big expense and I'm not in the financial position to pay for everyone. It will be hard enough for me to pay to get my immediate family there. The more I think of it, the more frustrated I get. What is my daughter thinking? And does that guy she's marrying have any money sense? You can tell that I am getting worked up, so before I blow up, I leave it to you to tell me how to break it to my daughter that Rio is out without breaking her heart.

Joe

Dear Father of the Bride,

Here's what you do. Tell your daughter that she can have her wedding in Rio with just the immediate family. I know it'll be a financial strain, but I mean immediate. It could be just you, your wife, your daughter, her fiancé, and his parents, who should pay for themselves. Then she can have some sort of party at home, celebrating her marriage. Not a party in a hotel ballroom, but a normal party. Okay?

You asked if the guy your daughter is marrying has any

money sense. That's a real worry for a father. You're watching your daughter get married to someone who seems to be frivolous. You're going to have to teach both him and your daughter the value of money. I truly believe that the first lesson can be about their wedding plans. It's a practical lesson that they won't easily forget.

If they sulk, buy a ladder and put it against your daughter's bedroom window. They might do you the favor of eloping.

Love, Gail, who is always bothered by destination weddings

Good solution, Gail. As the parents, we have to be careful not to get caught up in the young couple's dream of the exotic, unique wedding. It's easy for kids to come up with great, novel ideas for venues when they're not paying.

I hope that Joe's daughter and fiancé think a small wedding in Rio with a party later at home is a great option, or that they ditch the destination wedding and get married in their hometown.

In either case, Joe should make a financially responsible decision with his money. Joe should not look at it as breaking his daughter's heart. He should see it as breaking her and her fiancé into the real world of fiscal responsibility.

Susan

Cheryl's Birth Mother

Dear Gail and Susan,

I adopted my daughter right after she was born. Cheryl is now twenty-eight. About two years ago, she found her birth mother. They have seen each other occasionally. Cheryl is getting married and wants to invite her birth mother to the wedding and include her in the ceremony. I'm rather insulted. I raised Cheryl. I sat up with her when she was sick. My husband and I are paying for the wedding. The situation is torturing me. I can't sleep or eat. Please tell me how to deal with it.

Gloria

Dear Tortured,

Frequently, adopted children seek out their birth parents because it's a piece of the puzzle they've been missing, and the hard part for parents who have raised and loved their adopted children is that they frequently get insulted. I was at a wedding where a birth mother attended, but she wasn't included in the ceremony. So I don't blame you for feeling insulted. The only good news is you can't eat and will look really thin in the dress you buy.

You should tell your daughter it's fine with you that her birth mother comes to the wedding, but that you're not at all happy with her being involved in the ceremony. Try not to cry and be very brief. Make your point and end the discussion. If your daughter still wants it her way, you're going to have to live with it. It will be terrible, I know. But it's your daughter's wedding day, and as my mother always said, "You should always give a bride or pregnant woman anything she wants." I used to say to her, "What if the bride is pregnant, does that mean she gets everything forever?" My mother laughed. If Cheryl sticks to her plan, you're going to have to be a laughing mother, too, Gloria.

Gail, who feels bad

An adopted child may want to find her birth parent. Despite having good adoptive parents, an adopted child can have continuing angst about her adoption. Although she may have been told by her parents that she was "chosen" by them, the adopted child may also have feelings of rejection, thinking that for some reason she was not good enough to be kept by her birth mother. Remember, the child is young when she is adopted. She doesn't have the ability to understand why a mother might give up her child, and these early feelings stay with her.

Similarly, the adoptive mother has issues about having adopted. She doesn't feel fully and entirely entitled to her child. After all, she got her by taking her from someone else. She secretly fears that her child would prefer her birth mother, if she only knew her.

So, Gail, this is what I think is going on here. Cheryl wants her birth mother at her wedding to heal the wound of abandonment. If her biological mother is witness to her marital launching, Cheryl gets the acceptance she never had from her.

But the very presence of this mother exacerbates Gloria's secret belief that she took Cheryl away and has to give her back.

If Gloria can comprehend her own—as well as her daughter's—anxieties, she might feel compassion and empathy rather than confusion, anger, and fear. Gloria needs to recognize the falseness of her belief that she will lose Cheryl. If Gloria knows that the mother who raised Cheryl is the legitimate mother, she will be able to understand Cheryl's need to deal with her deep-seated feelings of abandonment and rejection. Then Gloria can more comfortably include Cheryl's birth mother as a guest who has a unique place in her daughter's history.

Susan

Family Photos

Dear Gail and Susan,

My son is getting married in a few months. We have sent an invitation to my daughter's boyfriend. They have been dating for a year. Do we have to include him in family photos? There's no guarantee at this time that he will become a member of the family. My daughter says if we exclude him, we are being rude. What do you think?

Ross

Don't Worry, Ross,

Professional photographers know who to include in formal wedding pictures. They're posing people and announcing who they want in the photos. It's their responsibility to get the bride and groom and then include the parents of the bride and groom and the bride and her parents and the groom and his parents. They have a routine. They're calling out for people to

join and unjoin the photo. Therefore, you won't be rude to
your daughter's boyfriend. If anything, the photographer will
be rude to him.

Maybe the boyfriend will end up in some of those candid
shots that the photographer takes, but I guarantee they won't
make it into the album. So relax, Ross. Have a good time.
Make sure your hair is combed.

Gail, who knows, because she's been
married more than once

*Ross's daughter is bringing a boyfriend to her brother's wed-
ding. Presumably, as a member of the groom's family, she will have
some obligations—being a member of the wedding party, posing for
photos, or being in a receiving line—that may leave her boyfriend
to fend on his own. She is concerned that he will be left out. She
doesn't want him to feel awkward and uncomfortable at a joyous
family event.*

*It seems to me that graciousness on the part of the family
would be to ask if he would like to have a photo taken with his
girlfriend or with members of the bridal party. Presumably, if he
feels that his presence in the family photo is inappropriate, he will
decline.*

*And as you say, Gail, the photo session is usually under the di-
rection of the photographer, and even if Ross's daughter's beau is in
a photo, the picture does not have to be displayed on the mantel or
in the photo album.*

*I have another idea, Gail, about why this has become an issue
between Ross and his daughter. Sometimes a wedding brings family tensions to the surface. The family is about to change. Ross's son
is leaving the nest. His daughter may feel rivalry with the new
young woman in the family who at this event is the center of everyone's attention. Wedding stress can cause the family to lose perspective, common sense, and manners. Arguing over details of protocol
may be a symptom of the stress.*

Susan

Cheating Fiancé

Dear Gail and Susan,

My daughter just found out that her fiancé cheated on her. The wedding is in two weeks. She doesn't know whether to call off the wedding and I don't know what to advise her to do. Everything is set to go, including out-of-town relatives with plane tickets and hotel reservations. I don't want to cancel, but is it the right thing to do?

Cynthia

Cynthia, Darling,

The wedding needs to be canceled. I know you know that, and I'll bet your daughter doesn't. Tell her that when a man is caught cheating, it means that he's cheated at least ten other times when he didn't get caught. He's not good husband material. As a matter of fact, he's not even bad husband material. We all know, even if he swears he'll never cheat on her again, that he will.

Give the relatives a choice of whether to come or not. Maybe some of them can get refunds. For the ones who come, throw a nice party. Having friends and family around you will really help. And having all your loved ones around might even help your daughter, because they'll all say the same thing that you've said: that she's way too good for him. She'll feel much better.

Make sure she stores the wedding dress properly. Most cleaners can do that. I guarantee she'll be getting it out for the right guy.

Gail, who postponed her
own wedding nine times

Gail, a wedding can be a lovely way to start married life. However, I have found that sometimes the year-long planning distracts the couple from addressing serious difficulties in their relationship. Often, the wedding planning brings an incompatible couple temporarily closer because they band together against an unreasonable parent or in-law. In addition, the wedding may become the rationalization for entering into a questionable marriage.

Weddings can and should be canceled if there is a serious problem in the relationship, and infidelity qualifies as serious. Avoiding embarrassment, returning gifts, and the discomfort of guests should not be reasons to go ahead with the marriage.

The good news in this case is that Cynthia and her daughter have open channels of communication, so they can discuss the problem. Luckily the daughter didn't keep her fiancé's cheating—a serious red flag—to herself.

When cheating comes to light in a long-term marriage, the parties sometimes work through the issues and decide to stay together. However, I agree, Gail. Why start out with a known problem that may never be fixed?

Cynthia, whose emotions are not as raw as her daughter's, is in a better position to think clearly. This is a marriage that should not take place. Cynthia should insist that the wedding be canceled.

Susan

CHAPTER SEVEN

Marriage

So your daughter got married. Nice guy. The wedding was lovely. And although she's been out of the house for five years (nine, counting college), in the past year you've had a lot of contact. Between visits to caterers and florists and discussing all the wedding plans, you've seen her or talked on the phone almost every day.

Now they're on their honeymoon—no phone calls, not even an e-mail. They return home to their new apartment. You call and they're out. When you finally reach them, they sound happy, but tell you they'll call to set up a time for dinner. They're busy with friends and work for the next few weeks.

Your married child's primary relationship is now with her husband. She and he get to set their boundaries. You have no power over the situation. You're no longer number one. You can sit around and wait for the call or you can remember what it was like when you were first married. You tortured your parents, too.

Or maybe your daughter gets married and calls every day to ask if she can drop over and hang out while her husband is at work, out golfing, or at his parents' house. It doesn't take too long before she's complaining about his never being home. How tempting for you to join in. It feels so right for her to be "home"—meaning your house—chatting with you. You and she against the world! But what about her marriage?

One of the major causes of the breakup of a marriage is that one or both of the young spouses has not emotionally separated from his or her family. The couple doesn't establish their own married unit. So, by letting your daughter hang out at your house, are you aiding and abetting her lack of separation and helping to undermine the marriage? You are. You need to tell her to go home—meaning to *her* house—and deal with the issues in her marriage: talk the problems through with her husband, get marital therapy, whatever is needed. You need to extricate yourself from being the place that tension is relieved without any problem being solved.

Freud said that there are six people in the marriage bed, meaning that parental dicta are internalized in the married couple's psyche. We can't do anything about our continuing influence, for better or worse, that we had over the many years our kids were under our care. But we can and should stay out of our kids' marriage problems and decisions unless we are specifically asked to contribute. It's not easy, since yesterday they were ours and now they're buying condos behind our backs.

Or perhaps you're the one getting married. You've been divorced for ten years and have finally met a woman to love. Up until now you've been your son's hunting companion, you had season basketball tickets together, you played racquetball once a week. Now you're busy with your fiancée, going to concerts, giving dinner parties, traveling. Your son doesn't like her. He thinks she's a gold digger. She's taking you away from him. He pouts when you are all together. You love your son. You love your fiancée. What to do? You don't want to give up this wonderful woman, but how can you get your son to come around?

Marriage, yours or theirs, means redoing the family structure. Boundaries and primary units change. Everyone needs to adjust. You can't hold on to the old power hierarchies and old expectations.

~~~~~~~~~~~~~~~~~~~~~~~~~~~~~~~~

Charlie, the Bully

Dear Gail and Susan,

My son-in-law Charlie bullies his wife and kids. My daughter Stephanie has a better job than he does and makes more money. I sense that Stephanie is getting ready to leave Charlie. I would really like to tell him how I feel about his behavior and maybe if I do, they can avoid a divorce. I would feel awful if they split up and I didn't at least try to fix the situation. What do you think I should say?

Lois

Dear Sensing Stephanie,

You can tell Charlie how you feel about his behavior but I doubt it will prevent a divorce. Bullies don't feel that they're bullies—so they rarely change and, if questioned, often get worse. What's going on now, which sounds like verbal abuse, can develop into physical abuse. My questions to you are: Why would you feel awful if they split up? Is this the type of man you'd want your daughter to be with forever? If anyone should be talked to, it should be Stephanie. Tell her how you feel about Charlie's behavior. And then leave it alone. Mothers can't possibly fix their grown children's marriages.

Gail, who hopes Stephanie leaves

Yes, that did catch my attention, Gail. Why would Lois want her daughter to stay married to a bully? Maybe the answer is that Lois wants her daughter to be married and thinks that she can talk Charlie into being a nice guy. Bullies have complex personality traits that don't change because someone points them out. Lois is being unrealistic to think that all Charlie needs is a good talking-to.

Stephanie seems to be handling the situation quite well. Deciding to divorce a bully isn't a bad decision.

Lois should not interfere with her daughter's working out her own marital problems.

Susan

Gina Gets It

Dear Gail and Susan,

My thirty-three-year-old son Robert is marrying a thirty-five-year-old woman with five children. I don't think he knows what he's getting into when he's committing to raising and supporting five kids. And I'm afraid he'll give up having children of his own. Isn't it my responsibility to talk to him about this undertaking, maybe get him counseling or something before he makes a huge mistake?

Gina

You Poor Thing, Gina,

Congratulations on your new grandchildren. You're right. Robert doesn't know what he's getting into. But he's marrying her, not dating her, not seeing her, not having an affair with her. I'm really sorry, but you have no power in this situation. You can try to talk to him, but I think you know deep down that's not going to do anything and he probably thinks he doesn't need therapy. Buy a dress for the wedding and be prepared to spend a lot of money on gifts for Robert's stepchildren at Christmastime.

I know you're worrying about your son not having children of his own. Maybe that's a good thing. You think he's out of his mind for doing this. That "out of your mind" thing can be inherited.

And don't forget to smile when the
wedding pictures are taken—Gail

No, Robert may not know what he's getting into. On the other hand, he knows more than he would if his wife were twenty-three and the children were yet to be born.

My impression from Gina's letter is that she wants to talk Robert out of his decision. Parents need to be careful not to set up a power struggle with their children. When that happens, oftentimes adult children feel that they have to go through with something they themselves have reservations about in order to hold on to their adult identity.

If Gina wants to help, she can offer information about child rearing and large families—the upsides and downsides—and then respect Robert's right to make his own adult decision.

Although we may think we can predict our children's futures, we really can't know how their choices are going to turn out. That's the adventure of life.

Susan

My Son Is an Unfaithful Slob

Dear Gail and Susan,

I bet this is the first time you've gotten a letter with my problem. My son Don is getting married to a lovely stockbroker named Tiffany. I love my son dearly, but he is also a slob, he doesn't help around the house, he doesn't stay at a job very long before he gets frustrated, and he's never been faithful to a girlfriend.

As a responsible citizen, I think I should tell Tiffany who she's marrying. I'm afraid she will get hurt and I will feel guilty for not having spoken up.

Rochelle

Dear Citizen,

I think you have to ask yourself a question. Are you a responsible citizen first or Don's mom first? By the way, you must have been a rotten mother to raise a son with all those faults. You should have at least made him clean his room. Maybe Tiffany will be able to straighten him out.

Your letter doesn't seem very motherly. It's clear you prefer Tiffany to Don. Perhaps you're hoping that she'll give you a good stock tip. In the meantime, keep quiet and pray for redemption.

Your only hope, Gail

Rochelle suggests that her son Don is incapable of sustaining a relationship. Perhaps she is right. Perhaps Tiffany can't, either. "Lovely" and "stockbroker" are not characteristics that guarantee marital maturity. There is a lot, good or bad, about Tiffany that

Rochelle cannot know. Don and Tiffany may be good for each other and work it out. They may divorce in a year or in twenty years.

As parents, we may think we know our children. But what we know is how they were when we were raising them. And depending on how clear-thinking we are, we may not even know that very accurately. There is a lot we don't know about how they will adapt to the adult world. And as I have said before, we cannot control our adult children or their intendeds.

Rochelle may be disappointed in how her son turned out. She may blame herself. But a "responsible citizen" pays taxes, doesn't run red lights, and calls 911 when he sees a crime being committed. Rochelle has no duty to warn Tiffany.

Gail, do you know the difference between rational and irrational guilt? If we do something illegal, immoral, or to hurt someone, then we should rationally feel guilty. All other guilt is irrational. It is irrational for Rochelle to feel responsible for Tiffany's marriage.

Susan

Always with the Kids

Dear Gail and Susan,

My daughter's marriage is falling apart and I know the reason. Betsy and Raul do everything with their kids: Clementine, eight, and Rodney, four. Weekdays, weekends, vacations—always with the kids. Betsy doesn't believe in babysitters.

My wife Marge and I weren't neglectful parents, but we had friends and a social life that wasn't about our children.

Raul has begun spending time away from the family. Is he playing golf or having an affair? I don't know, but I feel for him. Betsy is angry and hurt at his pulling away, but can you blame him? He and Betsy are never alone or even out with other adults doing adult things.

I want to try to save their marriage. Should I say something or keep my mouth shut and let nature take its course?

Trent

Dear Wanting to Save,

If you ever want a job solving people's problems like I do, let me know. You're good. You were able to put your finger on why the marriage isn't working. However, and this is why I think I'm better than you, I don't feel for Raul. He should be working on his marriage, not running away. Maybe he realizes that he needs to play with adults sometimes, but he should at least tell Betsy where he's going and when he's going to come home.

Obviously Betsy is letting you know she's angry. Usually I tell parents to stay away from their kids' marital problems, but next time Betsy conveys her anger to you, why don't you mention that Raul seems to need to be around grown-ups? Your daughter and son-in-law need professional help. I'm sure Susan is about to give it.

Gail, admirer of Trent

Gail, when a woman is pregnant and for some time after her baby is born, she is obsessed with her child. It is called "maternal preoccupation." It is a normal state and helps secure the essential bond an infant needs with its mother. A father can often feel left out.

However, maternal preoccupation should give way to ordinary "good-enough mothering." Good-enough mothering is not defined by spending all your time with your child and having no adult life.

Today, many young mothers are with their children all the time. No babysitters. Young parents may get together with other adults, but they all bring their children along. Little if any adult-only time exists. Little if any couple-only time exists.

Some couples institute a weekly "date night" to deal with the problem, because their natural inclination is to make life entirely about the children. Because date night is a discretionary activity, it often gets postponed. Parents shouldn't have to "date" each other to see each other. They should want and expect their marriage to include family time and couple time.

Children cannot grow unless their relationship with their mother changes. "Mommy and me" is for infants, not for growing children. Parents cannot grow if their whole focus is their children. Marriages cannot grow if couples do not spend grown-up time with each other.

Betsy and Raul are an example of a failing marriage because "maternal preoccupation" didn't give way. You are very wise, Gail. I don't recommend gratuitous interference in our adult children's problems. However, if Betsy is complaining to her father, then she may be open to advice.

Susan

A Lousy Wife

Dear Gail and Susan,

In my opinion, our daughter Carol is a lousy wife. She doesn't cook, clean, or have a job and confesses to her mother that she doesn't like sex and has it as infrequently as possible. I can see it in the cards . . . she will eventually lose her husband, who makes a good living and seems like a nice guy. What can I do to set my daughter straight?

Gerald

Dear Wants to Set Things Straight,

In your opinion, your daughter is a lousy wife. In my opinion, too. You sound like a real guy and you say you want to set your daughter straight. So there's no use in me telling you that you're not going to fix her, but you can try. Here's what you do. Sit her down and tell her that you have something important to say. You don't want or need a response from her; you just want her to hear you. Make it short. Make it sweet. And here's the last sentence: "I see it in the cards. You will eventually lose your husband." Then put your arm around her, let her know you love her, and thank her for listening.

Gail, who loves this method of communication

Carol's problem is bigger than being a lousy wife. Carol doesn't cook, clean, work, or like sex. Carol is seriously depressed. Is she depressed because she is in the wrong marriage? Is she developmentally stuck and not able to step into her appropriate role as an autonomous woman? Is she unable to cook and take care of a home and embarrassed to ask for help?

Gerald should consider all these possibilities and choose a proper time and place to talk to Carol about his concerns—not about keeping a husband, but about her not having a vibrant life. Sometimes out of anxiety, frustration, or despair, parents lecture or humiliate. Gerald needs to share his thoughts and feelings in a respectful way. He might suggest therapy.

If Carol's husband is a good guy, he may be willing to wait while she deals with her problems.

Susan

Darlene and Butch

Dear Gail and Susan,

My daughter Darlene, thirty-five, complains to me about her husband Butch. However, my son-in-law has told me in no uncertain terms to "butt out." But I want Darlene to have a person she can turn to, rather than deal with her marital problems alone. Shouldn't her mother be the one? Or should I pretend to comply with Butch and continue our talking in secret? I feel very mixed up about all this.

Renee

Dear Mother-in-Law,

Haven't you heard the jokes about mothers-in-law? We comedy writers consider mothers-in-law a good comedic well to dip into. Most of the time in comedies, mothers-in-law are made fun of because they're the ones who butt in.

You do realize, don't you, that Darlene complains to Butch about you as much as she complains to you about Butch. How else would he know that the two of you are talking behind his back? Don't continue talking to your daughter secretly. She obviously can't keep a secret. Tell Butch that it's perfectly natural for mothers and daughters to talk, but that you don't intend to interfere by telling your daughter what to do. I think that will convince even a man named Butch that you have no intention of trying to destroy his marriage. Tell him you're happy your daughter married him, even if you're not.

If Darlene brings a problem to you that she should be bringing up to her husband, stop her and tell her she's going to have to communicate with him. It would really be beneficial to their marriage if you could get them talking to each other as much as possible.

> Gail, who knows it's easier dealing
> with sons than daughters

Renee thinks she is helping her daughter by providing a sympathetic ear. But in reality Darlene has "triangled" Renee into her relationship with Butch. The triangling relieves Darlene's tension but doesn't resolve any of her problems. With her mother to complain to, Darlene can avoid dealing effectively with issues in her marriage.

Butch's language may not be elegant, but he is correct that Darlene's complaining to her mother is not in the best interests of the marriage.

As parents we have to be alert to being used in this way. As you say, Gail, Renee should kindly and clearly tell Darlene to deal with her disappointments or anger directly with Butch.

> *Susan*

Hal's Confused

Dear Gail and Susan,

My son Hal has been dating Melody for four years. Last week Melody told him that if he can't commit to marrying her, she is going to move on. She is ready to settle down and feels that she's given enough time to this relationship. It either moves forward or ends. I certainly understand where Melody is coming from.

The problem is that Hal doesn't know what to do. He and I are pretty open with each other. He would like to talk to me about his thoughts and feelings. He may ask for my advice. How can I make our talks useful and how should I advise him?

Audrey

Dear Mother of a Confused Boy,

I would advise my son to do nothing, especially when making such a big move. When Melody moves on, he will either be distraught or relieved. I don't want to confuse you any further, but he may be distraught at first and then relieved or more likely be relieved at first and then distraught. He's either going to turn toward Melody, begging her to come back, or get used to being without her. If he does get used to life without her, eventually he'll find someone he can't live without. This is not a logical situation, so there is nothing you can tell him to feel or do no matter how open he is to your opinion. His heart is going to direct him. In movies and books and songs, it's usually the woman who is pining for some man. But in real life, men get hit really hard when love goes away. So, Mom, you're going to have to listen more than you talk. Your listening will help him figure out what to do.

Gail, who would kill a woman who hurt her son

Hal is ambivalent about his relationship with Melody. However, now he is being asked to make a decision. In my opinion, when making a significant decision, if you can't say yes, then the answer is no.

Hal and Melody have been together for four years, so a breakup won't be easy for either of them. It's entirely possible that if Hal says no, Melody will have second thoughts. Or after a day of being alone, Hal may think he decided incorrectly.

Consequently, Audrey should advise her son to do the following: As I said, if he can't say yes, then he should say no. Since Melody and Hal are adults and are dealing with a serious decision, they should agree to a six-month moratorium on seeing or talking to each other. No exceptions! They should set a date six months ahead to have dinner and discuss their relationship rationally. At that time they can decide whether to continue as they were, make a commitment, or definitively separate and move on. During the six months they should date others.

I am strongly in favor of a strict moratorium on interaction so couples can get past the emotions of separation. It's not that a marriage decision is not in large part emotionally driven, but a young adult, even without much experience, should not discount his thoughts, insights, and instincts about himself and a prospective mate.

Susan

The Drop-ins

Dear Gail and Susan,

Our daughter Sylvie and her husband Todd live down the street. They have been married for a year and don't have much money since each is at the beginning of a career. Soon after they got back from their honeymoon, they began coming over around dinnertime. My wife and I would always ask them to stay. We enjoyed sharing a meal and having them around a few times a week. Lately, it's more like five times a week.

I understand eating here is a way of saving money, but I just don't think it's good for their marriage and, frankly, I don't like being used. I also don't like that the issues aren't addressed up front. What can I say that won't embarrass them but will put the situation up for discussion?

Phil

Dear Who Doesn't Like Being Used,

You say that you like to address issues up front, Phil, but it's too late for that. From your letter, I can tell that this has been going on for weeks, if not months. When I was a newlywed with very little money, my parents would have us over for dinner and when we left, they gave us bags of groceries to take home. We weren't going to starve without them but the gesture made me feel cared for. Many parents don't give newly-weds money but help them out in other ways. I'm avoiding your question because I want to say, "Feed them. Have them over for breakfast and lunch, too," but I know that's not the right answer.

You don't say in your letter whether the kids can afford to feed themselves. They shouldn't have gotten married if they couldn't, but it's too late for that now. A newlywed daughter could come to her parents' home for dinner for different reasons. One could be that she likes spending part of her time in what was her own house for many years. Even though she's married, she hasn't made a complete transition from your house to hers. However, this transition shouldn't go on for too long. How much is too long? I'd say anything over a month.

If she and Todd don't have enough money for food, that's another story. Are they getting paid very little? In that case, families should help each other out. However, if they're saving money by eating with you to go on a trip or buy something . . . that's not fair because in reality you are paying for the vacation or the purchase. Phil, you sound like a straight-talking guy even though you didn't straight-talk early enough. So reassure them that you love seeing them, but that you also think it's important that they have their own life. (They'll never get used to each other if they don't.) Invite them over for Sunday dinner and tell them you really want to see them another time during the week. They'll know exactly what you're telling them.

A sneaky way of doing this (and I kind of like sneaky) would be to tell them that sometimes you like to just have a big lunch and no dinner or that you like to sit in front of the television and watch sports while eating. (I might have hit on the truth.) The newlyweds may get insulted, but your comfort is important, too.

Gail, who wouldn't know what to do
if this happened to her

Gail, Phil says that Sylvie and Todd are at the beginning of their careers. So presumably they have jobs, just not high-paying ones. Phil has inferred that his kids drop over because they want to save money.

But I'm not sure the problem is money. In our day, the young stay-at-home bride wanted to step into her female, adult role and prepare a meal for her husband, even if it meant ground beef with Hamburger Helper. Nowadays, it's more likely that both the young bride and groom tackle the meal preparation. They share or take turns trying out new or family recipes or ordering in from their favorite takeouts.

Symbolically, mealtime at the end of the workday is when husband and wife reconnect with each other. Developmentally, the young couple should be establishing their own dinner style with each other and with friends.

Sylvie and Todd are off track. They have drifted back to being kids fed by Mom and Dad. It may be comforting after the grind of the work world to relax and have their parents feed them. And it's easier—they don't have to make decisions, go to the grocery store, prepare the food, or clean up the dishes. And they don't have to be only with each other.

I encourage Phil and his wife to bring up the subject with Sylvie and Todd. Phil can share his insight that they have all drifted into a regressive routine that is not encouraging the kids to set up their own life in their own household. Phil and his wife can suggest easy, quick meals for the working couple. They can propose a once-a-week meal at the parents' house and a once-a-week meal at Sylvie and Todd's. They can offer ideas for simple entertaining of their peers. In other words, Phil and his wife can set some boundaries and expectations. They can also provide leadership and practical advice to help the young couple establish their autonomous, adult married life.

Susan

Help for Amelia

Dear Gail and Susan,

I have a short question I need an answer to. I am desperate. I think my daughter Amelia is being physically abused by her husband Calvin. Is there anything I can do?

Benny

Benny,

There's something you must do. You know your daughter is being physically abused. You've seen her with a black eye or with her arm in a sling. You've seen her fearful eyes. Give her a big, long, hard hug and before you let her go, tell her you're going to help her leave Calvin and that it's going to be immediately. Don't let her go home. Rent a U-Haul right away, and get all of her things out of her house, preferably when Calvin isn't there. Talk her into filing a police report. Hopefully, he'll be picked up for battery.

She must get a restraining order. If he gets anywhere near your house, call the police. She's lucky she has you and doesn't have to go to a shelter for abused women. There may be times when she wants to go back to him because abused women get used to their abusers and interpret their actions as love. Do everything you can to keep her away from him. Her confidence is going to have to be restored, so do your best to get her into therapy.

My advice may seem extreme to you, but abuse tends to get bigger and bigger, and if you don't get her out of her situation, one day her husband may kill her.

Gail, who wants to cry for her and you

Parents, take note of these early warning signs that your child is with a potential abuser. The abuser looks like a man desperately in love. He wants to be with his girl all the time. He is very possessive and is jealous of any other relationship she has, male or female. He is overly sensitive to slights. He tries to isolate her from her friends and family. The courtship is fast and excessively exciting.

Clearly, Gail, we and Benny want Amelia out of the abusive household as fast as possible. But often that doesn't happen easily. The wife doesn't accept that her husband is an abuser, and/or she is afraid to leave because she fears he will find her and kill her.

I don't know how violent a man Amelia's husband is, but if she does leave, her husband may track her down. He may follow her from work or locate her when she uses her phone or computer. Given that possibility I would like to see Benny and Amelia have a safety plan. I would recommend that they contact the National Domestic Violence Hotline or a local crisis center to obtain expert advice on not only getting away from the abuser but also preventing the abuser from hurting her anymore.

Certainly, Amelia or Benny should call 911 if Amelia is in danger.

Susan

Unhappy Marriage

Dear Gail and Susan,

Our son Merv is in an unhappy marriage. He's told me that if it weren't for his two children, six and nine, he would leave. But he thinks he should stay until the kids are older, maybe in high school. He's miserable. Is he doing the right thing? If he stays, how can I help him get through the next ten years?

Bibi

Dear Mother of a Miserable Son,

This is not good. Your son is miserable, which means he's miserable in front of his six- and nine-year-olds. It's not fair for them to grow up with an unhappy father. And he can't just stay in this marriage until his children are in high school. That's when they need their father the most.

If Merv decides to stay, he is going to have to learn to smile. He's going to have to count his blessings, enjoy his children, and have some fun with friends. I usually wouldn't suggest a man have a separate social life, but I think he needs one.

Gail, whose son got divorced and remarried and things are better now, for him and his children and me

Gail, I'm going to say something that is not the prevailing conventional wisdom: I am of the opinion that divorce is not always bad for children. It always affects them, yes, and they need help getting through the emotional upheaval and changes in their family structure. But it is not always more damaging than being in an intact family in which there is enormous tension, arguing, or relationship deadness. Children in this kind of family are far more at risk than children of a reasonable divorce.

In a divorce, children often have to deal with two households and perhaps eventually stepparents. They may have more to manage than if they came from a happy intact family, but learning to cope with adversity and change can promote growth and emotional strength. It is my belief that how the parents handle *the divorce is a more important factor in the child's development than the fact of a divorce.*

That being said, Merv may do better for his children to divorce than to subject them to years of his misery in either a lifeless or an argumentative marriage. It's probably impossible to keep the children from being adversely affected by the truth even if the parents are fantastic actors. Bibi can advise him to contact a therapist who deals with children of divorce to help him help his kids.

Susan

A Good Marriage

Dear Gail and Susan,

My daughter Denise is married to a great guy. They seem to have a good marriage. They do lots together and work as a good team. The problem is that they keep everyone out, including my wife and me.

So first, is what they are doing healthy? And can we do anything to get them to open up and let other people in?

Norm

Too Bad, Norm,

Some couples just need each other and nobody else. I'm always trying to get a friend of mine to go out to lunch and shopping with me on a Saturday afternoon. She refuses to leave her husband alone. Some couples don't even have children because they don't want kids to interfere. You ask if what they are doing is healthy. I think it's healthy for them and not the rest of us, but Susan will know for sure.

Since Denise is always with her husband, what you are going to have to do is call her and have a one-on-one relationship over the telephone when he's not around. The man has to shower and go to the bathroom sometimes. Maybe as she gets older, she'll need you more, but I doubt it. Couples like this don't need anyone.

Gail, who still wants to have lunch with her friend

Gail, Norm is talking about a couple who are entirely dependent on each other to the exclusion of others. They are everything to each other and all each one needs. They have created a closed system into which new people and ideas cannot intrude.

I understand Norm's concern. Because his daughter and husband are not developing other relationships, they are at risk should something happen to either one of them. Since they have closed themselves off from dealing with other people, they will have limited skills in being able to do so.

I would guess that one or both of them have difficulty in coping with the emotions that outside people invoke and are dealing with their problem by restricting their interactions.

At this point Norm cannot do much about the situation. However, as time goes by, the changes and stresses of life may force the couple to need other people for support or advice. When that time comes, I encourage Norm to be open and not withhold a relationship out of anger about their current exclusion of him.

Susan

Nadine Is Pregnant

Dear Gail and Susan,

I have the worst problem. My twenty-five-year-old daughter Nadine is pregnant. The father of the child says it isn't his and he won't marry her. What should I do? How do I get him to marry her?

Sheila

Dear Worst Problem,

Shotgun weddings are called shotgun weddings because fathers used shotguns to force boys to marry their pregnant daughters. So here's what you do. Get a shotgun. Without one, a mother has never been able to talk someone into marrying her daughter, pregnant or not.

We're in a new millennium. Having a child out of wedlock doesn't carry the stigma it did a century ago, which is a good thing. Your daughter may love and want the guy, but if he doesn't love and want her in return, the best she can hope for is a loveless marriage. We all know where those lead.

Sometimes young women feel that they can get a man to be with them by having his baby or that the man will be attached to them because of the child. He will have to be attached, even if it's just financially. But it's no way to get a man or hold a man, especially when the father won't even acknowledge that the baby is his. Here's what to do. Once the baby is born, contact Child Support Enforcement in your state. If your daughter seeks public support and names him as the father, he will have to submit to DNA testing.

Be strong and supportive, no matter which direction your daughter decides to go. Another thing that wasn't around a century ago is legal abortion. Maybe Nadine will decide to have one. Hopefully, from now on, she'll be more careful.

Gail, who was terrified to get pregnant before
marriage because everyone would know

As you say, Gail, Sheila can't make a guy marry her daughter. But she can get Nadine professional and legal counsel about what her options are—about having the baby, about determining paternity (if Nadine's boyfriend isn't the father, who is?), about her legal rights to child support, and about birth control. Nadine needs to make informed decisions.

I can certainly understand Sheila's desire to put things into conventional order—father and mother marry and raise the child. But I advise Sheila to set aside her justifiable dismay and help her daughter get the guidance she needs. However, ultimately it is Nadine's responsibility to decide what to do.

And if Nadine got pregnant in order to snare this guy, then Sheila should suggest therapy.

Susan

On Being Honest

Dear Gail and Susan,

My son James married a decent girl. My wife and I like her a lot. Because James and I are pretty close, he tells me things—for instance, that he has secret bank accounts and I've known for a long time about a child he supports from a fling in college. His wife doesn't know any of this. I think James should be honest with her, but I don't know how to go about telling him that.

Jay

Dear Jay, Father of James, Father of a Secret Child,

You "think" James should be honest with his wife? Come on, Jay. You *know* he should be. You say you need a way to tell your son that. Just tell him. Here are the exact words: "James, you've got to tell your wife about everything: the bank accounts, the child, and the things you're probably not telling me. If she finds out about anything you're hiding, she will never trust you again. You could be making the most innocent trip to the grocery store and she won't be quite sure that's where you're going. When you tell her the truth, tell her why you hid it all in the first place. Swear you'll never do it again. Be near a stack of Bibles when you do."

If your son does what I've suggested and his wife leaves him, James will be mad at you. I know that you're going to tell him I told you what to say, so you'll think that he'll then be mad at me. He won't. He'll be angrier at you for taking advice from a book.

> Gail, whose head will rest easily

There is a difference between privacy and a secret. A spouse can have a private conversation with a friend about money, his children, a surprise birthday party for his wife. But hiding bank accounts, having affairs, and supporting illegitimate children are secrets. Secrets in a marriage are like time bombs. Eventually they explode. Sometimes the marriages get put back together and sometimes they don't.

Since James has made his father privy to his secrets, Jay has been included as a co-conspirator. Without realizing it, Jay has colluded with his son's behavior and in a way given it his stamp of approval. Jay has also helped James deal with the stress of having secrets by giving James someone to talk to about them.

Jay should tell his son that he doesn't want to be the holder of secrets, because he doesn't approve of the behavior. He should suggest that his son make full disclosure to his wife.

James, of course, may not do it. But whether he does or not, Jay can ask that James keep any discussion of secret activities out of their conversations. Without the outlet of someone to confide in (or brag to?), James will have the pressure of the secrets all to himself. Under those circumstances, chances are that James will find a way to let the secrets out to his wife—for better or for worse.

> *Susan*

Sixteen Years Younger

Dear Gail and Susan,

I was alone for twelve years after my divorce. I barely dated while my two children were growing up. Once they were both out of the house, I did online dating and met a great guy. We got secretly engaged. I finally introduced Kenny to my two children, Daria, twenty-seven, and Rudy, twenty-three. Rudy's okay with Kenny if he makes me happy, but Daria doesn't like him. She thinks he's too young for me. Kenny is sixteen years younger than I am, but we get along really well. I want to make this relationship work without losing my daughter. What should I do?

Holly

Dear Barely Dated,

It's nice that you barely dated while your kids were growing up. It's very confusing to children when parents bring lovers in and out of their lives. And when you have a lover, you have to have his favorite juice in the refrigerator. It's a lot of work.

Admit it, Holly. There's a reason you got engaged in secret. You knew that Daria wouldn't approve. You ask how you can make this relationship work without losing your daughter. That's coming from a very weak position. Tell your daughter that Kenny is someone you want in your life forever. And that's that. Let her worry about losing her mother. Maybe she'll get used to the idea of you and Kenny being together.

If you were a good friend of mine, I would ask you if you were sure you wanted to marry a younger man. It's nice if he'll take care of you if you're ill, but you'll have wrinkles and he won't. Be sure to have a prenuptial agreement.

Isn't it amazing that you can find a sweater, matching pants, and a fiancé online?

Gail, whose children have the same attitude Rudy does

Gail, the potential downside of Holly's not dating until her kids were in their twenties is that she and the children may have become overly dependent on each other. In particular, Daria may have made an unconscious bargain to stay attached. Now that her mother is moving on, in effect trading Daria in for marriage, Daria may feel betrayed.

Moreover, Gail, although we don't know Holly's age, she could be fifty, which means that Kenny could be thirty-four, an eligible-age man for Daria. Holly's marriage could feel to Daria like rubbing salt in her wounds.

That being said, Daria will have to deal with her sense of betrayal or jealousy. Perhaps she needs therapy to help her sort out her feelings and become more her own person.

Holly understandably wants her children to validate her new relationship, but she may not get it from her daughter. If Holly cannot go forward and marry Kenny without it, then Holly needs to rethink her reasons for wanting to marry him, or she needs therapy to help her separate from her daughter.

Susan

Hank and Stuart Are Wrong

Dear Gail and Susan,

A year ago, after a long illness, my wife died. Luckily, I met a very nice woman, Delia, a few months later and we have decided to get married. My two sons Hank and Stuart are very angry with me. They think I have lost my marbles marrying again so soon after their mother's death. I say it's none of their business. It's my life. I've lived eighty-five years and have earned the right to do whatever I want. I'm right, aren't I?

Thurston

Dear Eighty-Five-Year-Old Groom,

You have lost your marbles, but everybody in love has. Do Hank and Stuart think you should wait five years until you are ninety and then get engaged and then wait a couple of years until you're a ninety-two-year-old groom? Are they afraid that this woman will get some of their inheritance? You and this very nice woman have your whole lives in front of you. I'll pay for the Viagra.

A person who knows where marbles lie, Gail

I like your answer, Gail. You're a romantic. When a mother or father marries again, the children have to adjust. If the children are young, they have to accept a stepparent. But in this case Hank and Stuart are adults. Unless Thurston is mentally incompetent, Hank and Stuart are out of line. If Thurston had dementia, the sons would be concerned rather than angry, and considering legal action.

Thurston's wish for companionship is normal, and his marrying again does not dishonor the children's mother. Moreover, a parent is not required to take his grown children's opinions into consideration when making a personal decision.

That being said, I have the following observation to make. The reasons Hank and Stuart are angry are not revealed. All three of the family mentioned in the letter use provocative and uninformative language: "lost his marbles," "none of their business." I would encourage Thurston to have a meeting with his sons to ask them to articulate their concerns (are they worried that he is hooking up with a gold digger after their inheritance?), to explain his decision, and to invite Hank and Stuart to get to know his fiancée.

Susan

An Angry Daughter

Dear Gail and Susan,

Ten years ago my wife and I divorced. After we each had other relationships, we started dating and have decided to get married again. We both thought our children would be delighted to have the family reunited, but we were clearly naïve to think that. Our son is sort of okay with it, but our daughter is very angry. She in effect has said that we are crazy and are making her crazy. What's so crazy? My wife and I are older and mellower and have rekindled what brought us together in the first place. What can we say to get our daughter on board?

William

My Dear Sane William,

I'll bet there are other things besides you and your ex-wife getting remarried that drive your daughter crazy. She wasn't born angry, so something happened between then and now that has made her that way. You say that you and your ex-wife are older and mellower. Probably your daughter needs to be older and mellower in order to accept this rekindling.

I'd better be clear about what to do so that you don't make your whole family crazy. Your daughter doesn't have to be consulted about your plan. She needs to get used to it. Don't be upset with her. Keep talking to her but don't necessarily discuss your upcoming nuptials. When you speak to her, make her the center of the conversation. Ask her about her life and her work. Stay away from her relationships, because that will only remind her of your newfound happiness. She doesn't seem to want to know about that right now. Your ex-wife, her mother, should do the same. It seems your daughter needs nurturing.

Gail, who doesn't like crazy situations,
but sometimes creates them

Gail, we hope to raise our children to be independent. We can recognize lack of independence when our children want to move home, borrow money, or overly rely on us. But another symptom of lack of independence is always being angry with us. I would say that William's daughter qualifies as the angry dependent.

Although it is not usual for divorced parents to get back together, it is not unheard of. If the children are young, then divorcing, moving apart, remarrying, and getting together again would be confus-

ing and disruptive. But these are adult children. Independent children can accept their parents' choices because their own lives are full and demanding.

I agree, Gail. William and his ex-wife should do what they want to do. However, they should not demand that their decision be validated by their children. And in this family's case, the daughter still needs help in being more independent.

Susan

CHAPTER EIGHT

In-Laws

In-laws have been the subject of many jokes in television, in movies, among stand-up comics. They are dreaded, reviled, ridiculed. How did this happen? After all, they are only someone else's parents or children. They are just like you. Or you think they are, but then they do something like not invite you to an event you expected to go to, or the son-in-law you thought was so charming hardly says anything to you anymore.

Our child has new adults in her life, with different opinions, expectations, idiosyncrasies, and holiday rituals. We're not the one-and-onlys anymore and we have to deal with these former strangers. We acquire sons-in-law and daughters-in-law. They don't know what to call us. They think we interfere. It's not easy when your son- or daughter-in-law "suggests" you butt out.

But by the time our children marry, haven't we already lost that status to friends, roommates, and boyfriends? Not like this! The arrival of the in-laws makes it clear that the world order of our family has dramatically changed. The structure and dynamics are different. We have to rethink and readjust. We have to find a new place for ourselves. Or we try desperately to hold on to our old place—we're *the parents*, after all. Our son shouldn't consult his mother-in-law, the interior decorator, about his condo remodel; he should rely on his own mother, who hasn't redone her house since she moved in, because she's his mother.

The old cliché that we're not losing a son, we're gaining a daughter is true. However, any change brings stress and loss. In this case, considerable loss. Loss of the old way: The mother-in-law puts oysters instead of chestnuts in her turkey stuffing. Sacrilege! And what's worse, our daughter likes it. Loss of control: We call to invite our son to go on the annual family camping trip and find out that he and his wife are going to Hawaii with the in-laws. All we can do is hope they use sunscreen.

Loss requires mourning. Strange that with the happy event of a marriage we have to consider mourning as well, but emotionally we do. We shouldn't avoid mourning, either, but sometimes without realizing it, we try to. All our faultfinding with the in-laws or siding with our daughter against her husband—what better way to hold on to the old family power structure than to deprecate and discredit the intruders—*the in-laws*.

The in-laws can also ignite old rivalries. Instead of siblings vying for their mother's love, we and the in-laws may go to war over family holidays and the grandchildren. A lot of negotiations have to take place.

Then there are the sons- and daughters-in-law, those people our children married. The wonderful dentist or lousy bum our daughter calls her husband. The lovely woman or demanding princess our son married. Parents have to be careful here. How tempting for the mother of a now-married kid to become her confidante when she complains about the new husband who never picks up his clothes. Mom and daughter can rebond around the disgusting habits of men. Dad can be a hero to his daughter who complains about her husband's poor financial management. Dad can come to the rescue with money tips. We parents have to guard against trying to sneak back into our old roles and reassert control.

Getting to know our child's spouse may be easy or difficult. But we should try. If we are lucky, we will like him or her. But there's a chance we won't. However, accepting someone does not require that we like the person.

Sometimes the other parents-in-law become our new friends. They are new people to have dinner with, invite to parties, and visit. Our family suddenly expands. They are someone to exalt with when a new grandchild is born or when our son gets a promotion. The in-laws, like no one else, can feel and share our joy and anxiety. They're in it with us.

Whether or not the in-laws become friends or just new people who are an integral part of our child's life, they are here to stay. Accepting them is the challenge and definitely the way to go. However, the downside is that if we get along with the in-laws, comedy writers will lose a good source of material.

My Daughter-in-Law Stole My Son

Dear Gail and Susan,

I have a *big* problem. My daughter-in-law Cindy doesn't like me. We just don't get along. My husband Bill says it's because we're so much alike. Well, that's not the main problem—it's that she keeps my son Bill Jr. away from me. Junior and I were very close. I would help him pick out his clothes and we would go to the movies if Bill wasn't interested in a film.

I know that things change when your children get married, but our relationship has gotten distant because of Cindy. She insists we call and make a formal arrangement to see each other—absolutely no dropping in—and we don't get together that often. My heart is broken that my relationship with my son has changed so much.

Ruby

Dear Big Problem,

The one I feel sorry for is your daughter-in-law Cindy. It must have been really hard for her to pull Bill Jr. from your claws.

Here's what I think: You like Bill Jr. better than you like Bill Sr. and I'm not so sure Bill Sr. likes you. He thinks you and Cindy are so much alike. He thinks you are both controlling women. I would straighten out your relationship with your husband if I were you (and I'm glad I'm not).

Your daughter-in-law is right about you not dropping in. You say you need to make a "formal" arrangement to see them. *Formal* means an engraved invitation and wearing gowns and tuxedos. Picking up the phone and calling is the *decent* thing to do. You say your heart is broken. What I'm about to say will break your heart even more. If your son was a strong man and really wanted to see you more, he would override Cindy's decision to stay away. Enjoy the times when you do get together and try to give your heart, broken as it is, to your husband.

Don't try to drop in to see me either—Gail

When our children get married, we need to rewrite our relationships with them. We are no longer primary in their lives. We don't necessarily get to do with them what we did before or see them as often as we might like.

Although change brings something new, change also always involves loss. And if we suffer a loss, we need to mourn. Ruby wants to hold on to the past; she is angry about the changes in her life and blames her daughter-in-law for them. She needs to mourn the loss of her former relationship with her son and, as you say, Gail, work on her relationship with her husband.

Gail, I also think that given Ruby's prior relationship with her son, the young couple was wise to set firm boundaries to protect Bill Jr. from getting sucked back in by his mother.

Susan

Mason Never Attends

Dear Gail and Susan,

My son-in-law Mason never visits us. My daughter Chris consistently comes alone and makes some excuse that Mason is working or traveling. How should my wife and I handle this situation?

Herb

Dear Father-in-Law of Mason,

You know your son-in-law doesn't show up, but do you know the real reason why? Find out if he is overworked and overly tired. Maybe that's why your daughter visits you alone. Herb, you're a guy. Why don't you talk some guy talk with Mason? Ask if there's something you can do to make him feel more comfortable at your house. Maybe he stays home to watch football games; you can say that you'd be happy to have him watch a game or check the scores at your place.

I've got to tell you, you're lucky that your daughter shows up. She's a saint.

Gail, who hopes she's helped

There are many possible reasons for this family dynamic. Mason could be a workaholic who doesn't take time out for socializing. He could be boycotting visits to his wife's family because he doesn't feel comfortable with any family but his. Perhaps Chris discourages him from joining her, because she wants to be a kid again alone with her family. Maybe she doesn't check with her husband to see if he's free when she makes the arrangements for visits. Perhaps there's marital trouble.

Whatever the reason, I recommend that Herb and his wife issue a clear invitation to both Chris and Mason. If Mason still doesn't show up, Herb should accept the situation the way it is. It may or may not change over time.

Susan

Dresses Like a Hooker

Dear Gail and Susan,

Nina, my daughter-in-law, is sweet, but she dresses like a hooker. You know the look—low-cut bustiers, miniskirts, mesh stockings. I confess she embarrasses me. I know that people are talking. I've hinted to my son that Nina's such a pretty girl who could dress better, but he just brushed me off.

Is there anything I can do?

Bitsy

My Dear Overreacting Bitsy,

Do you know why your son brushed you off when you suggested his wife dress better? It's because he likes the way she dresses. They probably have a hot sex life because of all those miniskirts and mesh stockings. Isn't that what you would want for your son?

If you really want your daughter-in-law to be ladylike—and God knows why you would want that—when her birthday and Christmas roll around, why don't you give her some conservative clothing and see what happens? I'll bet if you give her a dainty little sweater, she'll unbutton the top buttons so that her breasts can fall out of it.

        Gail, who has wanted to look sexy her whole life

Gail, can you imagine what the Edwardian mother-in-law thought about her flapper daughter-in-law? Bobbed hair and short dress! Shocking! Is Bitsy overreacting to a modern style of dress she doesn't like? Maybe Nina is dressing like her peers. Every generation has its style that the older generation thinks is sleazy. Remember the Beatles and their long hair?

Or maybe Nina's style is a little—or a lot—on the provocative side. Her husband apparently doesn't mind. And besides, even Bitsy admits that Nina is sweet.

Maybe Bitsy has a little rivalry going with her sexy daughter-in-law.

In any case, I would advise Mom to focus on Nina's sweet nature and not criticize her to her son, although, Gail, I'm not sure Bitsy will be able to do that.

        Susan

Veronica's Day

Dear Gail and Susan,

My son Malcolm has been married to Veronica for four years. They don't have children yet. When Malcolm met Veronica, she was working as a secretary. Just before the wedding she quit her job and hasn't worked since. Malcolm is a teacher, so he doesn't make much money. He has told me that they don't have enough to buy a house. Frankly, I don't know what Veronica does all day and it irritates me that she isn't helping out financially. Any suggestions?

        Irv

Dear Intruder,

What's the matter with you? Why is it your business that Veronica isn't working? Your daughter-in-law quit her job before the wedding, so Malcolm knew before he married her that she wasn't working. It's not as if she was pretending to be a wage earner until after she got married. It's too bad Veronica irritates you, but there's nothing you can do about it.

I'm more concerned that your son told you that he doesn't have enough money to buy a house. He's telling you he wants one. Was he hinting that you should provide a down payment? I don't like it when adult children involve their parents with their financial situation. It reeks of immaturity.

I have no idea what Veronica does all day. I've never had days like that.

> Gail, who has a million suggestions, but not
> at the moment

There are three issues here. First, why doesn't Irv know what Veronica does all day? Apparently all he knows, or wants to know, about her is that she doesn't work. So we have to assume that after four years (or more) of knowing his daughter-in-law, Irv doesn't have a personal relationship with her.

Second, how his son and daughter-in-law decide to live their lives is up to them. Perhaps they want to have children, believe in stay-at-home mommying, and don't want to get used to living on two salaries. Perhaps Malcolm is irritated, too, and isn't saying anything.

Third, our children are their own people. They may be different from us. When they are living with us, we may not see the differences clearly. It's not until they reach adulthood and make their adult life choices that we can see their uniqueness. We may be surprised at the careers or the spouses they pick. Their choices may not jibe with our vision of how their lives were going to be. But we need to look and accept. Our adult children have become who they are.

In his letter, Irv reveals his hopes for his son—children, a house, and more money. Teaching is Malcolm's choice. Veronica is Malcolm's choice. Not being able to afford a house is the consequence of those choices. Irv needs to recognize his disappointment and let go.

Gail, I'm with you. I don't like it when children hint about wanting money. On the other hand, maybe Irv brings up the house and Malcolm is only informing his father that he can't afford one.

Susan

Dropping Over

Dear Gail and Susan,

My daughter Risa has complained to me that her in-laws are at her house all the time. They "drop over" every day and then hang around. My son-in-law Derek seems to like the arrangement. He never tells his parents to leave or to call first. My daughter says she feels left out in her own home.

Is there anything my wife and I can do? We're more formal. We don't believe in just dropping in.

Mack

Dear Mr. Formal,

Tell Risa that she's got to mix up her schedule a bit so that her in-laws don't know whether she (or Derek) is home or not. That way sometimes when they drop in, nobody will be there. Also, since you're more formal and considerate, you can call and ask your daughter if her in-laws are there and if you can come over, too. When you're all there together you can casually make remarks to your wife like, "I think we should go and let these kids have some time on their own." Do that a few times and see if your daughter's in-laws get the hint.

There's a bigger issue here. It's very sad that your daughter feels left out in her own home and that she seems unable to confront her husband or his family. She can't be happy in the situation she's in now. Does she feel bullied or inadequate? Why don't you try to find out? Then you and your wife can help her get her confidence back. Try to talk her into getting some therapy.

By the way, when we writers write for television, we make it so our characters always drop in on people. It takes too long for the doorbell to ring and then someone has to ask who it is and let them in, ruining the rhythm of the show. Remember *Seinfeld*? Jerry's door was always open.

Gail, who definitely calls ahead

This is such a simple problem to solve, I wonder why Risa hasn't solved it. Gail, you have one solution—don't be home all the time. Another is to talk respectfully to her in-laws about wanting some private time and making a schedule for seeing them.

My guess is that Risa and Derek have not fully separated from their families of origin. Risa and her parents side with each other about the inconsiderate, bad in-laws. And Derek doesn't mind having his parents around—it feels pretty much like before he got married.

Sometimes in an effort to be supportive of our children, we unknowingly encourage passivity and dependency. Sometimes our married children bring us into their conflict to perpetuate the status quo. In other words, as long as Risa has her parents to complain to, she doesn't have to do anything about her relationship with her in-laws. Mack should tell Risa that if she doesn't like the dynamic with her in-laws, she needs to talk to them, not complain to her father and mother.

Susan

Holding Hands

Dear Gail and Susan,

I am frantic with indecision. I know for sure that my son-in-law is having an affair. I saw him coming out of a restaurant holding hands with a coworker. Should I tell my daughter Nora?

On the other hand, affairs can just blow over and if I say something now, I could be causing unnecessary trouble.

Please tell me what to do.

Ariana

Dear Aggravated Ariana,

Indecision is the worst thing for you. Human beings need to decide whether to fight or flee. So you either have to get involved in this situation or get away from it. It's important for your health.

I have to take your suspicion seriously. You wouldn't be writing to us if your son-in-law was innocently holding hands with someone. Your daughter has a right to know. But be prepared, if you tell her, do it gently. Tell her exactly what you saw. She will kill the messenger. She'll cry and be angry at you. She'll confront her husband and he'll deny having an affair. He'll say he was walking out of the restaurant with a friend who had a problem and he was just trying to cheer her up. Your daughter will believe him and you'll be in even more trouble. She'll blame you for trying to mess up her marriage.

The reason I'm suggesting you tell her is because the two of you have had a relationship since her birth. Even though she'll be furious, you will have done the right thing. You will have planted a seed and that's important. Her eyes will be open.

You suggested that this affair could just blow over, but when men are unfaithful, they tend to stay that way, especially if they're not caught. Even though this affair may blow over, there will be others. The important thing to remember is that your allegiance is to your daughter, Ariana. She has to know that she'll always get the truth from you.

Gail, who would practice what she preaches

This is a tricky situation. I understand your point of view, Gail. We want to be supportive of our children and keep them from harm. But I don't agree with you that Ariana should immediately tell her daughter about her husband's infidelity. For several reasons I advise Ariana to say nothing to her daughter at this time.

Our children's marriages are their own, and there is a lot we parents aren't privy to. For instance, does Nora already know but want to keep it private and handle it in her own way? Is she having

*an affair and her husband's is in retaliation? Would she want to
admit that to Ariana? Is Nora ready and able emotionally and financially to deal with her marriage breaking up?*

*It would be another story if Nora brought her suspicions to
Ariana and solicited her opinion. Then her mother could more or
less confirm or at least reveal what she saw. But in the absence of
Nora's bringing it up, as difficult as it is to keep her counsel, that's
what Ariana should do.*

Susan

Tess Gets Everything

Dear Gail and Susan,

Tess, my daughter-in-law, is spoiled. She was not expected to
do anything around the house when she was growing up. Her
parents indulged her every whim. Not surprisingly, she expects
my son to treat her the same way. He does more than his share
of the shopping and housework. He takes Tess out to eat every
night, buys her presents, and takes her on trips. My husband
and I think he's being taken advantage of and we don't like it.
Can we do anything?

Carrie

Dear Crazy Carrie,

Does Tess expect your son to spoil her or does your son
enjoy spoiling his wife? There's nothing you can do about it,
and I mean nothing. It's their lives, their money, their time. If
I could, I would come to your house and tape your mouth
closed. That's how serious I am about telling you not to say
anything.

Think before you write again.

Gail, who thinks before she speaks

*Gail, you've said it all. I'll only add a little bit. As you say,
Carrie's son may like having a "princess" wife and doesn't at all*

feel taken advantage of. If he changes his mind, it's up to him, not Carrie, to do something about it.

Perhaps Carrie is envious of a young woman who not only got her son but gets him to wait on her. What do you think?

Susan

Susan,

You are so smart, it's scary.

Gail

Robbed

Dear Gail and Susan,

I agreed to watch my daughter and son-in-law's house while they were on vacation. One night I forgot to set the alarm and they were robbed. My son-in-law Roger is furious with me. I understand his being upset—I'm upset, too—but it was an honest mistake. At the moment Roger won't talk to me and my daughter says she doesn't want to be in the middle. Is there anything I should do?

Carter

Dear Forgetful,

Roger shouldn't be furious with you. You made a mistake. And you're not the one who robbed him. When someone won't speak to you, write to the person. Either an e-mail or a letter. Tell him you're upset, say you're sorry, and don't mention that it was an honest mistake. Be contrite.

Ask if they were insured for anything that was taken. If they were, Roger should give up his anger. If they weren't, and you can afford it, and with a name like Carter, I think you can, offer to replace some of their things. In addition to this, send a gift to replace something they lost. Do as I say and you will have bent over backward to please this immature man who's blaming you.

Next time someone asks you to watch their home, if you agree to do it, tell them that you hope they don't hold you responsible for anything that could go wrong.

I know you're distressed because you want harmony in your family. I do think that this will blow over, since you wrote, "At the moment Roger won't talk to me."

Gail, who knows when to hold people responsible

I think that Roger is lashing out at the wrong person because he has not yet come to terms with the event—the violation, the victimization, his vulnerability, lack of control, and loss. Making it Carter's fault means Roger doesn't have to think about conscience-less criminals taking advantage of innocent people and maybe getting away with it.

Carter should apologize, empathize, give Roger space, and wait. I predict that as Roger deals with the police about the crime, he will turn his focus and anger onto the true culprits and get past his fury at Carter.

Susan

Izzy and I

Dear Gail and Susan,

My daughter Sandra thinks that I'm too close to her father-in-law Izzy. It's true that Izzy and I get along great. We come from a similar background and have a similar sense of humor. When my husband and his wife are busy, we've gone out to dinner. My daughter thinks that our relationship is inappropriate and tells me so every chance she gets. What do you think? Is it? And even if it isn't, should I give in to my daughter and stop enjoying my time with Izzy?

Glenda

Dear Inappropriate,

Don't you know that a fellow parent-in-law is for nice, polite conversation with when the family is around, not for going out to dinner with? Don't not see Izzy just for your daughter's sake. Do it for the whole family. Remember that old warning, where there's smoke there's fire? You two are smoking. One or two drinks after dinner and there could be that polite kiss on the cheek that slides over to the mouth. Your lips will be locked and then there'll be no stopping you. Izzy isn't for you. Is he?

Gail, who doesn't want Izzy either

Phrases like "we get along great" and "enjoying my time with Izzy" make me suspect that Glenda's daughter is not overreacting. As does the fact that Glenda excludes any mention of her relationship with Izzy's wife.

If a mother is sexually inappropriate with her daughter's father-in-law, she is embarrassing her daughter and betraying her trust.

I agree that Glenda should drop her special relationship with Izzy and relate to the in-laws as a couple.

Susan

Wants to Be Friends

Dear Gail and Susan,

Estelle is my daughter's mother-in-law. She very much wants to be friends with me. She calls to have lunch and invites me to events she attends. I work and she doesn't, so she has more time to socialize. But more than that, we are very different. I really don't want to be that close to her. What can I do to keep our relationship distant without causing hurt feelings?

Sonya

Dear No Time to Socialize,

Unfortunately, you're going to have to account for your time. Let Estelle know in one conversation what time you get to work, how overworked you are, how tired you are, and how you have to go to business lunches and dinners. Hopefully she won't be hurt, and she won't be if your tone of voice is regretful rather than annoyed.

As a woman who has worked her whole life, I know how difficult it is to fit social events into a schedule. I've had to turn down a lot of people. Once when my kids were little, a friend of mine called on a Saturday and said, "Do you want to do something today?" The question confused me. I had never had a day where I could just do something.

If you can, go to an event with her. The two of you can enjoy something together without having to be friends. That would keep your relationship distant and you might even enjoy an evening out.

> Gail, who knows exactly what you're going through

Friendships with in-laws or new acquaintances may start out with one or both people pursuing more meetings. Over time the friendship either grows and the contacts become more frequent or the initial interest wanes and the relationship finds its own tempo—a once-a-year Christmas brunch, a Fourth of July bash. Or the people never see each other again. Of course with in-laws, there's a difference. They are here to stay.

Sonya sees Estelle as a pest pushing a relationship Sonya doesn't want. I'm going to suggest a different perspective on Estelle's behavior and a different way for Sonya to see the situation.

Perhaps Estelle believes that she's being a good mother-in-law by trying to make friends with Sonya. Maybe she will keep working at it until she thinks she's accomplished what she deems the right thing to do.

Instead of Sonya reacting with impatience to Estelle's overtures, I would encourage her to invite Estelle to something that might become a ritual together, for instance, a holiday afternoon girls' tea that includes Sonya's daughter. It's possible that if Estelle knows that her efforts to connect the two families have succeeded and are appreciated, she will not be so driven to get together.

> *Susan*

Unpleasant Evening

Dear Gail and Susan,

My husband Aaron and my son's father-in-law Del fight over politics whenever they get together. Last night after another unpleasant evening, my husband said, "No more." He doesn't want to see the in-laws anymore unless there are a lot of people and he doesn't have to talk to Del. What should I do?

Essie

Essie, My Love,

A lot of people fight over politics, but it's gotten worse. People have dug in and Republicans and Democrats think along party lines. There's no middle ground.

It's normal for parents-in-law to see each other among a lot of people. It's rare for them to get together on their own. So either stick to a "no speaking about politics" rule or listen to Aaron, for once in your life, and just see Del and his wife when there's a lot of family around. I'm sure you can talk this over with Del's wife. The two of you understand what it's like to have husbands who fight over politics. At least there hasn't been a food fight.

Gail, who loves a good food fight

Politics, religion, and money used to be inappropriate topics for dinner table conversation for just this reason. That rule of etiquette has fallen by the wayside. Depending on the kind of guy Del is, Aaron might be able to get him to agree to no political talk when they are together. If that doesn't work, then Essie and Aaron will have to discontinue the intimate dinners and stick to meeting at family events.

Susan

Tahoe

Dear Gail and Susan,

My daughter's in-laws have more money than my wife and I do and they invite my daughter and son-in-law on trips or to a condo they own on Lake Tahoe. My wife feels left out. She thinks that the in-laws should invite us along at least to Tahoe when they all go. I'm not so sure she's right. Because my wife is hurt, she doesn't want to get together with the in-laws at all. Is there anything I can do?

Luke

Dear Husband of a Hurt Wife,

A mother should be happy that her daughter gets to enjoy some luxury. Your wife is abnormal. She's jealous of your daughter. Tell her to stop being a bitch or get rid of her. It's up to you, Luke.

Explain to your wife that when people have a vacation condo, they don't necessarily have room for in-laws, nor do they particularly want a woman under their roof who resents her daughter.

It's obvious there's nothing you can do. Tell your wife when she's in a good mood, if she ever is, that seeing in-laws is an obligation.

Gail, who is angry at the woman you married

Luke's wife thinks she's entitled to what her daughter gets, in this case an invitation to the in-laws' condo. And when she doesn't get what she wants, she's angry. Not seeing the in-laws (in effect killing them off) is her spiteful way of dealing with her hostile envy.

What can Luke do? He can tell his wife he thinks she's wrong, make it clear that he will see the in-laws with or without her, and suggest that she get therapy to deal with her envy and resentment.

Susan

Saying Grace

Dear Gail and Susan,

I never thought I would have a problem with in-laws, but I do. My daughter-in-law's parents are very religious and I am an atheist. The in-laws insist on saying grace at every meal we have together, even though they know how I feel about religion. It's beginning to annoy me. Why should their religious beliefs trump my lack of them at every dinner? Should I say something to them?

Benedict

Dear Atheist,

Do you know there's a whole order of monks named after you? You have a very strange name for an atheist. What's the big problem? They're thanking God for food they eat, and since you don't believe in God, you realize that they're thanking something or someone that doesn't exist. Stop being annoyed.

My suggestion is: at your house, start eating before they can say grace and at their house, you're going to have to put up with it. Stop being a baby.

Gail, who had in-laws that said grace,
even though she didn't

Politeness would dictate asking, Do you mind if we say grace? Benedict's in-laws apparently haven't done that. They are, I guess, overbearing. However, Benedict shouldn't get into a power struggle over the short ritual.

He can try to talk to the in-laws about sometimes forgoing grace. Depending on how flexible they are, they may or may not be able to occasionally give it up.

The bottom line is that we have to tolerate a lot of differences and annoyances when in-laws join the family and, unless they do something harmful, we should just get through the moment.

You're right, Gail. Benedict is an unexpected name for an atheist.

Susan

CHAPTER NINE

Grandchildren

Grandchildren are a treat for us grandparents. Unlike their own parents, we have the time and space to observe and reflect on their growth and development. We don't have to buy diapers and we can buy a cute little party dress, which is more fun. We're not on the firing line, having to make myriad decisions each day the way our kids do. When we're tired, the grandkids go home. We put our houses back in order and keep them that way until the much-loved grandchildren come for another visit. It's perfect, isn't it? Well, not exactly. When we were growing up, grandparents were often part of the child-rearing team. They were consulted and involved. They were respected for their wisdom.

Some adults today don't want grandparents' advice. They join Mommy and Me classes, talk to their friends, and search the Internet. They want to do it on their own. They don't want to consult their own parents even though they were raised by them and survived. Why did this change?

Some parents of our generation were permissive and indulgent and erroneously believed that if we made our children feel special and never said no, our kids would have great self-esteem and confidence. Ironically, needing to feel exceptional and not wanting to hear "no" made them narcissistically vulnerable. So some of our kids are unsure of limits and boundaries and they experience advice as criticism. In addition, having grown up thinking they were remarkable, they suffer blows to their self-image when they discover that someone knows more than they do. We have come to realize that what we thought were superior child-rearing techniques were really an overreaction to our own parents and upbringing. Now that we know the errors of our ways, we could teach our kids something about raising children, but that's not what they want from us. They still only want our approval and admiration.

Our kids are involved in their children's school and sports activities, know CPR, do background checks on nannies, and are able to maneuver luggage, backpack, stroller, and three kids through an airport and onto a plane with seeming ease. Too bad they can't keep them quiet during a flight. Some of our grandchildren have too many toys, are plopped in front of videos from infancy, are stuffed with the wrong kinds of food, have too many electronics, lack structured family mealtimes, and are oversched- uled and overprotected by overinvolved mothers. It's horrible to watch.

We grandparents talk among ourselves about our grandkids' lack of independence and creativity, about their having too much power in the family, about how they're growing up without separating, without enough grit and self-direction. But what can we grandparents do? We can refrain from advising our children, because that doesn't work. However, when we are with our grandchildren, we can set limits and boundaries, restrict electronics and television, and encourage creative activities and social interaction. We can also expect orderliness, personal responsibility, and respect. Good luck.

Children need grandparents. Especially those who love uncondition- ally. There is no safer lap than the one a grandparent has to offer. If only our children realized it.

~~~~~~~~~~~~~~~~~~~~~~~~~~~~~~~~~~

My Granddaughter Has Talent

Dear Gail and Susan,

My son Michael is a doctor who works for an HMO and his wife Amy is a stay-at-home mom. They have two children, Sean, four, and Amanda, six. Amanda is very bright and talented and would do well at the excellent private school in town.

Here is the problem: Amy's parents got into financial trouble. Her father is grandiose and a gambler. He overextended, his business went belly up, and he has a lot of debt. Michael and Amy have agreed to help her folks out financially. That means Amanda can't go to private school. My husband and I live very frugally so we never have to depend on our children. It is eating me up that Michael is giving money to Amy's parents and my grandchild can't go to private school because of it. Should we say something to Michael?

                                                                    Ruth

Dear Grandmother of a Maybe Gifted Child,

Not only should you not say anything to Michael, you shouldn't have written to us. I hate letters like this because what you are really telling me is that since you live frugally, you feel morally superior. Speaking of hate, do you hate your son? Bringing up this issue is just going to make him feel unhappy and stressed.

Michael and his wife have already agreed to help her parents out and now you want to tell him that it's not fair that little Amanda, who is bright and talented, according to you, her grandmother, a prejudiced woman, is being deprived of a good education? Barbra Streisand is bright and talented. She went to a public school in Brooklyn. Keep quiet, Ruth. I'm guessing it's almost impossible for you, since your letter has a lot of extra words in it. Write me again in twenty years if your granddaughter becomes the superstar you think she is now.

                                                    Gail, who knows talent

Gail, what does the parent of a dependent child have that the parent of an adult child does not have? Control! Parents have no control over their adult children's lives. Or shouldn't have.

Michael and his wife have made a decision about how they spend their money and how they school their children. Michael and Amy have the right and responsibility to do so. Although Ruth thinks she knows what's best for her grandchildren, she may be wrong. Besides, being an autonomous adult includes the freedom to make your own blunders. Ruth needs to accept Michael's decision and say nothing.

                                                                    Susan

Evil M.

Dear Gail and Susan,

Help! My daughter-in-law Madeline (I call her Evil M.) won't let me see my grandkids. Whenever I call the house, Evil M. says it's not a good time. It's never a good time as far as she's concerned. I told my son that his wife is boycotting me, but he says I'm being paranoid. He says that as a family, they are very busy and that I should not take it personally. But don't you think that my son and daughter-in-law owe it to me and their children to make sure we get together?

Magda

Dear Mad Magda,

Your son and daughter-in-law don't owe you anything. However, they should be getting you together with their children because grandparents play an important part in children's lives. My grandparents were sweet and nonjudgmental. I smile when I remember them on holidays.

Magda, I think you haven't gotten to the bottom of this. There's some reason that your daughter-in-law is torturing you. Could it be that Madeline knows you call her Evil M.? Is it possible that she calls *you* Evil M.? Have you said or done anything to her that would make her not want you around? If you have, apologize even if you don't want to. Take the high road, Magda. And no more talking to your son behind her back. The worst thing you could do is put him in the middle of the two women in his life who are both alpha females.

I know what you should do to make the family cohesive again. If there's any children's theater near where you live, why don't you buy tickets for the whole family and say you'll meet them there? Part ways after the show. It doesn't have to be theater tickets. It can be any event that's interesting and fun for kids. A movie? If you happen to live near an amusement park, get everyone tickets for that. Maybe one of your friends is having a backyard picnic that the family can be invited to. What I'm suggesting is that you don't try to go over to their house or ask them to come to your house. You have to include them in a bigger event.

Once you and your daughter-in-law have been together a few times around a lot of other people, maybe you can get together with just the immediate family.

If none of my suggestions work, just take your son's assessment of the situation literally. Young families are very busy and so tightly scheduled, they don't have time to do anything they haven't put on their calendars.

Gail, who is pleased with her answer

Gail, I want to present you with a scenario. Someone calls you every day when you're in the middle of something—preparing breakfast, getting dressed, writing a book on a deadline—and they want something that takes time and energy on your part. And because your life is scheduled and your time accounted for, you can't give them what they want when they want it. So you find yourself always having to say no.

You know, Gail, I don't think that Magda's primary goal is to see the grandchildren. I suspect that what Magda really wants is for her son (and us) to see Madeline as victimizing her and for us to agree with her that Madeline is Evil M. Magda thinks she is entitled to call the shots and have control over her son and daughter-in-law's life and she plays the victim when she doesn't get her way.

If Magda really wants to see her grandchildren, she will call her busy daughter-in-law and invite her and the kids over for a barbecue at a time convenient for them both. Madeline will put it on her calendar and the get-together will take place.

Susan

Bribing

Dear Gail and Susan,

My son-in-law Chaz does not know how to parent. His way of dealing with every situation that comes up with the kids is to buy them something. If he wants to get them to do something they don't want to do, he bribes them with the promise of a trip to the toy store. In my opinion, our grandchildren aren't being taught good values. Should I say something to Chaz or to my daughter Penny?

                                                        Alan

Dear Not Knowing What to Do,

You tell me what your son-in-law is doing wrong, but you don't mention your daughter's part in all this. Shouldn't she be the one to tell Chaz that he shouldn't always bribe the kids? Does she just sit back and watch or is she actively bringing up her children? If she hasn't tried to correct Chaz, could it be that she likes the kids quiet, too, and that's her way of dealing with them? I think you're going to have to sit back and wait a few years, Alan. Adolescents need bigger bribes than young children. So if your daughter and son-in-law don't want to be broke, they will have to change the way they parent. Say nothing. Watch.

                Gail, who believes in bribing occasionally

I can well understand why Alan is disheartened by Chaz's parenting style. Teaching a child frustration tolerance and to accept "no" is a good idea. Bribing him to do what you want is a bad idea, because a manipulative parent is in effect teaching his child to manipulate rather than to accept boundaries and limits.

However, Alan has no control over how his son-in-law parents. What he can do is use more appropriate parenting techniques with his grandchildren and hope that Chaz and his grandchildren catch on.

                                                    Susan

Free Babysitting

Dear Gail and Susan,

My daughter Margo and her husband Dan expect me to be on call for the weekends. They drop off their children, sometimes for the whole day. My husband Benny says we are lucky that our daughter trusts us. That may be true, but it feels to me that she wants us totally available to her. I love my daughter and grand-children, but I don't want to give up my whole weekend to them. What should I do that won't hurt anybody's feelings?

May

Dear May, the Unwilling Babysitter,

Guess what? Next weekend, you could put a note on your door that says you're away or that you've moved. Or you could not answer your phone. Better still, you can tell your daughter how you feel. In that conversation, mention that you're excited about doing something on the weekends. Then add that you know she depends on you, but there are times that you'll be busy. This doesn't have to be one of those big discussions where you sit her down and talk about your true feelings. No one has to get hurt. No one has to cry. She'll get the idea quickly. Then you can start making plans and she can start making plans to get another babysitter or, better still, to be with her kids.

Your husband is the one who should be sat down and talked to until you bring him to tears. Tell him that if he really wants to be available for his daughter and grandchildren, he can babysit. Some men are scared to be left alone with little kids. They don't know what to do when children get upset. They don't have a clue about what to give them to eat. So I'll bet he'll be joining you for some weekend fun.

A grandmother myself, Gail

Gail, what's missing in this family system is the ability to communicate in a straightforward way. May feels used when her daughter drops the grandchildren off every weekend. We don't know why Margo and Dan do it. Are they selfish and want free babysitting? Or do they erroneously think that their parents expect it?

May should thank her daughter and son-in-law for allowing

them so much time with the grandkids. She should also request that a pattern not be established, that each week May and Margo discuss the upcoming weekend and whether May is available for babysitting.

Susan

ADHD Frustration

Dear Gail and Susan,

My daughter-in-law told me that my seven-year-old grandson has attention deficit hyperactivity disorder and she is giving him Ritalin. I've learned that my son and daughter-in-law don't want any advice from me. However, I have it to give. My son George was what we called then an overactive kid or a kid that couldn't sit still. I got up every morning with him at six and took him swimming for an hour and a half before school started. This seemed to get rid of a lot of excess energy. And, although he still moved around and squirmed a lot, we never drugged him. He got through school fine and became an engineer. He still exercises every day and he's a successful adult and didn't have to take drugs. What my son and daughter-in-law do is take my grandson to Spanish and Chinese lessons. They give him piano lessons and take him to the opera. These sedentary activities are not the things that will help him. I started to give advice on the ADHD subject and was stopped by both of them. Is there anything I can do?

Ben

Dear Frustrated Ben,

Once your children make it clear they don't want to hear what you have to say, it's impossible to confront them. They think they're doing a great job. You're going to have to do what no other grandparent has been able to before. You're going to have to be quiet.

Gail, who doesn't believe in drugs

Attention deficit hyperactivity disorder is not simple to diagnose. There are no relevant medical tests to do. Hyperactivity and inability to complete tasks can be caused by other factors—depression, anxiety, an under- or overdemanding school environment, a chaotic home life, an oppositional disorder or other mental problem, and even some medications.

In the absence of any kind of test to confirm a diagnosis, clinicians turn to reports from multiple sources—parents, teachers, babysitters, parents of friends, and grandparents—to get an accurate picture of the child's behavior. Unfortunately, Granddad Ben was not part of his grandson's diagnostic process.

Ben voices concern about his grandson's being given drugs. Some professionals who treat children agree with him. They suspect that ADHD is being overdiagnosed and are concerned about administering psychoactive drugs to young children.

What is surprising and sad for this family is that there is apparently no open dialogue about the welfare of a seven-year-old child whose impairment is sufficient to warrant psychiatric intervention.

What to suggest to Ben and other grandparents in this situation? First, I would advise that they have empathy for the parents of the disturbed child. In order to be diagnosed with ADHD, a child must show serious behavioral symptoms and functional impairment in at least two settings. We can infer that Ben's grandson has a behavior problem at home and in school, perhaps even in social situations. It is stressful to live with a hyperactive child, whatever the cause. It is stressful to hear complaints from your child's school. To their credit, these parents sought and obtained professional help. Ben can congratulate them for that. Ben then needs to proceed slowly, because the parents hope they have found an answer. At this point, they don't want to hear that they made a mistake.

Ben can show interest and concern—ask them how the program is working—without being critical. He can request that he be kept informed. In other words, he can begin to lay the foundation of an open dialogue.

If the medication works, then his grandson will begin to focus, become more organized, and be able to learn. If the stress on the

*family from his hyperactivity is mitigated, the parents may be
more open to talking and listening. If the medication doesn't work,
then they may need Ben's advice and seek it.*

Susan

Cassy's Crazy Kids

Dear Gail and Susan,

My daughter Cassy and her two sons have temporarily moved
in with my husband and me. Cassy's husband Ken is in the military and was sent overseas. Cassy moved in with us so she
wouldn't be all alone while her husband was away. We are happy
to help out, especially since Ken isn't making much money. The
problem for me is that her boys, five and eight, are uncontrol-
lable. They run around the house leaving havoc in their wake.
When they are not running, they are punching each other. I may
be slightly exaggerating, but not much. Cassy doesn't seem to be
able to discipline them. My husband and I have talked a lot
about the situation, but neither of us knows if we have the right
to discipline them since we are not their parents. What's the
correct way to handle this?

Arlette

Oh, My Dear Arlette,

I'm sure you're not exaggerating. First of all, be sure to
store anything breakable where the kids can't reach it. Second
of all, listen to me. You have a daughter. I have no idea if you
raised any sons. Young brothers are like baby tigers. They
snipe at each other. They growl. They run. They're noisy. And
it doesn't end until they go to college.

I have two boys and I have said the following words: "I've
told you a thousand times not to throw a pencil at your brother.
He can lose an eye like that." You can replace the objection-
able activity with any number of things, including "I told you
a thousand times to stop running around like a wild animal.

You can lose an eye like that." It takes saying those things a thousand times before they get it.

Here's what you must do! You're going to have to teach Cassy how to discipline her children. We think that since our children are grown, they know the things grown-ups should know. Sometimes they don't. The kindest way to teach adult children is by example. Do it and then help her do it, and then she'll do it without you.

> Gail, a mother who has said a thousand times,
> "I can't wait until your wife has to deal with you"

In this particular family situation, Cassy and her kids have suffered a loss over which they had no control. Husband, father, and their old life have temporarily disappeared. I recommend that Arlette verbalize how hard the loss must be for her daughter and offer to help make a plan to integrate her and the grandchildren into their new environment.

Arlette should also make it clear to Cassy and the kids that there are house rules that may be different from the ones they are used to. Cassy may have allowed jumping on furniture and having toys all over her own house. Arlette may not want her antique sofa used as a trampoline nor want her living room to be a playroom. It's her house—her rules.

As Gail suggested, boys will be boys. Actually, kids will be kids. They will break the rules. Violation of house rules requires discipline. Either Mom does it or Arlette and her husband do it.

I think the problem may be that Cassy has moved back to her childhood home and is unclear who's in charge. Her children may not know, either. Arlette's letter suggests that's exactly what's going on. Arlette needs to take back her role as head of her house, which includes rules and discipline. That may help Cassy take on her role as boss of her children. The children may calm down once they know that the adults are in charge.

Susan

Lily Rules

Dear Gail and Susan,

My daughter Norma is doing something to her teenage girls that I think will damage them. She often contradicts them in front of people, which humiliates them. If they object to her criticism, she punishes them for disobedience. How can I get Norma to see what she's doing and to treat her children more respectfully?

Lily

Dear Right Lily, Who Has a Daughter Who's Wrong,

It's rare that a letter comes in where the writer is perceptive. Norma is doing something that can damage her adolescent children. This is the time when they start to imagine their future without their parents. They're in the first stages of breaking away. However, if they're criticized enough, they'll never have the confidence to leave. There is hope, and you're it. You're going to have to compliment and praise them behind Norma's back. Applaud them for every little thing. And you're going to have to invest in a lot of greeting cards—not the birthday kind but the ones that say "You're the Best" or "Thinking You're Great." I did some research in my local drugstore so I know that there are lots of them out there. Some even have smiley faces. At least your grandchildren will know that somebody thinks they're wonderful.

Gail, who applauds your
sensitivity

Gail, an issue that may be at play here is that sometimes the mother of a teenage girl feels hostile rivalry toward her daughter. Mom's getting wrinkles and cellulite just as her daughter is blossoming, and men, including Dad, are smitten with the budding beauty. Norma may be depressed and irritable and unaware of the reason. I suggest that Lily find ways of supporting and validating

Norma, ways of praising or complimenting her. If Norma feels better about herself, she may be less critical of her daughters.

Susan

Susan,

All your answers are good. This one is great.

Gail

Beautiful Baby Belle

Dear Gail and Susan,

Here's one for you. My gay son Luke married a guy named Perry in Michigan. Then they adopted a beautiful Chinese baby named Belle. I went with them to China to pick her up and fell in love immediately. About three months ago, Luke and Perry got divorced. Perry left the state but sends money. Luke is so devastated by the breakup he's barely functioning. So I am taking care of Belle. Should I take this to court and try to become Belle's legal guardian or should I insist that Luke and Perry figure out what to do about their daughter?

Martha

Dear Tired Martha,

You're not going to believe it, but your situation is more common than you can imagine. Gay married couples have children and get divorced like everyone else. The most important person in this is Belle, and I see that you know that or you wouldn't be taking care of her. I think the next most important person is you. If you're young enough and strong enough to become Belle's legal guardian, do it as soon as possible. Your son is a jerk, not because of the breakup, but because he's so devastated by it. Gay or not, he's Belle's parent and should be taking an active role in raising her. He is an abusive parent for abandoning his daughter. I am against physical punishment, but I would like to punch him. And I know how to punch. I learned to on the set of *The Main Event*, a movie about boxing, which I co-wrote. If you feel you can't raise this beautiful girl, then you're going to have to insist that Luke and Perry figure out what to do with their daughter.

Gail

Gail, I have little to add to your answer, except to suggest to Martha she encourage Luke to get professional help. Luke should deal in therapy with his poor coping skills and depression. Belle has already lost one parent, Perry, who moved away. Even if Martha gets custody, Luke will undoubtedly be in Belle's life. Without therapy, Luke is likely to fall apart again, which will enormously stress his daughter.

Susan

Play Ball

Dear Gail and Susan,

Our son Ben is my husband's from his first marriage. I married Joe when Ben was eighteen and going off to college. Now Ben has asked me to babysit for his children, four and five and a half. I have never been around little children, so I don't know what to do with them. Do you have any suggestions or can you tell me where I can get some guidance? Better yet, can I tell Ben I can't babysit?

Lena

Dear Grandmother Lena,

Can we tell you where to get some guidance? You're kidding me, right? Susan and I give the best advice in the world. Our middle name is guidance.

Like it or not, you're a grandmother now. And sometimes adult kids have to rely on their parents to take care of their children. Don't tell Ben you can't babysit. He'll hate you for that and I'll hate you, too.

Here's a suggestion: keep them physically active. A friend of mine who is a grandmother came up with a perfect solution for her four-year-old grandson, and your five-and-a-half-year-old will love it, too. My friend's grandson wanted to play basketball. She doesn't have a basketball net, so she figured out a different way for him to do it. She opened her first-floor bathroom window. She stood outside with her grandson and her housekeeper stood inside the bathroom. He threw the ball in the window and the housekeeper returned it. My friend is a genius. Most people don't have housekeepers to do that for them. So, Lena, you're going to have to stand in the bathroom. Good luck.

For meals, give them juice boxes and finger foods. Make sure they're seated at a table.

Love, Gail, who strives to be the perfect grandmother

Gail, I want to talk about the relationship between Lena and her adult stepson. I don't recommend that a mother or stepmother tell a young and dependent child of her anxieties. A young child needs to idealize parents to feel safe. But Ben is a grown man. I would encourage Lena to discuss her worries with her stepson and husband. She can ask for guidance or suggest that she spend some hands-on time with the grandchildren when their parents are around before she solos.

Susan

Following Frank

Dear Gail and Susan,

My wife and I moved to San Diego to be near our son Chris and his family. I was retired, so we could relocate. Even so, it was a big adjustment. It took a while to feel part of the community and to make friends. But my wife and I know it was worth it. We so enjoy being around our grandkids and I think we have been helpful. Now Chris is moving to Colorado to take a new job. The question is, Do we follow him? Chris says he realizes that it would be hard for us to move again. Is that code for he would rather we stay put? I know we will feel bereft without them all near us. Colorado isn't that far, but it's a plane trip. So should we follow him? What do you think?

Frank

Dear Following Frank,

If you had written to me the first time you moved, I would have warned you that your son and his family might not stay in San Diego. You say it took a while to feel part of the community and make friends. It's great that you have new friends. My parents moved to Los Angeles when my father retired so that they could be near their children and grandchildren. And I was thrilled when they made new friends. It was that same thrill I had when my kids were young and made friends.

Do you really want to make another big adjustment? Chris and his family are likely to move again. Are you going to keep following him? I say stay in sunny California. San Diego is warm. Colorado is cold. Your grandchildren, once they're old enough to travel, would love to visit a place like San Diego with that great zoo and that fabulous SeaWorld, especially since they lived there once. You'll have wonderful vacations with them.

You ask if I think that Chris's comment is code for you to stay put. I think it is. He might be insecure about relocating and starting the new job. Moving his family is difficult enough without having to worry about his parents' move, too. Don't burden him right now by bringing up your dilemma with him. It'll only cause him anxiety, which he doesn't need right now. Keep remembering this, Frank: if you stay in San Diego, you won't have to buy a winter coat.

Gail, who has winter coats, even though
she lives in sunny California

Sometimes parents move to be near their children and grand-children in order to share experiences and help out. Frank says that he and his wife moved for those reasons. Parents sometimes move because they are dependent on their children or they want to control the family.

An adult child is on his own life journey. Change is an inevitable part of that journey. Chris's career, as an example, requires that he move again.

Frank doesn't say that he's always wanted to live in Colorado and learn to ski. So he would be following his son to try to control the family system—to keep it the same forever. Frank needs to accept that he can't. As you've already said, Gail, he and his wife should invest in their life in San Diego. And visit.

Susan

Paula's Problem

Dear Gail and Susan,

My grandchildren are raising themselves. My daughter is divorced and often leaves the two younger kids alone with their twelve-year-old sister. My daughter is a nurse who works the late shift and is gone from 10:00 p.m. to 8:00 a.m. I know it's hard to get babysitting for those hours. I'm not sure I want to babysit, but should I offer? Should I say something to my daughter about what I think is irresponsible behavior?

Paula

Dear Irresponsible Paula,

You're writing to me about your daughter being irresponsible. You're being irresponsible, too. You're asking me if you should offer to sit for your young grandchildren. You should run right over to your daughter's house and volunteer. It may appear that a twelve-year-old is capable of taking care of younger siblings once they're all asleep, but it's not true, and I'm pretty sure it's not legal. A twelve-year-old does not have the ability to take care of emergencies. Period. I can think of a long list of dangers that can arise that a child would have a hard time handling. (I'm really good at thinking of dangers. Ask my kids.) A fire starts in the hallway. Do you leave the apartment? The doorbell rings at midnight and the person on the other side says she's a friend of your mother's. Do you let her in? You've got to look out for these kids, Paula, if your daughter has to work and can't find a reliable babysitter.

And where's the father? Your daughter and her ex-husband can live in the same house and, if he works during the day, they'll never even see each other.

Gail, the intelligent alarmist

I don't usually advise that grandparents intervene without being asked, but this case is different. A twelve-year-old should not be in charge of her younger siblings. She is a child herself. Gail, something doesn't add up here. Paula's daughter has a responsible job with a reasonable salary. Why wouldn't she arrange and pay for babysitting? Is she spending her money on drugs? Is she paying off debts?

Whatever the reason, when Paula first learned of this situation, she should have done something. She should have either become the babysitter, hired a babysitter, or insisted her daughter hire one. As hard as it might be, if the arrangement isn't changed immediately, Paula should call Social Services and file a report.

Susan

Gladys, the Spoiler

Dear Gail and Susan,

I invited my son and daughter-in-law and their three children to visit for a week. My son and the kids are coming, but not my daughter-in-law. She says she has to work. I was disappointed and a little apprehensive. I figure that I will have more responsibility with the kids if their mother isn't with them and they may be more difficult because they miss her. But I am saying nothing and I plan to enjoy the week, no matter what difficulties arise. My friend Gladys says I'm nuts. That I should say something to my daughter-in-law to make sure she knows I am displeased. Gladys thinks I'm being taken advantage of. I don't look at it that way, but maybe I just don't stand up for myself enough. What do you both think?

Marla

Dear Saying Nothing but Writing a Lot,

I am assuming that your son will be there to take care of his children during his vacation and that you won't have much more responsibility. Your son seems to be a good father since he's willing to deal with his three children in a car or on a train or on a plane on their way to you. Don't anticipate that the kids will be unhappy and they'll miss their mother. This is an adventure for them.

As for your friend Gladys, she's filled with bad advice. To tell your daughter-in-law that you're displeased will definitely upset her, which in turn can upset your son, which will upset you. Gladys is at best a troublemaker and at worst a poison. Maybe you don't stand up for yourself enough. I can't tell from your letter. But I know a surefire way to make you feel better about yourself. Get rid of Gladys.

Gail, who thankfully doesn't have a Gladys in her life

Gail, Marla's got it right. Marla's son and daughter-in-law made a responsible plan for Mom to be able to work and for Marla to see her grandchildren. There may be more stress for Marla—if her son is not skilled at laundry or dishes or the kids have separation anxiety—but Marla has realistically accepted the situation and expects to enjoy the visit.

Gladys is a troublemaker wanting there to be a problem where there isn't one.

Susan

Victoria Is Horrified

Dear Gail and Susan,

What are your views on spanking as punishment? My son-in-law Alan believes in it. He spanks both his son and daughter. Alan says he doesn't do it hard so it hurts; just hard enough to make his point. I am horrified. My husband and I never spanked. Can I stop Alan?

Victoria

Dear Victoria,

I'm so sorry that your grandchildren are getting spanked. Hitting children is usually handed down from generation to generation. Alan must have come from a family that did. You and your husband should tell him together to opt for time-outs. A united front might help. You might even enlist your daughter. You may be surprised to discover that she's on your side.

It's really hard to see your children hurting your grandchildren. Give them extra hugs when they're around.

Give them a hug for me, Gail

This is a tough question. I don't advocate spanking as a form of discipline, but in and of itself, it is not illegal. Hitting has to meet several criteria to be considered child abuse. I am going to assume that Alan would not be deemed a child abuser.

Spanking not only hurts but is humiliating to the child. The child is helpless, often in an undignified physical position, trying not to be a baby and cry. Spanking is also a violation of the child's body, his personal property.

Disciplining children is not easy. Parents can become so frustrated that they feel like whacking the kid. Some even occasionally do. But Alan has adopted spanking as his only form of discipline. I would guess that his parents spanked him. He may not want to admit that he was hit and that he doesn't know how to control his children any other way.

Victoria and her husband can attempt to open a dialogue with Alan and their daughter about the subject of disciplining children. They can offer their perspective on the matter. They can suggest a parenting class—local community colleges and hospitals usually offer them.

I don't often recommend that grandparents intervene between daughter and son-in-law, but I agree with you, Gail, that in this case, it's worth a try. If Victoria and her husband ascertain that their daughter is being bullied into going along with spanking, they can privately recommend she take a parenting class and get therapy to enable her to stand up to her husband and protect her children.

This is a problem that will not be solved quickly. Perhaps over time, changes in the family system will compel Alan to change as well.

Susan

Sperm Bank

Dear Gail and Susan,

My daughter Mara is unmarried. She decided that she wanted a child and went to a sperm bank behind my back. It was such a big step to take. Why didn't she talk to me about it before she did it? Should I tell her how hurt I am that she didn't want me to be part of it?

Kaylee

Dear Wants to Butt In,

Would you care if your daughter went to a regular bank behind your back? I'm kidding about that, but I was born to kid. When I was on *David Letterman*, I talked about sperm banks and how you could get the sperm of Nobel Prize winners and that it cost more than regular sperm. I got a big laugh when I said, "Sperm used to be free."

Kaylee, I know you're not laughing and I get that you're

hurt. I really do. There's a couple of reasons why your daughter didn't tell you about her big decision. Maybe she felt you wouldn't approve. There's a good chance Mara thought you might try to talk her out of it. There's a possibility that Mara felt she wanted to do this on her own. In any case, she had a reason why she didn't tell you.

This is not about you, Kaylee. This is about your daughter wanting a baby. Your feelings are not important in this, so don't tell her how hurt you are. Stop being a drama queen and support your daughter. She included you when she wanted to include you.

Gail, who loves talking and writing about sperm banks

We use the phrase "behind my back" to imply that somebody did something secret and treacherous. Trying to have a baby, however you do it, is a private act, not a treacherous one. Mara did not betray her mother. Mara, as an adult, apparently didn't want to include her mother in the decision and the process and she had a right not to. Raising a child alone is a big responsibility. When adult children get around their mothers, sometimes they feel like kids. Perhaps Mara wanted to take her most adult self to the sperm bank and not risk any childish, dependent feelings rising up and getting in the way.

I can understand Kaylee's being surprised or even uncomfortable and worried about Mara's going to a sperm bank. Sperm banks weren't part of Kaylee's generation. But why is she hurt?

Gail, young children are egocentric and feel angry and hurt by others' autonomous actions. Young children want to believe that they have control over everyone. It makes them feel more secure. But adults should not be hurt if they are not included in another person's decision, even if the person is their child. Kaylee is unhappy because she isn't in control of her daughter's life. I hope she can get beyond her childish feelings and enjoy her grandchild and her daughter's motherhood.

Susan

Praying Grandchildren

Dear Gail and Susan,

We have a situation in our family I hope you can help me with. My husband and I are churchgoing people. When our two grandchildren stay over, I get them to say their prayers at night. My husband and I had to teach them how to do it, because their mother is a nonbeliever and our son has given up his faith. Our problem is that the oldest told her mother that they were saying prayers before bedtime and now the children are not allowed to spend the night.

We want to solve the problem. Do we have to give up our beliefs to get the grandchildren back? We just want to expose them to another way.

Melody

Dear Unstrung Melody,

How dare you do something behind the back of your non-believing daughter-in-law! You want to solve the problem? Well, you're the one who created the problem. You knew you were doing something wrong. You don't have to give up your beliefs, but you will have to stop imposing them on your grandchildren.

The only way to solve this situation is to gain your daughter-in-law's trust again. You've got to promise her that if she lets you have *her* children—and they are *her* children—you won't impose your religion on them. Maybe she'll believe you. But I doubt it.

You write that you just want to expose your grandchildren to another way. Melody, you're not allowed to. I think you should be ashamed of yourself.

Gail, who sees right through you

Grandparents, like schools, can have house rules. But grandparents, like schools, cannot make a kid pray without parental consent. Melody stepped over the line. She argues that if she can't make her grandchildren pray, then she has to give up her beliefs. What non-sense! Actually, what manipulation! Melody doesn't have to forfeit her beliefs to see her grandchildren; she has to forfeit trying to in-doctrinate her grandkids with them.

What should Melody do "to get the grandchildren back"? Understand and admit that she was wrong, apologize to her daughter-in-law, and not do it again.

Susan

Lucille's Blood Pressure

Dear Gail and Susan,

I don't like one of my daughters-in-law. My blood pressure goes up when I'm around her. I don't like the way she treats me or my husband, nor do I think she's a good wife to my son or that she's a good mother to their children. She is on the phone or texting when we are out for dinner and our grandchildren are unkempt and run wild. My husband nevertheless wants to see them a lot. How can I make the time we are together tolerable for me?

Lucille

Dear Unlucky Lucille,

Your son married a bad woman. We don't want your blood pressure out of control because of it. The way you make the time you are together tolerable is to tolerate this bad woman. You're going to have to tell yourself that there's not a damn thing you can do about this. When I first told some of my friends that I was working on this book, they all shared with me a similar version of what a mother-in-law's job is: to keep quiet. It's in the job description. The one thing you can do is not go out to dinner with them. Children running wild in a restaurant would give any grandparent high blood pressure.

Gail, whose blood pressure is good

Lucille should not just suffer and complain, but rather she should take some initiative. She can talk to her daughter-in-law and suggest ways of making the family times feel more organized, people-connected, and fun. She can plan activities that are more flexible and kid-friendly than going out for dinner—a picnic, a barbecue, an afternoon at a park. Lucille might also try to find some common ground between her and her daughter-in-law, something they are both interested in and can talk about.

However, if nothing changes and Lucille still can't stand being with her daughter-in-law and grandkids, then she can pick the family events she can tolerate and opt out of the others.

Susan

Everything under the Sun

Dear Gail and Susan,

My daughter-in-law's parents buy our grandchildren everything under the sun. My wife and I not only can't afford what our in-laws can, but we don't approve of kids having so many toys. Our grandchildren are being spoiled, but we don't know what to do about it. Do you have any suggestions?

Gary

Dear Grandfather Gary,

Children don't care who buys them toys. Young kids don't remember where their toys came from. Also, they don't connect toys with money because they haven't really learned what money is about. Believe me, they're totally unaware about what a person has in the bank. So if you give them love and attention, that's all they need from you. There's nothing you can do about the other grandparents spoiling your grandchildren. However, you can enjoy them in your own way. Take them to the zoo, because children remember experiences more than they remember toys, which usually break.

Gail, who tries to have grandchildren experiences

In his letter Gary raises two issues. First, too many toys don't spoil a child; they confuse and overwhelm him. Each toy makes a demand on a child for performance. So Gary's discomfort is warranted. But unfortunately, he can't do much about it other than limit the number of toys when he plays with his grandchildren.

The other issue is that Gary compares himself to the in-laws, which means he is feeling competitive with them. If he stays self-absorbed in his rivalry instead of establishing real relationships with his grandchildren, the grandkids will prefer the in-laws, because the kids will conclude that Gary is not really interested in them.

Susan

CHAPTER TEN

Divorce

"Until death us do part." We all know that line from the marriage vows. It's memorable and compelling, a solemn pledge. However, in actuality, the marriage vows, reality, and the law are not in sync. Couples get divorced. There are divorce laws governing the dissolution of a marriage. "Until death us do part" should really be viewed as a sincere hope, not a binding promise. If it were really binding, we might have less unemployment among hit men.

When our children get divorced, we wonder where we went wrong. We cry almost as much as they do. Should we have talked them out of it? Are we going to have to move them in with us? Anger, profound loss, custody battles, financial problems, disorganization, and despair may all become issues. Our child has to pay a lawyer; maybe find a new place to live; and possibly deal with depression and loneliness. Perhaps our daughter-in-law left our son for a woman, leaving him humiliated and full of self-doubt. Maybe our daughter's husband cheated on her and she finally had enough—but still has the anger and a legacy of mistrust. Our children may turn to us for solace, financial help, or advice on how to keep their lives together. They're in our lives again.

We may want to turn away from the pain and loss. We may feel un-equipped, that our image as the good parent or perfect family is tarnished, or that we don't want to lose our relationship with our son-in-law or daughter-in-law. Or we may want to rescue, take away the pain, make everything okay again. We need to deal with our shame, confusion, and heroic fantasies privately, and realistically be there for our child. We proudly told our friends that our child was getting married. We're not so proud that the marriage is breaking up. It's rare, but it happens, that parents are happy about a divorce. If we felt our daughter was mentally abused or our son's wife was a bitch—we're happy when those marriages dissolve.

Parents also get divorced, and, even though our children are grown, they are affected. Our child may blame us; may not want to deal with a temporarily needier, more dependent parent; or fear that she will have to deal with Dad's loneliness or new girlfriend or Mom's anger and dating.

Believe it or not, although divorce is like a family earthquake, it can also be an opportunity for growth. A mom who never wrote a check, when her husband leaves, gets a job and becomes a financial tycoon. A dad who stuffed his feelings, when his wife divorces him, gets therapy and finds a new, more satisfying relationship. A son who was a workaholic and left the parenting up to his wife, now single, is forced to become an involved dad. A daughter who yearned for a career, but was thwarted by a controlling husband, now on her own, fulfills her ambitions.

We learn in the face of frustration. When there's a divorce, we can easily get caught up in picking up the pieces, making finances work, just keeping the family from spinning out of control. But if we have the realistic perspective that mistakes, frustration, and loss are a chance for learning, we can better help our children and ourselves weather the storms and become more mature.

My Son Is Impotent and I Don't Want to Know

Dear Gail and Susan,

My son Terrence divorced last year. I feel bad for him. I know he was devastated when his marriage broke up and he is lonely. The problem is that now I am his confidante. He calls me several times a day about work, about dating, about his sex life! I don't really need to hear he has been impotent for several weeks.

What can I say to him that wouldn't hurt his feelings? I dread it when the phone rings.

Bobbie

Dear Bobbie,

I don't know what to tell you.

All my love, Gail

Gail without words! Unimaginable! But I can understand feeling stymied, because there are several ways to look at Bobbie's problem.

Bobbie says that Terrence was divorced last year. If in fact a whole year or more has gone by and Terrence has not found a way to work through his devastation, then he needs professional help. Bobbie can explain to Terrence that she doesn't have the expertise to provide him proper guidance. She can suggest that therapy would be a better choice to alleviate his pain.

If "last year" really means a few months ago, then Terrence may just need someone to listen while the healing takes place. However, as a mom, Bobbie may feel uncomfortable hearing about her son's sex life. If so, she can tactfully ask Terrence to confine his conversation to less intimate topics. In other words, parents can set boundaries even when their children are having problems.

We need to remember that it is not our job to make our child happy. Frustration and loss are part of life and we need to encourage our children to learn to cope.

Susan

Hey, Susan,

Maybe Bobbie should rip out her phone.

All my love to you, Gail

Ex-Wife's Anger

Dear Gail and Susan,

I have been divorced for many years, but my ex-wife has never forgiven me for leaving her. My two grown children don't live near either one of us. Because of my ex-wife's anger, the children sneak into town when they see me and I presume do the same when they visit their mother. I feel bad for the kids and would like to help them be more open and not so secretive. What should I say to them, if anything?

Roger

Dear Never Has Been Forgiven,

I know you may not like hearing this, but your ex-wife is going to live forever. Have you noticed that angry people live very long lives? When I was writing for *The Golden Girls*, Sophia, the old lady, said anything she wanted to. She once called Blanche, the sexy one, a human mattress. I didn't write that line but love it. Women like that don't die.

I suppose I should answer your question. You'd like to help your kids be more open. (You sound like a guy with a gray ponytail who was a hippie during the '70s.) Just let them know you don't mind hearing about visits to your ex. They still might have to be secretive when dealing with your wife, but there's nothing you can do about that.

Peace, Gail

When children are young and their parents divorce, we help them adjust. We set new boundaries and encourage them to talk about their feelings. But when they are adults, they get to make their own decisions about how they want to cope with their parents. Actually, that's also true when there isn't a divorce.

Roger's kids seem to have figured out a way of seeing their parents that works for them. Roger can tell them exactly what he said to us, Gail—that he regrets that they have to be secretive—but he should then let it go and enjoy their visits.

Susan

Rick Is Dating

Dear Gail and Susan,

Our son and daughter-in-law are separated. Tracy asked Rick to move out. Rick has been staying with us going on six months.

He brings the children here when it's his weekend with them. He says that he and Tracy are close to getting back together, which of course my wife and I would prefer. But Rick is dating! He says otherwise he'd be too lonely and depressed to function. I guess I have two questions: Can Rick be dating and really be serious about getting back with Tracy? And how long do we let him stay here?

Jeff

Dear Two Questions,

Allow me to answer your last question first. You never should have let Rick stay with you. If he wasn't living with you, you wouldn't know about him dating and you wouldn't be aggravated. A separated man is allowed to do what he wants.

Adults and their adult children really shouldn't be living together. Have you ever heard of the alpha male? Only one leader of the pack should be allowed to stay under one roof. I can tell by your letter, Jeff, that you are the alpha male.

Your instinct is absolutely correct. Rick is not doing the right thing if he really wants to get back with his wife. Dating tends to get in the way of a husband and wife's relationship, whether they're separated or not. Since he's living with his mommy and daddy, I give you permission to yell at him and punish him for doing the wrong thing. Next time he makes a date, tell him to go to his room.

I hope I've answered your questions, because I'm too angry at Rick to go on.

Gail, who knows all about alpha males

When parents separate, they have to clearly set new family boundaries and rules. They need to clarify their marital status, either by divorcing or by trying marital therapy for six months and then making a decision to get back together or proceed with dissolution.

Rick, however, has created anything but clarity. He has created incredible ambiguity. He has moved into his childhood house with his parents. He is keeping the door open to reconciling with his wife while dating and looking for a new partner in case his marriage doesn't work out. And he's using his parents for room, board, and babysitting to boot. In essence Rick seems unable to function on his own and is willing to sacrifice his children and parents to his problem.

So what should Jeff do? First he should tell Rick that he and the children have to move into their own place ASAP. If Rick moves into his own apartment, with more responsibility and no free babysitting, he will find it harder to date.

However, I would wager that having to move and take care of his children himself will motivate Rick to go back to his wife, if she will have him. I don't think he will opt for creating his own family life.

Susan

The Minnie Question

Dear Gail and Susan,

My son Perry and daughter-in-law Cindy are getting a divorce. Cindy and I have always been close. I only have a son, so Cindy was like the daughter I never had. I want to stay friendly with her, but Perry told me that he doesn't want me to. He's too hurt and wants me to be on his side. Children don't have to take sides when their parents divorce. Do I have to?

Minnie

Dear Perry's Mom,

Perry seems to need his mother right now. Tell your son that you have always been and always will be on his side. And throw in that you love him. Sons are never too old to hear that. You don't mention whether Perry and Cindy have children. If they do, you have to try to convince your son that you want to stay friendly with the mother of your grandchildren. If grandchildren aren't an issue, tell Cindy your relationship with her is important but that you must support your son.

When our children get divorced, it can be very hard on us. First of all, we don't like to see them unhappy. Second of all, divorces can get ugly. And third of all, we as parents can lose out on things also. In your case, it seems as if your son and daughter-in-law are fighting for custody over you.

> Gail, who didn't realize what she did to
> her parents when she got divorced

Divorce means loss—for everyone. Relationships that once were are no more. Boundaries change. The structure of the family changes.

Minnie wants to know if she has to take sides. It's not a matter of taking sides. Her son needs her help to cope with his loss. A parent who stays "neutral" in a child's divorce is not there for the child when he desperately needs the parent's support.

I understand that parents also suffer loss in a divorce. In this case, Minnie may lose "the daughter she never had." However, her son Perry has lost more—his family and his dreams for his future.

Perhaps over time, when Perry gets over his anger and has moved on with his life, Minnie and Cindy will rekindle their relationship, but probably they won't.

> *Susan*

Grandma's a Lesbian

Dear Gail and Susan,

My wife Mary and I have been married for thirty-five years. About five years ago Mary told me that she is gay. We agreed to stay married but live separate lives. A few months ago, Mary said that she met a woman she wants to live with. She wants a divorce and to move out. We have never told our grown children about our situation. Now we will have to. And how do we tell

our two- and four-year-old grandchildren that their grandmother
is a lesbian?

Rob

Wow, Rob,

You don't have to tell your two- and four-year-old grandchildren anything. Their small minds wouldn't get it anyway.
What kids really care about at that age are their own feelings
and how safe they feel.

I agree with you. It's a huge problem that you never told
your grown children about your situation. Tell them immediately. When you keep a huge secret like this, children tend to
resent it and may have a hard time trusting you again. After
you tell them, I would apologize that you've kept such important information from them and say that you'll never do it
again. They'll be skeptical about everything you do now, and
you're going to have to give it time.

By the way, congratulations to Mary. She's going to live the
life she always wanted.

Love, Gail, who adores men

*I agree, Gail, the grandchildren need not be told that their
grandmother is gay, but they will need help with the change in the
family structure. Grandma will be living elsewhere, and not with
Grandpa. There will be a new person in their lives.*

*But I don't agree that Rob and Mary should have told their chil-
dren earlier. After all, parents' sexual and marital arrangements
are their own private business to reveal when they choose to, especially when we are talking about grown children who are out of
the house. Rob and Mary have decided to tell now because they
have to.*

*Certainly, I encourage them to allow their children to ask ques-
tions and express their feelings.*

Susan

Ex-Wife and Daughter

Dear Gail and Susan,

I've been divorced for a year and a half. Lila, my twenty-two-year-old daughter, wants me to get back with her mother. I know my ex-wife wants that, too, and is pushing Lila to pressure me. Believe me, a reconciliation is just not in the cards. I know why I divorced and I have moved on. What should I say to my daughter?

Lucas

Dear Being Pushed,

I don't think a twenty-two-year-old whose parents have been divorced for a year and a half still needs the security of them being together. She may long for her whole family once in a while, but hopefully she isn't any more involved than that.

You say you know why you divorced. Does your ex-wife also know? If you're still speaking to her, why don't you remind her why the two of you aren't married anymore. And you could also throw in that she should leave Lila alone. Tell her I said your daughter should not be forced to be a spokesperson for her. Hopefully, she'll stop the big push.

You don't have to tell your daughter exactly why you got divorced. However, there must be a simple explanation you can give her, if she doesn't know already. And while you're at it, tell your daughter that you're absolutely not getting back together with her mother. Trust me. She doesn't really expect you to. Lila is starting her own life and looking around for a guy to love and to be loved by. She is most likely more interested in her own love life than in her parents'. If you're a sentimental guy, you can add that you were in love with her mother when she was born.

Gail, who hates being pushed

Gail, I suspect that although Lucas has been direct with us, he has not been explicit with his daughter. Sometimes parents are

vague and general about important matters, especially if they relate to something their children don't want them to do.

Divorce is one of those areas of life that parents should be very
clear and up-front about. Lucas needs to tell Lila that he is never
going to reconcile with her mother and that the subject is off the
table for reconsideration. If Lila wants to know the reasons for the
split, Lucas should be equally clear. Lila is an adult and can understand the truth.

Susan

Derogatory Things

Dear Gail and Susan,

My daughter Roseanne was married to Len for ten years before they divorced. They have two young children. Roseanne is
still very angry with Len. I hear her say derogatory things about
him to the kids. I'm afraid that she is poisoning my grandchildren against their father, which I don't think is good. Is there
anything I can do?

Patricia

Dear Good Grandmother,

It's futile for you to try to reason with your daughter. Angry
ex-wives want everyone to be equally as mad at their ex-
husbands. You're right to be concerned about the children.
Young children believe their mothers. If she keeps reinforcing
how horrible Len is, the kids will incorporate that into their
thinking and feel guilty when they have a good time with him.

I'm happy to inform you that there is something you can
do. When you're around your grandchildren, say some nice
things about their father. Fortunately, children believe their
grandmothers, too. Your daughter won't like hearing any
praise for Len, but I'm sure you can do it casually behind her
back. I usually don't advise subterfuge, but in this case, I advise it strongly.

Also, you can suggest that the children get therapy. Tell

your daughter that it helps children get through difficult times. Don't mention Len.

> Gail, who knows you can be sneaky—you wrote the letter to us behind her back, didn't you?

I find this issue not as straightforward as some people would like to make it. Divorce gurus advise that you never say anything bad to the children about the other parent. I agree that a parent should not gratuitously disparage her ex to the kids. However, sometimes the other parent is bad, for instance, a father who promises to pick his son up on Saturday mornings and routinely never shows. There's a difference between saying "Your father is a jerk" and "It must make you sad and angry that Daddy didn't pick you up when he promised to." I don't advise the former, but I do advise the latter kind of statement.

If Roseanne is bad-mouthing her ex for unwarranted reasons, Patricia can suggest that she stop and encourage her to join a divorce support group where she can appropriately vent her anger.

But if Len does in fact treat his children badly, Patricia can suggest that Roseanne articulate the kids' feelings in the way I have suggested above.

Susan

Maybe Things Could Work Out

Dear Gail and Susan,

My ex-son-in-law Darren was the one who wanted a divorce. My daughter CeCe was crushed. Now Darren says he's changed his mind. He keeps calling me to enlist my help in getting back with CeCe. My feelings are mixed. On the one hand, I'm angry with him, too, but then again, I don't like to see CeCe alone and miserable. Maybe they could work things out if she gave him a chance. Should I get involved?

Lana

Dear Mixed Feelings,

The one thing you don't mention in your letter is how CeCe feels about Darren. You told us she's alone and miserable, but that doesn't necessarily mean she still has any love for Darren. I suggest you find out if she does. If she has feelings for him, the two of them should talk. The next time Darren calls you, tell him never to call you again, because you're not going to be the go-between. Then . . . you know what, Lana, I don't want to get involved with this situation, either. They were old enough to get married and old enough to get divorced. Let's both of us leave them alone.

Gail, who's had it up to here with Darren and CeCe

If Darren really wanted to get back with CeCe, he would have found a way to communicate with her. He might have suggested marital therapy to see if they could heal the wounds. Darren is calling his ex-mother-in-law in order to bind his anxiety about his decision and not have to do anything risky about it.

Lana should definitely not get involved and she should stop taking Darren's phone calls.

Susan

Catholic and Divorced

Dear Gail and Susan,

My son Hector told us last week that he is getting a divorce. As Catholics, my husband and I don't believe in divorce. I have tried to talk Hector out of it, but he is insistent. I'm angry and torn. I don't want to lose my son, but I don't think I will be able to have a relationship with him.

Carolina

Dear Angry and Torn,

Let me tell you my mother's philosophy: If you can, you can. If you can't, you can't. If you do, you do. If you don't, you don't. If you will, you will. If you won't, you won't. Enough said.

Gail, who always listened to her mother

Carolina says she cannot retain her faith and have a relationship with her son. Why not? Gail, do you think that she avoids all relationships with non-Catholics and people who are divorced?

Hector's divorce does not compromise his mother's faith in any way. Hector and Carolina are separate people. So what's up? I wonder if we have the answer in Carolina's letter: she says she is "angry and torn," meaning she is debating about whether to withhold from her son in order to punish him for not complying with her wishes.

In my opinion Carolina has a choice to make. She can throw away her relationship with her son or set aside her anger and accept his right to make his own decision.

Susan

Susan, Isn't that what my mother said?

I think so, Gail

Divorce Settlement

Dear Gail and Susan,

I hate my daughter's divorce settlement. Her husband got primary custody of their three children. Doris has them only every other weekend, so I can't see them whenever I want to. My grandchildren are young. I'm afraid that I will miss out on their growing up.

Francine

Dear Can't See Them,

I hate to tell you this, but something is really wrong with Doris. It's common nowadays for couples to have joint custody of their children. It's uncommon for a mother not to get custody and extremely rare for a mother not to want custody. So what's up with her?

If your daughter can't see her own children except for every other weekend, then you, of course, won't be able to see them whenever you want to. When there's at least one parent in the picture, grandmothers have no rights. You *will* miss out on them growing up and that's too bad. Children need grand-parents. You sound like a very good person despite the fact that you raised a lunatic.

Perhaps you can work out a deal with your son-in-law.

> Gail, who thinks a grandmother's feelings
> should always be considered

I agree, Gail, there is important information left out of this letter. Judges don't routinely take custody away from mothers if they want it. Therefore, I speculate that Doris didn't want primary custody—which means that she didn't want the responsibility of raising her kids full-time.

Francine wants to see her grandchildren whenever she wants to. But Francine is not entitled to visiting-on-demand no matter who has custody. In fact, Francine's letter reveals a pretty self-centered parent. She tells us about how she feels, what she wants, and how her daughter's divorce affects her. Francine's self-absorption and lack of boundaries may have something to do with Doris's feeling unable to cope with her children.

Francine will just have to accept the reality that she can see her grandchildren when either her daughter or her ex-son-in-law arranges visits.

> *Susan*

Manipulating Alimony

Dear Gail and Susan,

My daughter Vera was divorced eleven years ago. She lives with a man but won't marry him because then her alimony will stop. The arrangement doesn't sit well with me. It seems manipulative. Should I have a talk with Vera?

Louis

Dear Doesn't Sit Well,

You can have all the talks in the universe with Vera, but she won't listen to you. She wants a live-in boyfriend and she wants the money from her ex. It doesn't concern her how it sits with you. The only thing she's interested in is her own comfort level.

Be happy, Louis, that you didn't marry a woman like your daughter. She's just not nice.

Gail, who's sorry about how you feel

When children become adults and take on their own lives, parents learn things about them they may not have known or may not like. Louis has found out something about Vera he doesn't admire. Just as children need to de-idealize their parents, likewise, parents need to de-idealize their children. Louis is going to have to accept this character trait in Vera. It's her life, and what she is doing is not illegal.

Susan

Divorced and Dating

Dear Gail and Susan,

My grandchildren are three and seven. My son is divorced and dating. He includes his dates in activities with the kids and sometimes brings his dates back to his house overnight. I don't think it's good for the kids. Am I just being old-fashioned?

Myron

Dear Not Old-Fashioned,

Myron, there's old-fashioned and there's decent. Your son shouldn't include his dates and activities with his kids because his children can grow attached to the women. This can have an adverse effect on them temporarily and permanently. It's not good for anyone to have people coming and going from their lives. The kids can feel abandoned and, as adults, may not want to get attached to anyone for fear of losing them. Why doesn't your son realize this?

Also, having women sleep over is a bad idea. It's a terrible lesson for kids. It's so much better when they grow up with morals that they can later break. But if they don't have them to begin with, they're at a big disadvantage. At three and seven, they may not know all about sex, but they know it's not good to be naked with someone you don't know really well. They will be nervous to go into their father's bedroom, fearing they will be told to get out. Or if he locks his door, they will feel scared that they can't get to him. You know that and I know that. So why doesn't your son know this?

Myron, you're not old-fashioned. Your son is a jerk. The most important thing to him is his own immediate satisfaction. Let him know your point of view. Somebody should embarrass him.

> Gail, who feels sorry for you, your grandchildren,
> and the girls your son gets involved with

For me, the issue is not about being old-fashioned. The issue is what is appropriate for children still living at home. My rule is that parents should not in any way involve their children in their dating lives. Dates and children shouldn't even meet. When a parent and his girlfriend decide to make their relationship permanent, then and only then should he introduce her to his children.

The reasons are many. A child of divorce has already suffered a big loss. It is not in the child's best interest to attach again and suffer another loss. Moreover, no matter what we say to a child, he always believes he was in some way responsible for the divorce. If the child is involved with a parent's dates, he may feel it's up to him to make the relationship work or it's his fault if it doesn't. In addition, a child shouldn't have to deal with liking or not liking a woman who is only around temporarily.

So Myron is correct. But what can he do? He can tell his son everything Gail and I have said and hope that his son listens.

Susan

Divorced Three Times

Dear Gail and Susan,

Ashley has been married and divorced three times and has kids from three different husbands. She says she wants to get married again, but how can she find a husband who will take on three kids and three ex-husbands?

Loretta

Dear Crazy Ashley's Mother,

I can totally understand why you think it will be difficult for Ashley to remarry. Not many men want the noise that three kids make. Even when they're quiet, they're loud. Also, your daughter doesn't seem like a good risk. If I were a guy, I would wonder why this woman keeps getting divorced.

On the other hand, a man married her with two kids and two divorces. So maybe she can find another husband who she'll divorce. Then you'll get to enjoy your four grandchildren.

If Ashley gets married ten times and has ten kids from ten different husbands, she could probably get her own reality show. Let's not mention this to her.

Gail, who wishes you, your daughter, and your
grandchildren well

Gail, you've said it all. I would only add that Loretta suggest therapy to her daughter. Ashley needs to learn how to make better husband choices and to cope with the relationship called marriage.

Susan

Not Marrying Clara

Dear Gail and Susan,

I am a divorced man. I divorced my wife fifteen years ago. It was an ugly time and cost me a lot of money. I am now dating a nice woman named Clara, but I have made up my mind that I will not marry again. My adult daughter Renee wants me to marry Clara. Renee says she's embarrassed by my arrangement. She doesn't like introducing us as "my dad and his friend." How can I help Renee get over it?

Alec

Dear Renee's Dad,

This is one of those situations where no one ever changes their mind. You are not going to get married and your daughter will not stop being embarrassed.

Unless.

You realize that it's not Clara's fault that your ex-wife and you had an ugly time. She deserves to have the same security and happiness that most women want. One day you might decide that Clara is the one. Then you, Clara, and Renee can all be happy. Until then, tell your daughter to introduce you as "my dad and the woman he loves."

Gail, who loves love

Renee says she's embarrassed by her father's relationship. Embarrassment means shame. Shame means self-depreciation. So Renee depreciates herself because her father has a love life with no marriage. I am guessing that Renee feels shame that she comes from a divorced family. Her own self-image is adversely affected by her father's lifestyle. If her father married again, the fact of his divorce, in Renee's mind, wouldn't be so apparent.

Alec needs to make clear to his daughter that he does not want to marry again and that he expects his daughter to respect and accept his choice. In other words, the topic is off the table for conversation or debate.

If Renee's self-esteem remains affected by her father's decision, then Alec should encourage her to get therapy to help her separate.

Susan

A Mess

Dear Gail and Susan,

My husband and I stayed together until our daughter Myra went to college. It was not easy but we had decided that it would be better for Myra if we stuck it out until she left home. Now we are getting a divorce and our daughter is falling apart. She's angry, mostly at me, and is threatening to stop talking to me. Should we put the divorce proceedings on hold? I don't want to, but I'm having a hard time knowing what to do with our mess.

Dina

Dear Stay Together,

What's the matter with you people? Here's where you really went wrong. You thought that you did a good thing by sticking it out until Myra left home. She didn't leave home. When a kid is still in college, "home" is the home of her childhood. So what you did is pull the rug out from under her. It's almost as bad as moving while your child is away at college and not giving her a forwarding address. It's too late now to stop the proceedings. She's going to come home either to separated parents or to parents who no longer want to live together. Those are terrible options.

Myra has threatened to stop talking to you but hasn't yet. You're going to have to listen to all the anger she has. Your daughter is falling apart. You're going to have to provide an extra safety net for her, so I think the two of you should go visit Myra at school. You both should explain exactly how the new arrangement will work. Tell her one of you will be living in the home she knows—don't you dare sell it yet. Tell her that the other will hopefully live nearby. Tell her how much you love her and that you're going to keep her life as together as possible. If she's really falling apart, bring her home for a semester.

You and your husband are unthinking and very selfish.

Gail, who hates parents who put themselves first

Myra is away from home for the first time—her big developmental step. She assumed that Mom and Dad were home, together, rooting for her. Now she finds out that they were actually breaking up the family and the house.

Parents who wait to divorce until their kid goes to college rationalize that if they do it while she's away, she'll be spared the disruption. But it seems to me that they really want to sneak the divorce through to be spared their child's grief.

Divorce is always hard on a child, but if the child is still at home, parents can be there to help her with the feelings, changes, and loss. So I don't recommend that parents wait until their child goes off to college. They should divorce either earlier or later.

That being said, Dina and her husband should proceed with the dissolution of the marriage. As you say, Gail, Dina needs to accept her daughter's anger, but it should not have the power to stop the divorce. Accepting a child's anger never means letting it rule the family. They should keep Myra informed as changes are made regarding living arrangements, money, etc. No more sneaking. In addition, Myra's parents owe their daughter a sincere apology for making a dramatic mistake of timing.

I wouldn't, however, rush to bring her home. Myra should see the campus psychologist for help. Perhaps there can be some family sessions. It would be a shame for Myra to lose her family, her home, and also her first year of college.

Susan

Marty Says

Dear Gail and Susan,

My thirty-five-year-old son Marty told me to divorce his father John. I was embarrassed, but not that surprised. My husband and I haven't gotten along for years. We either don't talk to each other or argue. Marty says he can't stand being with us and that I have given enough of my life to this marriage and I deserve better. What do I say to Marty and what should I do?

Anna

Dear Miserable in Marriage,

Why is thirty-five-year-old Marty giving you advice about your marriage? Is he with you that often? Marty is the type of person that other people scream at. They scream, "Get a life."

You asked what you should say to your son. Tell him to worry about himself. You also asked what you should do. You and your husband haven't gotten along for years. It's the way you coexist. But have you really considered leaving him or is that just thirty-five-year-old Marty's suggestion? Maybe the two of you can stay under the same roof—the roof that you and John learned to live under—but from now on, you don't have to be with your husband twenty-four/seven. Get involved with things outside of the house. Go on a vacation with a girl-friend. See thirty-five-year-old Marty alone so you won't annoy him. Once you've done things on your own, you can decide whether to be on your own permanently.

Gail, who is happy she's not
thirty-five-year-old Marty's mother

Gail, the letter speaks to Anna's passivity. Her son tells her to divorce and she asks us what to do. Her passivity is probably what frustrates Marty. A son wants his mom to be happy and engaged in life.

What Anna should do is make her times with Marty pleasant and upbeat—either not fight with her husband or see her son alone. She should apologize to him for subjecting him to her dysfunctional marriage and tell him that she will stop doing it. Then Anna should get therapy to decide what she wants to do about her marriage and her life.

Susan

Not Invited

Dear Gail and Susan,

My wife and I divorced when our kids were twenty-eight and thirty-three. My daughter Darlene—she's the older one—invites her mother but not me to dinner and birthday parties and other gatherings. I've told Darlene that I don't mind being at the same party as my ex, but she still won't invite me and I don't understand why. Am I missing something?

Chuck

Dear Missing Something,

Your letter is difficult to answer because it doesn't give crucial facts, but I'm going to guess why you're left out. You probably left your wife and she suffered because of it. Your children saw their mother cry and you be happy. Then you went out and got some young chick who wears push-up bras. (Weren't you surprised when you saw her naked the first time and she had no boobs?) On top of that, you probably thought that your twenty-eight-year-old and thirty-three-year-old didn't need any comforting. You figured they were old enough to understand. You probably haven't called them enough or asked them enough questions. I bet you don't know what's going on in their lives. You've become a stranger, which is why you're not on Darlene's guest list. Yes, you are missing something. You're missing a chance to be close to your family. The above is all hypothetical, but you're a hypothetical kind of guy. Pick up the phone and get rid of the chick. Then there might be a place for you at Darlene's table.

Gail, who's always invited

Just because Chuck doesn't mind being with his ex, it doesn't mean that his ex-wife feels the same about being with him. Darlene may be closer to her mother and more protective of her, so she invites Mom, not Dad.

Chuck wants to know if he's missing something. Yes. He's miss-

ing the maturity to just ask his daughter the question he wants the answer to. He may not like the answer, but then he'll know. And if he wants a relationship with his daughter, he should stop focusing on what she invites him to and concentrate on what he can offer her.

Susan

CHAPTER ELEVEN

Aging and Illness

We all know people in their nineties or hundreds. Perhaps your own parents have reached that age. Maybe you have. Now that we are living longer, aging issues are numerous and complicated. One question is where we will live as we get older—whether we remain in our own home, move to a retirement facility, or move in with one of our children. Hopefully not. How do we make the decision? And what happens when our adult children don't agree with our choices? Do we have to take their requests into account? All of a sudden they want to parent us and we don't want them to. We have to keep Queen Elizabeth in mind and not relinquish our thrones.

And then there's the reality that families have spread out all over the country. There was one sixty-two-year-old daughter who moved into her eighty-four-year-old mother's retirement home, but that's rare. It's not a given anymore that our children will be near us if we are sick. Or even if they are, what can we expect from our children in the way of help and care? Do our children owe us something when we get older? As harsh as it may sound, our children don't owe us anything when we are sick any more than we owe them an inheritance when we die. Our job is to raise them. Their responsibility is to live independently and well. Just as we may choose to leave them money, they may choose to take care of us when we are old. Each is a decision, not a requirement.

What if we do need help? Can we ask? How should we approach our children? Being direct and up-front is always best, provided we accept that our children may not be able to give us what we want, and that they are free to turn us down. It's tempting when we get older to try to manipulate. After all, we've given so much for so long and we're tired and maybe impatient. But manipulation is never the right way. It may temporarily get us what we want, but it breeds resentment.

Dementia is another issue that affects us and our children as we get older. If a parent has dementia, the stress on a family is enormous. There are lots of decisions to make and losses to mourn. Families should educate themselves about the disease and join together to deal with a parent who is suffering from brain deterioration. They should also avail themselves of community resources and support.

What if our child is sick? He's at college and doesn't want to come home. Do we insist that he leave school and see the doctor we know? Our child is obese and we worry about her compromised long-term health. Should we pester her into going on a diet?

Our adult children are separate from us. We can no longer control what they do or the decisions they make, even about their health, even if we think that they are entirely wrong and we fear for them. We can offer opinions, but we need to respect their right to make their own choices.

~~~~~~~~~~~~~~~~~~~~~~~~~~~~~~~~

Living Alone

Dear Gail and Susan,

I am ninety-two and still living in my own home. I have a weekly poker game, occasionally go to a concert or movie, and keep up my walking. My unmarried fifty-five-year-old daughter helps me out by driving me to doctors. She just told me she thinks that I should not live alone and that she wants to move in with me. I don't want her here. I love her, but she's a micromanager and I like my independence and privacy. How should I handle this?

Don

You Know What, Don?

There's more to this than your daughter moving in with you. Fifty-five-year-olds, married or unmarried, don't want to live with their daddy. At this moment in time, she needs you more than you need her. Maybe she needs to be taken care of monetarily or emotionally.

And living with a micromanager is impossible. She'll alphabetize your canned fruits and vegetables. She'll insist your coffeemaker not be on the counter. She'll put the television remote in its proper place. It'll be hell, Don.

You have to retain your position as the dad and tell her that it's not good for either one of you if she moves in. Enjoy your independence. Write to me when you're a hundred so I can see how you're doing.

> Gail, who knows there's much more to this

I agree, Gail. Although Don may need some help—apparently he has stopped driving—his daughter's motives for wanting to move in with him may not be his failing faculties.

Don should thank his daughter for her offer but respectfully decline it. So long as he has his mental faculties (and his letter suggests that he does), Don can and should make his own decisions. However, he should also be realistic about what assistance he might need and make sure he gets it.

Once he makes his decision known to his daughter, he can ask her if she needs anything. If she does, Don can try to help her with her problems. However, if she says no, he should respect her privacy.

> *Susan*

Lisa Is Not Well

Dear Gail and Susan,

I just found out that my daughter Lisa has ovarian cancer. She didn't tell me about it. Her husband Jack called me because he thought I should know, even though my daughter was adamant that I not be told. I am beside myself with worry about Lisa. As her mother, I feel I should be there to support her. My dilemma is whether to call and tell her I know or respect her wishes not to tell me.

> Sara

Dear Sara,

I have always had a hard time respecting someone else's wishes. I have an idea for you. Why don't you go visit her? Once you are in close proximity to her, I'm sure she'll tell you what's going on. There are times when adult children need their mother. This is one of them.

Gail, who is sad, too

This is a difficult situation to sort out and advise about, but let me offer my perspective. We don't know why Sara's daughter Lisa is so adamant that her mother not be told about her ovarian cancer. Does Lisa want to protect her mother from worry or does she want to protect herself from a mother who falls apart and is not helpful in the face of illness?

Since Jack betrayed the secret, Sara should ask him to come clean with his wife. Knowing that her mother has been informed, Lisa may now welcome Sara's support. But if Lisa is still determined to keep her mother away, then Sara (and Jack) should respect her wishes.

Susan

My Daughters Don't Agree

Dear Gail and Susan,

I am seventy-nine and have cancer. I have decided that I don't want chemotherapy. I have heard all the doctors' statistics, probabilities, etc., and have made my decision to do surgery but not chemo after. My two daughters don't agree and keep trying to get me to change my mind. If my cancer doesn't come back and I'm not hit by a bus, I might live many healthy years. I don't want to spend whatever time I have left fighting with my daughters about chemo. What can I do to stop their nagging?

Corinne

Corinne, Dear Corinne,

I'm sorry about your health and I hope you live many happy years. By the way, mothers teach their daughters how to nag and I can tell they learned well from you. Just remember, nagging is their way of loving you. Don't take it so seriously. And since you've checked out statistics and probabilities, I have faith that you are doing the right thing. However, I'd like to do a little nagging myself. Bring your daughters to your next doctor's appointment. Women, no matter how old they are, will listen to an authority figure.

> Gail, who doesn't blame you

I can understand why Corinne's daughters want their mother to do everything medically possible. They love her and they are not seventy-nine. The daughters could be in their fifties. In your fifties, with many years left to live and a younger constitution, you might very well opt for the most aggressive treatment. At fifty, Corinne might have. But older people sometimes factor in their age, their potential time left, and quality of life and choose a more conservative protocol.

I suggest that Corrine empathize with her daughters' intentions but remind them that age makes a difference and that they need to see the decision from the point of view of a seventy-nine-year-old. I hope that the daughters are mature enough to understand and will stop bugging their mom.

> *Susan*

My Health Is Failing

Dear Gail and Susan,

I am eighty-five with three daughters who live in different states than I do. None of them lives anywhere near me. My health is failing. My children want me to move near one of them. They say they can't take care of me unless I do. But I don't want to move. I appreciate their concern, but I just can't think of uprooting and resettling in a new place and becoming dependent on one of them. Do I have to?

Irene

Irene, Irene,

Talking to your daughters won't do any good. So keep quiet.

Remember those T-shirts that said "I'm the mom"? You should be wearing one. In a script I wrote for *The Golden Girls*, the dialogue supports my point. Dorothy is very sensible and in her sixties. Sophia is a tough little Italian woman in her eighties.

DOROTHY: Ma, I forbid you to do this.

SOPHIA: Dorothy, sometimes you forget, I'm the mother here.

DOROTHY: That has nothing to do with this.

SOPHIA: It has everything to do with this. In the twenty-five years I have on you, I've learned something. [*searching*] I just wish I could remember what it is.

Another writer wrote *King Lear*. It's about a king who has three daughters, just like you. Since he's old, he gives them all his money and they promise, in return, to take care of him. Only—surprise, surprise—they don't. He visits each of them in her castle. Today they would be expensive condos. And since the play is a tragedy, he ends up poor and alone. What I want you to do is send your daughters a copy of the play. They won't read it but they might skim it. It's by a far better writer than I am . . . Shakespeare.

Gail, who writes and reads

I empathize with Irene's children. They want to be able to provide more hands-on attention. They may feel guilt for not being more diligent caretakers. Some old, childhood feelings of rejection may have surfaced—Mom would rather be alone than with me. But uprooting and resettling an older person can often hasten deterio-

ration. So it's not always a good idea anyway. Therefore, Irene should stay where she is if that's what she wants to do. She should also make sure she has adequate health care and support for herself. Health-care facilities and doctors will speak with relatives, so Irene's daughters can be involved in their mother's medical care via phone or e-mail. And perhaps they can visit.

Irene says her health is failing. Presumably she is thinking about the end of her life. We all like to have control over as much as we can for as long as we can. Since Irene's mental faculties seem fine, she should exercise her right to control where she lives until the end of her life. Perhaps if Irene explains her desire to maintain her independence and dignity, her daughters will come to understand and validate her choice.

Susan

Overweight Daughter

Dear Gail and Susan,

My daughter Claire is overweight, bordering on obese. She always had a weight problem, but since the birth of her two children, she really let herself go. I'm afraid she will develop serious medical problems—diabetes or heart disease. Also, she's not a good role model for her two daughters. Is there anything I can say to her that will get her to do something about her weight? She looks terrible.

Merv

Dear Merv, Who's Worried about Weight,

I truly believe it's impossible to say anything to overweight daughters. Friends tell me that when they do, their daughters screech and vow never to speak to them again. They slam down the phone and don't speak to them for long periods of time. The truth is, they know they're fat. They're angry at themselves and the rest of the world. However, their bodies are in their hands. They've gotten information on television, in magazines, and from doctors who warn about the ills of obesity. So, Merv, nothing you do or say is going to help. I know someone who offered to send her daughter to a spa and/ or to pay for a weight-loss doctor and/or to stock her refrigerator with wholesome things. Her daughter angrily told her never to bring up the subject of her weight again and didn't speak to her for months. I strongly advise you not to mention Claire's weight even once. I'm afraid she will kill you.

Gail, who goes on diets herself

As you say, Gail, no one who is overweight needs to be told it. And as you also say, there is lots of information out there about dieting and weight-loss programs.

Overeating and obesity are not simple problems. Depression, unresolved childhood issues, and unexpressed anger are some possible underlying factors in overeating. Because low self-esteem and self-destructiveness are also part of the problem, berating or lecturing the overeater doesn't help.

People with eating disorders often focus on food management as a way of life. It can become their life. Merv would be well advised not to participate in an already well-developed obsession. I would counsel him to concentrate on who his daughter is rather than on how she looks and what she eats. Supporting and validating other parts of her personality will help her fill up with something other than food.

Susan

Fertility

Dear Gail and Susan,

Todd, my son, and Reba, my daughter-in-law, want children very badly, but they have had no luck. They have been referred to a fertility clinic and are now paying a fortune to try to get pregnant. They are stressed and in financial trouble. Is there anything I can do?

Mona

Dear Maybe to Be a Grandmother Soon,

No. There's nothing you can do. Supposedly Todd and Reba are adults, and having children is a very important decision. It only takes two to make a baby, not three. So stay out of it, Mona.

You know what's crazy? In our generation, it was the woman who got pregnant. It amazes me that today both the future mother and future father say they're pregnant. Is he going to go through labor? Are his ankles going to be swollen? Will his nipples be tender once the baby is born?

> Gail, whose children never consulted her about
> having kids and who is glad they didn't

Todd and Reba have made a decision to spend their money on fertility treatment. It is their decision to make. Wanting children with the biological clock ticking is stressful, as can be paying for fertility drugs. But in the case of pregnancy, time is a factor. Todd and Reba may not be able to wait until their financial situation is better.

Mona should be supportive and encouraging, which may ease her son and daughter-in-law's stress.

> *Susan*

Mono

Dear Gail and Susan,

My son Johnny is in college and has mononucleosis. I want him to come home to recuperate. He refuses. I am concerned about his health care and would be more comfortable if he saw doctors I know. Am I overreacting?

> Daryl

Dear Concerned about Your Son's Health Care,

When I was in college, kids got mononucleosis and each had a different way of handling it. Some left school for a semester.

Others went to doctors connected with NYU. All of them survived, so relax. Whatever doctor gave Johnny his diagnosis will be around for him. Doctors near college campuses are used to dealing with mono. Tell him not to kiss anyone. That's probably how he got it in the first place.

We're used to taking care of our kids and taking them to the pediatrician whenever anything is wrong. It's hard to let go of that responsibility, but you're going to have to. Don't pediatricians just handle kids until they're eighteen? So now that he's on his own and taking care of this illness himself, why not try to celebrate his independence rather than trying to drag him home?

Gail, who would probably feel the same way you do

As you point out, Gail, because we are used to taking care of our kids, it's hard to let them make their own medical decisions. However, mono is a pretty common illness on college campuses. University health clinics have experience treating it. Daryl can stay in touch and monitor Johnny's recovery, but he should respect his son's decision to stay in his own world and cope rather than run home to Mom and Dad.

Susan

Telling Children

Dear Gail and Susan,

I have terminal cancer with only months to live. I don't want to tell my children I am dying. My husband says I have to. I just can't imagine how to tell them. Is my husband right that I should?

Juliana

My Dear Juliana,

I am so sorry that you have to struggle with this problem. I'm glad your husband is by your side and smart. He's right.

You should tell your children. If you don't, then they'll never get the chance to resolve things with you or to tell you how much they love you or get to say good-bye. If you do tell them, it will make the loss a little easier for them and maybe it will even do some good for you, knowing that you mothered them until the end.

Here's how you do it. Tell them you need to see them; don't say you'd like to see them, say you *need* to see them, because you don't want to give them a choice. When they arrive, give the family some time to enjoy themselves. Get into the issue gently. Your husband might want to do this so you don't have to. State the truth. Give them proof of the truth by telling them exactly what your doctor has told you and say that you'd be happy to answer any questions they might have. They'll want you to try another doctor or get another treatment. Tell them you're not going to and that you feel confident in what you're doing. Expect tears, but also expect hugs. The warmth they will give you and the warmth you give them will be worth it. You'll realize that telling them was the right thing to do.

Families tend to get closer at a time like this, and that's exactly what you want. You've raised your children and you want them to be able to survive without you. That's the whole point of life.

> Gail, who with her sisters actually had some
> good times together with their mother
> in the last few months of her life

Although the end of life is inevitable for all of us, how to handle it may be confusing and frightening. Juliana doesn't want to share the news of her impending death with her children. Is she withholding the news because it helps her maintain some denial about the reality? Will telling her children force her to face what she is not yet prepared to deal with? Does Juliana feel more in control if only she and her husband know her secret? Juliana may feel that she will be giving up control by telling. Her children will express their emotions and opinions.

Nevertheless, I agree, Gail: Juliana should tell her children.
They should be given the opportunity to say good-bye. Although we
are not obligated to help our children with our death, I think it's a
mature parental thing to do. I hope that Juliana tells her children
the medical truths and financial arrangements. That she reminds
them that death is part of life and that she expects them to carry on
well. And I also hope that she tells them that she was privileged to
have known them and to have been their parent.

Susan

Susan, that was the hardest question I've had to answer.

Face-Lift?

Dear Gail and Susan,

My children asked me what I wanted for my seventieth birthday. I said a face-lift. They said they would buy me a car but not a face-lift. Don't you think they should give me what I want since they asked and I told them?

Elaine

Dear Almost Seventy,

Do they have a reason they don't want you to get a face-lift? Do they think you're pretty enough? Do you think you're pretty enough? Do they want their mother to look the same as she always did? Do you think they might not want their mother to look younger than they do? Are they afraid of the consequences of plastic surgery? Do they think you may get a messed-up face or die on the table? Do they think unnecessary surgery is wrong?

Do you think I made any attempt to answer your question?

Gail, who's glad her mother never got a face-lift

We might ask our college kid what he wants for graduation. He
might say a Porsche. That doesn't mean we have to give it to

him. Our kid needs to accept that we give what we are comfortable
giving. So does Elaine. I understand that her children asked, but
telling someone what you want does not obligate them to give it
to you.

For whatever reason, Elaine's children do not want to buy her
plastic surgery. They prefer to spend their money on a new car. If
Elaine doesn't want a car, she should work out a compromise with
her children so they can give her something they want to give that
she wants.

Susan

Celia Needs to Be Stopped

Dear Gail and Susan,

My daughter Celia lives alone. I think she's a hypochondriac.
She calls constantly to tell me about every cold, sore throat, and
stomach pain. How can I get her to stop being so focused on her
health?

Natalie

Dear Mother of a Hypochondriac,

My guess is Celia needs attention. She obviously hasn't
separated from you and there's a good chance she's lonely. I
would talk to her about anything but her health. When she
brings it up, steer the conversation in another direction and
don't talk to her too often or for too long. She needs to transfer
her attachment from you to her friends and, hopefully, someday to a man.

You'll be surprised how soon her health will improve when
she doesn't have complete access to you.

Gail, who didn't tell her mother that anything
was wrong, ever, because she didn't want
to alarm her

Preoccupation with one's body and one's health is a symptom of someone with narcissistic issues. If your suggestions don't work, Gail, Natalie should suggest that Celia get therapy.

Susan

Larry Is Fixed

Dear Gail and Susan,

My son Larry was married to a woman who didn't want children, so he had a vasectomy. Now they are divorced. What if he meets someone who wants kids? What if a woman won't even go out with him when she finds out that he can't have children?

Sophie

Dear Worrier,

Good news, Sophie. Vasectomies can be reversed. I have a friend who had one, then reversed it, had two kids (of course they're smart and beautiful), then had a vasectomy again so he could enjoy sex with his wife without protection. Yes, there were days when he was sore and walking funny but it all worked out fine.

Larry will never have to worry about getting together with someone who wants kids. He'll just be sore and walking funny for a day or two like my friend.

Gail, who doesn't have to worry about protection anymore

Gail, you have the solution to Larry's problem as defined by his mother. His mother's issues are another story. Sophie is overly involved with Larry's procreative choices. He married a woman who didn't want kids. Perhaps he didn't, either. In today's world, couples are making choices about having a family and some are opting not to. Maybe Larry is looking for another woman who doesn't want kids. Or as you say, Gail, if Larry does want children, he can have the vasectomy reversed. I recommend that Sophie let go of the issue of Larry's issue and see what happens.

Susan

Straightening Up

Dear Gail and Susan,

I've been in and out of the hospital in the past few months. Every time I am gone from my house for a few days, my daughter Ann rearranges things and tidies up. I appreciate her efforts, but I really would like my house to stay the way I left it. What can I say to her that won't seem ungrateful or hurt her feelings?

Myron

Myron, My Man,

Tell your daughter that you can't find anything (and I'm sure you can't). She sounds like she wants to be helpful and take care of you. So don't blow your relationship with her by being critical. Thank her over and over again for her effort and ask her nicely to leave things where she found them.

To tell you the truth, Myron, you're a very lucky man. It would be a fantasy of mine that my kids would come and straighten up. It's not going to happen. They're boys. Tell Ann she can come to my place anytime she wants. I'll supply the sandwiches and Diet Coke.

Gail, who hopes your latest visit
to the hospital was your last

Myron's daughter wants to do a nice thing for her dad. Sometimes we want to be helpful and, not knowing what to do, we guess or do what we know how to do. Myron would help himself and his daughter by telling her specifically what she can do that would really be useful—bring him books, DVDs, or food; file papers; or just visit and keep him company.

Being up-front about what we need is always the way to go. Myron will get what he wants and his daughter will feel good about doing something really appreciated. Both parties will win.

Susan

Redecorating

Dear Gail and Susan,

My second husband—we've only been married for three years—has just been diagnosed with Alzheimer's. I would love to redecorate the house—it desperately needs it—but his daughter tells me that keeping everything the same is better for her dad and that changing things around will be confusing to him. I feel stuck. Can you help?

Noreen

Dear Feeling Stuck,

The father of a friend of mine had Alzheimer's. His new wife took him traveling because she wanted to go places, and she had part of the house redecorated every time they went away. My friend went nuts because her father was disoriented all the time. That's what happens, Noreen, when you take the familiar away from a person who is trying to hang on to the familiar. How about not redecorating or changing anything? Just refresh the place. Paint the walls the same color they are now. Get some new linen and put one of those flat-screen TVs in.

It must be very difficult for you to have married someone, expecting to have a really nice future with them, and then they get an illness where they slip away. You must be disappointed. Instead of changing the house, why don't you indulge yourself? Buy some new clothes, maybe a new car, if you can afford it. But leave the house alone. It'll help you out in the long run.

My big message to you is take care of yourself.

Gail, who understands how difficult it is

There are several issues here: a man with Alzheimer's, a conflict between a stepmother and stepdaughter, and a newlywed who has become a caregiver. First, Gail, you and Noreen's stepdaughter are correct that in the case of someone with Alzheimer's, keeping the house as much the same as possible is strongly advised. There should be established routines and places for things like keys and eyeglasses. Decorating changes are disorienting and upsetting.

Second, Alzheimer's is very hard on the caregiver and family members. Therefore, it's helpful for the family to be united and supportive of each other. But sometimes the enormous stress of a parent or spouse with dementia creates schisms and conflicts in the family, as seems to be happening here. Since the disease and dysfunction will inevitably worsen, I urge Noreen and her stepdaughter and other family members to find an Alzheimer's support group in their community to help with decision making and securing resources for the Alzheimer's patient. Stepmother and stepdaughter will be better able to cope if they work together and are supportive of each other.

Gail, you have great ideas for how Noreen can deal with her disappointment and need for some cheer and creativity in her life. As a caregiver, she is in for a hard road.

Susan

Ungrateful?

Dear Gail and Susan,

I broke my hip and am recuperating. My daughter Susie wants me to move in with her. I would prefer to stay in my own home and have her help me out with the shopping, the errands, and cleaning my house. I feel that since I put her through college and supported her after her divorce, it's the least she could do for me. When I told her what I just told you, she said I was being selfish. But isn't she being ungrateful?

Simon

Dear Recuperating,

It was very nice of Susie to invite you to move in with her. It was an outstanding invitation and probably the best way for her to be your caregiver.

We're supposed to put our kids through college and support them when they need us. But our children don't need to be grateful to us for doing what we're supposed to do. If you had said that your daughter was ignoring your illness, I would have said yes, she's being selfish. So if you need help, ask her to assist you in getting someone. An aide could come in every day and take care of your needs. It may not be as expensive as you think and it certainly would preserve your relationship.

I know how scary it is to have to depend on someone else, but believe me, it'll be less scary to depend on a stranger than it would be to depend on a reluctant daughter. Daughters have been known to yell.

Gail, who is saving up for her old age

I agree, Gail, we should not believe that because we did things for our kids, they owe us. If we send our children to college, we are making an investment in their future. All they "owe" us is to do well in school, find a career, and live independent lives. They are not obligated to be our caregivers when we get sick.

If Simon supported Susie after her divorce, it was his choice to do so. Unless they made a contract for remuneration, Susie owes him a thank-you and gratitude, but nothing else. She certainly is not obligated to be at his beck and call when he's in need. There's no quid pro quo. We're supposed to give altruistically. We shouldn't give to our children in order to stockpile credit and then call in our markers. That's not giving; that's manipulation.

Simon should either accept what Susie is offering, which is a lot, or ask her to help him secure further assistance from outside resources.

Susan

Dementia

Dear Gail and Susan,

My wife Lauren has dementia. She's at the point where she doesn't recognize our children. Although we have discussed what it means to have dementia, my children still feel confused and rejected. They were close with their mother and I can tell they don't know how to deal with her. How can I help them?

Liam

Dear Father Who Wants to Help,

I would tell my kids to remember all the good times. I would bring out photo albums and videos of when the family was close and happy. And then I would tell them that that's their real mother.

It's very difficult to see someone with dementia and expect her to react like she always did, because she doesn't look any different. Encourage the kids to give their mother a hug; tell them she may not recognize them, but the hug will feel good.

I think you're a wonderful guy, Liam, for trying to make this difficult situation work.

Gail, who will, if necessary, follow her own advice

Good suggestions, Gail. When a parent has dementia, the children suffer a unique kind of loss. The person may look the same, but since the brain is deteriorating, she is not the same. On the one hand, because the disease develops slowly over years, the family has time to learn to cope. On the other hand, because the course of the illness is so protracted, the family stress is enormous.

In addition to what you suggested, Gail, I would recommend that the family learn as much as they can about the disease. Knowledge of how the brain degenerates and how the disease progresses can help Liam's children better understand their mother's behavior. There are support groups to assist family members in coping.

Susan

Treating Me Fragile

Dear Gail and Susan,

I had a heart attack eight months ago. My doctors tell me that I've made a good recovery. My problem is that my children still treat me as though I'm fragile. We always played touch football at family reunions. They don't want me in the game anymore and they won't let me have the hamburgers and hot dogs that are served, even though I watch my diet very carefully. They call me all the time to see how I am doing. I'm happy that they care, but they're driving me a little crazy with their attention and worry. What can I say to them to get them to stop being so concerned and let me get on with my life?

Bruce

Dear Good Recovery,

Bruce, you're going to have to get very specific and technical with your children. If you can, march them into your doctor's office and let him explain how you are. Then take them to lunch and reassure them that you're doing everything you can to take care of yourself. (Don't forget to order something healthy.)

Here's what you're going to have to say when lunch is almost over: "I love you for caring. I'm supposed to have as little stress as possible. Your overreaction to my condition is making me crazy. I love hearing from you. So when you call, let's talk about other things. Who wants dessert?" (And then don't order it yourself.)

Gail, who sometimes hits it right on the head

I agree, Gail, a visit to the doctor is in order for Bruce's children. They should find out exactly what Bruce can and cannot eat and do and what medications, if any, he is taking. Since there is no mention of a wife, I infer that Bruce lives alone, which may be a reason his kids worry and call so often.

Bruce should make it clear by his behavior that he is vigilant about his health, devise emergency plans in case he needs assistance, and make reasonable arrangements for checking in with his children. I also suggest he try to be a little tolerant of their worry (maybe eat his hamburgers when they're not around) and encourage them to get on with their lives.

Susan

Conclusion

Mort gave us the perfect ending to our book. When we read his letter, we realized he was asking the question we are all asking, one way or another.

~~~~~~

Being Wise

Dear Gail and Susan,

I'm fifty years old with a lot of life experience. I know lots of things that my twenty-five-year-old son Martin doesn't. I want to pass on my wisdom and save my son some of the heartache I had to live with when I made bad decisions. But whenever I start to give Martin advice, he gets tense and changes the subject. How can we have a relationship when he doesn't want what I have to give?

Mort

My Dear Mort,

Your question is the reason this book will sell well. I think through the 1950s, children of any age were happy to get wisdom from their parents. Parents were respected and remained the head of the family until they died. The only situation I know that's like that today is that of Queen Elizabeth II and her son Prince Charles, who's around your age. She's a really bad parent of an adult child. The woman won't give up the crown and is keeping her son an adolescent.

Why things have changed, I'm not sure. I think it might have to do with the fact that we started dressing like our kids and the generation gap went away.

I'm sorry to say that when I was twenty-five, I felt I was smarter than my parents about a lot of things, including how to raise my children. I didn't take advice easily until I got old enough to realize that my parents might know something. Your son is still young, Mort, so maybe someday he will come to his senses and want your advice.

My mother always told me that the older you get, the more you realize how much your parents know. My mother was right.

Gail, who appreciates the question

As parents, we want to save our children from hurt and from making bad choices. But a lot of learning comes from trying things and making mistakes. Moreover, we say that wisdom comes with age, meaning life experience. If that's true, then our children may need more experience to understand or make use of our advice, even if we give it.

Gail, I'm also not surprised that Martin tenses up when his father offers advice. At twenty-five, Martin is still struggling to find his identity as a man. Mort thinks he's offering help. But Martin, like other kids his age, hears something different—that his father doesn't think he can do it on his own.

The last sentence of Mort's letter points to another problem. Mort says that he doesn't know how to have a relationship with his adult son if he can't give him advice. I guess he wants to continue to be the all-knowing parent caring for the inexperienced child. Mort needs to find other ways of relating to his grown son. I recommend sharing experiences—such as golf, sailing, bowling, watching ball games, or discussing (not giving advice about) Martin's job or friends.

Susan

Mort's struggle is the struggle of the parent of the adult child. We have spent years thinking we were supposed to advise and protect our children. Now we have to let go of our old role so our child can take on his new one. It's not easy. While the transition is taking place, there is inevitable tension. The parent, who still wants to cling to the authoritative role, sometimes steps over the line and invades the autonomy of the adult child. The adult child, used to soliciting advice and being dependent, can easily fall back into being a seemingly scatterbrained adolescent. When he does, we are seduced into thinking that we can't leave him on his own when he is so off the mark. We're sure we have to rescue him.

Separating and fundamentally forging a new relationship can be messy and fraught with anxiety and aggression. Sometimes to avoid the tension and anger, both parents and child want to stop the process and keep things the way they were.

Don't back off just because you and your adult child get into uncomfortable situations. Expect your adult child to be an adult and expect yourself to respect his autonomy. If you do, you will not only have an independent, well-functioning adult child, you will also have a new, gratifying relationship with him. Thank you, Mort, for giving us the perfect way to end this book.